QUICK LOOK NURSING:
LEGAL and ETHICAL ISSUES

QUICK LOOK NURSING

LEGAL and ETHICAL ISSUES

Susan Westrick Killion, JD, MS, RN

Professor
Department of Nursing
Southern Connecticut State University
New Haven, Connecticut

Katherine Dempski, JD, BSN, RN

Attorney at Law
Old Saybrook, Connecticut

SLACK
INCORPORATED

An innovative information, education and management company

6900 Grove Road • Thorofare, NJ 08086

Publisher: John H. Bond
Editorial Director: Amy E. Drummond

ISBN 1-55642-505-8
Copyright © 2000 by SLACK Incorporated

The procedures and practices described in this book should be implemented in a manner consistent with the professional standards set for the circumstances that apply in each specific situation. Every effort has been made to confirm the accuracy of the information presented and to correctly relate generally accepted practices. The author, editor, and publisher cannot accept responsibility for errors or exclusions or for the outcome of the application of the material presented herein. There is no expressed or implied warranty of this book or information imparted by it.

Care has been taken to ensure that drug selection and dosages are in accordance with currently accepted/ recommended practice. Due to continuing research, changes in government policy and regulations, and various effects of drug reactions and interactions, it is recommended that the reader review all materials and literature provided for each drug, especially those that are new or not frequently used.

Any review or mention of specific companies or products is not intended as an endorsement by the author or the publisher.

Published by: SLACK Incorporated
                    6900 Grove Road
                    Thorofare, NJ 08086 USA
                    Telephone: 856-848-1000
                    Fax: 856-853-5991
                    World Wide Web: www.slackbooks.com

Contact SLACK Incorporated for more information about other books in this field or about the availability of our books from distributors outside the United States.

Last digit is print number: 10   9   8   7   6   5   4   3   2   1

Contents

PART V. ETHICS

Preface

Creating a book for the nursing community in the *Quick Look Series* presented a timely challenge, especially with such important and far-reaching subjects as those included in *Legal and Ethical Issues*. But more than ever, it is an idea whose time has come. Never have nurses been more acutely aware of the explosion of information that must be dealt with on these and other topics, in the face of ever-shrinking resources and time. And yet nurses must deal with these realities, in both the practice of nursing and the education of nurses.

Quick Look Nursing: Legal and Ethical Issues as part of the inaugural books in this series for nurses fills a gap for a much-needed resource. Already successful in other markets for veterinary and medical students, the series comes to nursing students with the same purpose: to provide a scholarly yet concise presentation of material that is essential for professional practice. Each chapter condenses content that would normally be included in an hour-long lecture and incorporates the essentials of that topic. A schematic presentation, checklist, or supplemental information accompanies the topic as a visual learning tool.

All chapters are written by nurse attorneys who were solicited from the Connecticut Chapter of the American Association of Nurse Attorneys (CTTANNA). As the primary authors and editors, we have extensive experience in nursing education and legal practice involving health care and nursing issues. We have backgrounds as practicing nurses and are invited speakers and authors of other works on legal and ethical issues in health care and nursing. All contributors are experts on the topics on which they wrote; most are practicing attorneys or risk managers in health care. Each brings a wealth of knowledge and a unique perspective from the blending of the professions of nursing and law.

The topics chosen for this book range from basic legal concepts to bioethical issues. They are based on issues raised in nursing practice, interactions with nursing students, continuing education topics, curricular requirements for nursing programs, and work experience as nurse attorneys. These topics are widely taught in nursing curriculums and include some cutting-edge content and discussion.

Part I discusses subjects related to legal risks in nursing practice and presents a review of the legal system, negligence and malpractice, the standards of care, insurance, regulation of practice, and an assignment. Part II examines topics related to liability in patient care including confidential communication, informed consent, pain control, patient teaching, patients with AIDS, abusive situations, reproductive services, and organ transplantation. Documentation issues, presented in Part III, include use of computerized records, implementation of orders for incident reports, and forensics. Employment issues are dealt with in Part IV and include contracts, unionization, employment status liability, sexual harassment, violence, employees with AIDS and needle sticks, and the Americans with Disabilities Act. Ethical issues, presented in Part V, include reporting illegal or unethical conduct, patients' rights, maternal versus fetal rights, futile treatment, assisted suicide, advance directives, and life-ending decisions.

As the primary target audience for this book, nursing students will benefit from both its relevance and presentation. In focus groups held by the publisher, nursing students repeatedly stated they did not have time to read the extensive and comprehensive texts assigned for so many courses. Thus, a book with the format of the *Quick Look Series* can be especially helpful in gaining the knowledge they need in important areas. The text includes selected references, most of which are readily available if further reading on the subject is desired. As an important adjunct and learning strategy, multiple-choice review questions focusing on application of the material are included for each topic. The rationales provided for correct and incorrect answers will help students gain a thorough understanding of the material.

Nursing faculty will find this book useful as it covers most topics in the curriculum and in individual courses on legal and ethical subjects. It is well known that nursing faculty without a legal background often find many of these topics especially challenging to teach. An authoritative book on these topics assists in this effort.

Additionally, practicing nurses will find the book useful as both a resource and a review. It includes some updated topics that nurses may not have covered in their nursing curriculums or that they may want to be more familiar with, to enhance their practice.

As with all works of this nature, we offer the usual caveats about the ever-changing and dynamic nature of the law. The book incorporates legal concepts and analyses as we know them today, with the realization that they may become outdated or modified by tomorrow.

We are pleased to offer this book as an addition to the growing body of scholarly work written by nurses with legal expertise. However, the real challenge of using this information to enhance the education of nurses, to improve practice, and ultimately to benefit patients remains with the members of the nursing profession.

S.W.K.
K.D.

Contributing Authors

Diana C. Ballard, JD, MBA, RN
Of Counsel Susman, Duffy, and
Segaloff
New Haven, CT

Doreen J. Bonadies, JD, RN
Attorney at Law
Biller, Sachs, Raio, and Bonadies
Hamden, CT

Regina M. DeLuca, JD, BSN
Koskoff, Koskoff, and Bieder
Bridgeport, CT

Barbara Dunham, JD, RN
Attorney at Law
Delaney, Zemetis, Donahue, and
Dunham
Guilford, CT

Susan B. Ramsey, JD, BSN
Gary, Williams, Parenti, Finney, Lewis,
McManus, Watson, and Sperando
Stuart, FL

Roberta G. Gellar, JD, BS, RN
Scheirer and Geller
Hamden, CT

Cynthia Keenan, JD, BA, RN
Law Offices of Cynthia Keenan
Stratford, CT

Melinda S. Monson, JD, MSN, RN
O.Brien, Tanski, and Young
Hartford, CT

Lynda L. Nemeth, JD, RN
Norwalk Hospital
Norwalk, CT

Joanne P. Sheehan, JD, RN
Friedman, Newman, Levy, and
Sheehan
Fairfield, CT

Maureen Townsend, JD, RN
Danaher, Tedford, Lagnese, and Neal
Hartford, CT

Abbreviations

AAP	American Academy of Pediatrics
ADA	Americans with Disabilities Act
AHA	American Hospital Association
AHCPR	Agency for Health Care Policy and Research
AIDS	acquired immunodeficiency syndrome
ANA	American Nurses Association
ANCC	American Nurses Credentialing Center
BSN	bachelor of science in nursing
CAPTA	Child Abuse Prevention and Treatment Act
CDC	Centers for Disease Control and Prevention
CMV	cytomegalovirus
CPR	computerized patient record
EEOC	Equal Employment Opportunity Commission
EMTLA	Emergency Medical Treatment and Labor Act
FCA	False Claims Act
FDA	Food and Drug Administration
FMLA	Family Medical Leave Act
FOIA	Freedom of Information Act
FTCA	Federal Tort Claims Act
HCFA	Health Care Financing Administration
HIV	human immunodeficiency virus
HMO	health maintenance organization
IV	intravenous
IM	intramuscular
JCAHO	Joint Commission on Accreditation of Healthcare Organizations
LPN	licensed practical nurse
NCSBN	National Council of State Boards of Nursing
NLRA	National Labor Relations Act
NLRB	National Labor Relations Board
NPA	Nurse Practice Act
OBRA	Omnibus Reconciliation Act

OPO	organ procurement organization
OPTN	Organ Procurement and Transplantation Network
OSHA	Occupational and Safety Health Act
PCA	patient-controlled analgesia
prn	as needed
PSDA	Patient Self-determination Act
RN	registered nurse
STD	sexually transmitted disease
UAP	unlicensed assistive personnel
UNOS	United Network for Organ Sharing

PART I
Legal Risks in Nursing Practice

1

The Legal Environment-Part I

Susan Westrick Killion, JD, MS, RN and
Katherine McCormack Dempski, JD, BSN, RN

Civil and Criminal Court System

Federal

U.S. Supreme Court
- Appeals from U.S. Court of Appeals
- Appeals from State Supreme Courts
(involving federal or constitutional law)
  - Lawsuits between states

U.S. courts of appeals
- Appeals from lower district courts

U.S. district courts
- Civil lawsuits or criminal acts involving federal law
or between litigants with diverse citizenship

State

State supreme court
- Appeals from state appellate courts
final decision in that state
(unless constitutional issue)

State appellate court
- Appeals from state trial courts

State district courts
- Criminal (divided by geographical area)
- Civil (divided in jurisdictions)

Definition of *Law*

Law has been defined as the formalization of a body of rules of action or conduct prescribed that is enforced by binding legal authority; or as the sum total of rules and regulations by which society is governed. Because law reflects society's values, it is by definition an ever-changing concept subject to modification. The law reflects the will of the people as represented by legisla-

tive or judicial bodies (almost all of whom are elected) that enact the law or interpret the law.

Sources and Types of Law

Constitutional law is the organizational framework of a system of laws or principles that govern a nation, system, corporation, or other organization. It forms the basis of how that entity will be governed. The U.S.

Constitution (and its amendments) is the supreme law of the United States and sets forth the general organization of the government and the powers and limitations of the federal government. The best-known limitations on the powers of the government are the first 10 amendments, known as the Bill of Rights. These incorporate such concepts as free speech, freedom of religion, and the right not to be deprived of life, liberty, or the pursuit of happiness without due process of law. Any rights not expressly granted to the federal government are reserved to the states.

Also established by the U.S. Constitution are the three branches of government: executive, judicial, and legislative. These serve as a system of checks and balances, with powers distributed among them.

Individual states have constitutions as well and are an important source of legal rights. If there is a conflict between federal and state law, the federal law would take precedence as the supreme law.

Enactments by the legislative branches of government are known as *statutes,* the written laws that are "on the books" and codified or available in writing. Examples are the U.S. code that contains federal statutes, state statutes (such as the Connecticut General Statutes), and ordinances passed by city or municipal government representatives. The nurse practice act (NPA) is an example of a statutory law that is available for review in the written statutes of each state.

Administrative agencies (e.g., National Labor Relations Board, state board of nursing), are empowered by legislative bodies to implement a certain area of law, called *administrative law.* The administrative agency has delegated power to make administrative rules and regulations and to adjudicate disputes within the area of delegated power. Decisions by these agencies are subject to judicial review but on a very limited basis, and the agency is considered the expert decision-maker in its area of expertise. Administrative rules, regulations, and decisions are subject to administrative procedure acts, which also govern their activities.

Attorney generals' opinions are another source of administrative law. An attorney general may be asked to render an opinion related to an important aspect of administrative law. This will stand as binding until it is overruled by a specific statute, regulation, or court order. These opinions serve as an important source of guidance in interpreting statutory or common law.

The *common law,* or *case law,* is the result of judicial decisions made from disputes that arise and are decided in courts of law. Case law is an important source of guidance for others who may be in similar circumstances, as it serves as legal precedent in the jurisdiction where the decision was made. Even though case law is not precedent for other jurisdictions, courts often look to case law for guidance in similar situations. Important case law (usually that which has been appealed) is reported in case law books, which are available at law libraries.

The Court System

Courts in the federal, state, and municipal systems are organized in a tierlike structure (see **Figure**). The lowest level is the trial court where cases are first heard. The second level is the intermediate court, or court of appeals, where the case is taken if one of the parties is not satisfied with the outcome in the trial court. The highest level in the system, the supreme court, often makes the final decision, but higher courts do not automatically take all cases that seek an appeal. The trial court for the federal system is called the *federal district court,* and the intermediate courts are divided into circuits that cover several states. It is important to know in which court a case is decided to determine if it is applicable as precedent in a subsequent case.

Many special branches of trial courts have a particular area of authority or jurisdiction (e.g., probate court often is the designated court for decisions related to competency of patients, family court may handle termination of parental rights).

Procedural and Substantive Rights

Procedural laws (e.g., evidence and jurisdictional laws) prescribe the manner in which rights and responsibilities are exercised and enforced in court. They provide the form and manner of conducting judicial business before the court. *Substantive laws* (contract, criminal, and civil laws) define and give rights that the court administers.

The due process clause in the 5th and 14th amendments provides citizens with *procedural* and *substantive due process. Procedural due process* applies when a citizen has been deprived of a life, liberty, or property interest. The person is entitled to be heard in a proceeding (hearing right) and must be notified of such a right before the deprivation (notice right). Substantive due process requires fair legislation that should be reasonable in context as well as application. No one should be unreasonably or arbitrarily deprived of life, liberty, or property.

2 The Legal Environment–Part II
Susan Westrick Killion, JD, MS, RN and
Katherine McCormack Dempski, JD, BSN, RN

Civil and Criminal Court System

Federal

U.S. Supreme Court
- Appeals from U.S. Court of Appeals
- Appeals from State Supreme Courts
(involving federal or constitutional law)
  - Lawsuits between states

U.S. courts of appeals
- Appeals from lower district courts

U.S. district courts
- Civil lawsuits or criminal acts involving federal law
or between litigants with diverse citizenship

State

State supreme court
- Appeals from state appellate courts
final decision in that state
(unless constitutional issue)

State appellate court
- Appeals from state trial courts

State district courts
- Criminal (divided by geographical area)
- Civil (divided in jurisdictions)

Civil Law

Civil law such as torts, contracts, and property is society's rules for dealing fairly with litigating parties. Tort law establishes liability on socially unreasonable conduct. The wrongdoer (tort-feasor) is liable when acting in departure from the standard of care (how people should conduct themselves while carrying on daily activities). Professional malpractice is a failure to perform professional duties and falls under the tort system. The injured party institutes the court proceedings.

Criminal Law

Criminal law seeks to protect the public from harmful acts by punishing those who break the rules imposed by society. The state (not the harmed party) brings the criminal action against the wrongdoer. Crimes are punished even if the lawbreaker is not aware of the law; thus, "ignorance is no excuse." Most crimes involve the wrongdoer's intent to complete the criminal act. However, there are crimes where the wrongdoer acted not with intent to harm but with such a reckless disregard for others' safety that it constitutes a crime. Recently, several states have applied this criminal definition to health care providers (both nurses and physicians) for professional negligence that is a "reckless" disregard for patient safety.

Liability

Vicarious liability is the liability of the employer for the negligent acts of the employee in the course of his or her employment. Also referred to as *respondeat superior* (Latin for "look to the man higher up"), vicarious liability is based on the theory that the employer has fictitious control over the employees and the injured party should not bear the burden of the injury without compensation. Vicarious liability is an allocation of risk and is considered the "cost of doing business." It provides incentive for employers to make a careful selection of employees and supervise them to conduct business safely.

Vicarious liability also applies to acts the employee performs in the course of employment. Stepping outside the scope of employment leaves the employee open for *individual liability* for his or her acts.

Generally, employers are not vicariously liable for the negligent acts of *independent contractors* because they are not employees. Independent contractors have their own enterprise and are responsible for preventing negligent harm to others while performing their business. This is a form of individual liability. Nurses who are independent contractors are always encouraged to carry their own liability insurance.

Although independent contractors are individually liable for their own negligent acts, corporations hiring contractors are sometimes liable for negligent acts of their employees and their hired contractors as well as for negligent corporate policies and procedures. *Corporate liability* was formed on the basis that corporations market themselves to serve the public, and the public seeks those services based on the corporations' resources including their independent contractors. Under corporate liability, corporations are liable for the negligent acts of independent contractors, for negligent supervision of the contractors, and for negligent hiring of contractors. Hospitals have been held liable for negligent selection and negligent retention of incompetent physicians who are independent contractors.

Interaction Between Law and Ethics

Laws and the legal system provide a framework for the shared values of people within a society. Ethical codes (as a reflection of professional values) and behavior become a guiding force for professional decision-making and continuously interact with the law. While laws do reflect the values of the majority of people, they also often require only a minimum standard of conduct.

Good ethical behavior should reflect lawful behavior, but sometimes the two can conflict. Usually if the act is ethical, it fulfills the legal duty as well, but fulfilling the minimal legal duty may not always incorporate ethical principles.

Legal duties are binding and enforceable, whereas ethical duties may not be. However, courts will look to ethical codes and conduct of the profession when determining the proper standard of care required under certain circumstances.

3 Regulation of Nursing Practice

Susan Westrick Killion, JD, MS, RN

A Licensure

Enables nurse to work as an RN and use this title

↓

Mandatory (all states):
Anyone performing nursing activities
and using title RN must be licensed

↓

Multistate licensure
- Practice beyond state borders
- NCSBN proposed Nursing Licensure Compact
- Some states have entered into compact voluntarily
  as a pilot project

B Nurse Practice Act

- Entry requirements
- License renewal
- Disciplinary actions
- Scope of practice
- Advanced practice
- Special provisions

C Credentialing

- Recognition of knowledge and skills exceeding basic practice
  (performance, knowledge, and preparation requirements)

- Recognition by specialty organization

- Can use initials with title RN, e.g., certified oncology nurse (CON)

Licensure

Licensure is the process by which a governmental agency (state health department through the board of nursing) entitles a person to practice a certain profession (see **Part A**). Licensing laws derive their power from the police power of the state to protect the public. In addition to protecting the public, these statutes regulate the profession. Licensure of an individual as a nurse or a registered nurse (RN) assures the public that the person is qualified to assume the duties as specified for this professional practitioner. However, licensure only assures minimal safety and competence and does not specify a particular educational background or degree, unless specified in the state statute.

All states have *mandatory licensure*—all persons compensated for nursing services and performing the duties of an RN must be licensed. Both the designation *RN* and the actions of RNs are protected by the statute. Exceptions to this rule include student nurses providing nursing services while enrolled in educational programs.

Violation of these statutes or practicing nursing without a license is a crime, as is aiding or assisting another to practice nursing without a license. Penalties may include fines or more severe sanctions such as confinement. Those who harm patients may be liable for civil damages in suits alleging negligence.

Multistate Licensure

Regulation of nursing practice across state borders has become an increasing concern of professional nursing organizations. With the advent of telenursing, many issues have been raised concerning the "site" of practice and which state's NPA would prevail in questionable situations. In 1998, the National Council of State Boards of Nursing (NCSBN) proposed the Nursing Licensure Compact to address interstate licensure. This compact basically calls for recognition of persons licensed in another state, similar to the procedure used for drivers' licenses. However, professional organizations such as the American Nurses Association (ANA) and individual state boards of nursing have expressed multiple concerns about this proposal. A few states have agreed to adopt the compact on a trial basis.

Nurse Practice Acts

NPAs are individual to each state. However, they typically follow model NPAs as defined by the NCSBN or the ANA. NPAs define entry requirements for the profession (such as graduation from an approved educational program for nursing), duties and composition of the state board of nursing, scope of practice, grounds for disciplinary action, license renewal and fees, and other regulatory rules (see **Part B**).

State legislatures modify and update NPAs in what is often a long and challenging process. Changes usually are initiated by the state nurses association in response to a need identified by the professional community.

Provisions

- Scope of practice. These provisions are broad in nature and provide guidance for nursing actions. They provide the legal boundaries for practice. Most statutes incorporate language for nurses to "diagnose human responses to actual or potential health problems" and to "assess needs of patients." Many also specify "health counseling, referral, patient teaching, and prescribing nursing actions" as nursing activities. Nurses need to check the scope of their practice as related to the licensed practical nurse (LPN). Most often the LPN works under the supervision or direction of the RN. Independent nursing actions are identified along with those that are interdependent or dependent, such as administration of medications prescribed by other practitioners. These provisions are purposefully broad so that the practice act does not become outdated as nursing practice continues to evolve.
- Advanced practice. Many NPAs have separate sec-

tions for advanced practice nursing that often permit diagnosis of certain medical conditions, prescription of medications following practice protocols, and treatment of some conditions. Some specify that these nurses have written agreements with supervising physicians or work under the supervision of a physician. Some specialized advanced practice nurses such as nurse midwives and nurse anesthetists have separate statutes that regulate their practice.
- Special provisions. Some states have passed provisions for mandatory continuing education for license renewal, to ensure continued competency. Two states, North Dakota and Maine, have provisions or regulations specifying a bachelor of science in nursing (BSN) as the entry criterion for initial licensure of RNs. Each nurse needs to check the state NPA because the requirements for practice vary among states.

Interaction with Related Health Care Practitioners

Other health care practitioners (e.g., physicians, physician's assistants, social workers, etc.) have separate practice acts that can potentially affect nursing practice. Practicing outside the scope of one's practice can have serious consequences, including successful malpractice claims if patient injury results. The person who acts outside the scope of practice usually is held to the standard of the other practitioner for purposes of malpractice. Thus, if an RN removed a patient's cast and this action was outside the scope of practice for an RN, the nurse would be held accountable to the standard required by the practitioner (herein an MD). Other actions may be sustained as well including other tort actions for fraud, crimes, or disciplinary actions by the state board of nursing or other regulatory bodies.

Credentialing

Another means to regulate practice is by credentialing (see **Part C**). Credentialing usually involves endorsement or recognition by a specialized organization or specialty group that the nurse has certain qualifications that exceed basic competence. The nurse has met additional standards of performance and preparation and can then use initials appropriate to the credential or certification after the title RN. As an example, on behalf of the ANA the American Nurses Credentialing Center (ANCC) certifies nurses in certain specialties such as nursing administration or oncology nursing. Often, educational, practice, and testing criteria have to be met. For advance practice nurses, the nurse practice act may require certification by a national certifying organization such as ANCC. Certification is often for several years; thereafter, the nurse must become recertified. Many other specialty organizations, such as the Emergency Nurse Organization, certify nurses for specialty practice.

4 Nurses in Legal Actions

Joanne P. Sheehan, JD, RN and

Katherine McCormack Dempski, JD, BSN, RN

A

Most Common Grounds for Disciplinary Charges

- Fraud or deception in obtaining a nursing license, or falsifying insurance claim forms or patient hospital records.
- Physical or mental impairment such as loss of motor skill or mobility and mental illnesses such as schizophrenia. Having a physical or mental impairment doesn't necessarily mean that the nurse's license will be in jeopardy; however, the nurse must be able to perform the job. The board may request that the nurse undergo a physical or psychological examination to determine ability to practice nursing.
- Illegal conduct, incompetence, or negligence in carrying out a nursing function. A nurse can be disciplined even if the acts did not cause injury to the patient.
- Drug or alcohol abuse. Many state boards recognize the problems of chemical dependency and will require participation in a rehabilitation program.
- Abusive behavior, either physical or verbal.
- Conviction of a criminal offense.

B **Disciplinary Process**

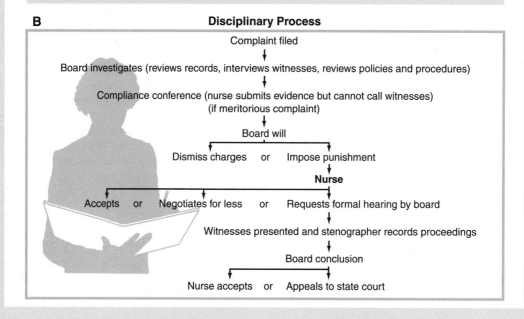

Complaint filed
↓
Board investigates (reviews records, interviews witnesses, reviews policies and procedures)
↓
Compliance conference (nurse submits evidence but cannot call witnesses)
(if meritorious complaint)
↓
Board will
┌─────────────┴─────────────┐
Dismiss charges   or   Impose punishment
↓
Nurse
┌──────────┬────────────────┬────────────────┐
Accepts   or   Negotiates for less   or   Requests formal hearing by board
↓
Witnesses presented and stenographer records proceedings
↓
Board conclusion
┌─────────────┴─────────────┐
Nurse accepts   or   Appeals to state court

Nurses may become involved in different types of actions within the legal system, including criminal actions, administrative law actions, and civil actions. A nurse who makes an error administering medicine is susceptible to a civil malpractice action by the patient injured and a disciplinary proceeding by the licensing board. The same nurse may be subject to criminal charges if the error was so egregious that it constituted negligent homicide or manslaughter.

Criminal Actions

Criminal actions are brought by the state against a defendant accused of breaking a law. Nurses have been prosecuted for crimes such as negligent homicide, manslaughter, theft of narcotics, insurance fraud, and falsifying medical records. A nurse who attempts to conceal a negligent nursing action (civil action) by entering false information in a medical record commits fraud and falsification of a record and could face criminal charges for these crimes.

When a nurse's professional negligence rises to the level of "reckless disregard for human life" (a legal standard of conduct), the nurse may face criminal charges of negligent homicide or manslaughter. Each charge is defined in the state criminal statutes and requires certain elements the state must prove.

Administrative Law Actions

Administrative law agencies are created by state statutes that define the agencies' purpose, functions, and powers. The state board of nursing is an administrative law agency. The governor of the state typically appoints members to the board of nursing, and most state statutes determine the number of board members, the professional requirements, and the length of appointment. The board of nursing is empowered by the NPA to administer and establish the rules and regulations of nursing practice, educational requirements, licensing for practice, licensure renewal requirements, and approval of schools of nursing. In addition, the board enforces the state's NPA and is responsible for disciplinary actions.

Disciplinary Actions

Each board of nursing is charged with the responsibility to maintain the standards of the nursing profession within the state and to protect the public. The board may conduct an investigation to determine whether a nurse has violated the NPA. This is a disciplinary procedure and differs from a civil action or criminal action. **Part A** lists the most common grounds for disciplinary charges.

Investigation and Disciplinary Process

Anyone (patient, patient's family member, coworker, or employer) can file a complaint with the board of nursing. The board will notify the nurse in writing that a complaint has been filed and an investigation has been started, and may request a written response from the nurse. The response should be provided in an objective manner. Before submitting a response, the nurse should consult an attorney. Some nursing malpractice policies now cover attorney fees in disciplinary matters.

A schematic outlining the investigation and disciplinary process is provided in **Part B**.

If the board imposes a punishment, it can take one or more of the following disciplinary actions:

- Revocation of the nurse's license
- Suspension of the nurse's license
- Letter of reprimand (published in the board's reports and means action has been taken against the nurse's license)
- Letter of admonishment (in the nurse's file but isn't made public)
- Probation (fulfilling certain requirements to continue practice)
- Imposition of a fine

Administrative Due Process

The nurse has a constitutional right during the administrative process called *due process*. Due process ensures that nurses receive a hearing where they have the right to be heard and defend any charges brought against them before the board can terminate a "liberty" (e.g., practicing nursing). In certain situations, however, the board has the right to summarily revoke or suspend a nurse's license when the nurse presents an immediate danger to public safety.

Civil Actions

Civil actions deal with disputes between individuals. Civil law is designed to monetarily compensate individuals for harm caused to them. Nurses can become involved in civil actions such as malpractice actions, personal injury lawsuits, and workers' compensation. Nurses also can become involved as a witness in a patient's personal injury case against another person. Workers' compensation laws prevent employees from suing their employer for injuries received on the job. Cost of the injury and lost wages due to the injury must be settled through the workers' compensation benefits plan the employer provides for the employees.

Malpractice is the negligent conduct of a professional. It is defined by (1) duty—established by a professional relationship; (2) breach of duty—an act or omission in violation of the nursing standard of care; (3) a physical injury; and (4) causation—nurse's breach of duty caused the plaintiff's injury.

Most plaintiffs (person initiating the lawsuit) will hire a lawyer to pursue a malpractice claim. To establish the claim, pertinent medical records and opinions of expert witnesses (nurses with experience in the same field of nursing who will testify as to the standard of care) will be obtained to support the allegations of malpractice. The parties then exchange information (discovery phase) about the plaintiff's claims of negligence and damages (injury and any costs incurred due to the injury) and the defendant's defense to such claims. The exchange is done through documents filed with the court and depositions. The defendant nurse may also be required to give deposition testimony. A deposition is a legal proceeding where questions are asked and answered under oath and recorded by a stenographer. When the discovery phase is complete, the case will either settle or proceed to trial. Any money paid to the plaintiff may come from the nurse's malpractice insurance policy or from the nurse if the judgment amount exceeds the policy amount, the nurse is uninsured, or the malpractice carrier has denied coverage. Malpractice coverage is denied when the nurse acted outside the scope of employment.

5 Standards of Care

Katherine McCormack Dempski, JD, BSN, RN

A Definitions

Standard of care: degree of care skill and judgment practiced by a reasonable nurse; may be established by expert testimony

National standard: under same or similar circumstances	vs	Locality rule: in the same or similar area

National standard: under same or similar circumstances   vs   Locality rule: in the same or similar area

Standards: authoritative statements that evaluate the quality of practice   vs   Guidelines: outline for professional conduct (usually based on scientific evidence or expert opinion)

Procedure: step-by-step guide on implementing a policy   vs   Policy: plan for meeting agency goals

Ordinary negligence: act or failure to act that is below standard of care   vs   Gross negligence: negligent act that is a reckless disregard for human life

Nursing negligence: unreasonable nursing care or conduct for the circumstances   vs   Nursing competency: level of care required for a nurse to avoid disciplinary action

B Sources for the standard of care

1. Professional organizations (e.g., ANA, American Association of Critical Nurses)
2. Nursing literature (e.g., journals, periodicals)
3. Agency policy, procedure, and bylaws (must be updated to reflect changes in standards)
4. Federal administration codes (e.g., nurse-patient ratios for federally funded institutions)
5. Joint Commission on Accreditation of Hospital manual
6. Court decisions (sets precedents for future cases)
7. Experts and expert testimony (e.g., published authors, nursing professors)
8. State statutes and administrative regulations (e.g., Nurse Practice Act)

In most states, the professional standard of care is defined by statute or case law. When they breach the standard of care, nurses can be liable for nursing negligence in a civil court. They also can face the restriction or revocation of their nursing license in an administrative proceeding by the licensing board. Having a definition of the standard of care gives a clearer view of when nursing negligence has occurred and allows the injured party to be compensated for the harm done. It also allows the nurse to avoid a nursing malpractice claim when a bad result occurs despite due care by the nurse.

National Standard of Care versus the Locality Rule

The national standard of care (see **Part A**) is the degree of care, skill, and judgment exercised by a reasonable nurse under the same or similar circumstances. A nurse has the duty to practice nursing using the standard of care. This does not require the nurse to render optimal care or even possess extraordinary skill. Likewise, the rule that a nurse must exercise best nursing judgment does not necessarily hold the nurse liable for an error in nursing judgment. However, the nurse's error in judgment must not be below the standard of care. Good nursing care does not guarantee the patient a good result.

The *locality rule* holds that a nurse must practice with the degree of skill and care possessed by other nurses in the same or similar area (locality). How a nurse in a rural emergency department performs will be compared to nurses in other rural areas. The locality rule is followed in a minority of states.

The *national standard of care* holds a nurse in a rural community hospital to the same standard of care as a nurse in a metropolitan medical center given the similarity of the situation. The national standard takes into consideration that the emergency department at a metropolitan medical center has more resources and technology than a rural emergency department. The majority of states follow the national standard.

The national standard (or locality rule in a minority of states) is used in a malpractice civil action, whereas a nursing board disciplinary action looks for a nurse's level of competency. State regulations define the level of competency required of a nurse. Falling below the level of competency can result in a disciplinary action by a state board even when no harm was done to a patient.

How the Standard of Care Is Applied

A nurse is liable for nursing malpractice when the nursing standard of care is not followed. As the definition implies, the standard for nursing conduct varies in each situation. For example, an emergency department nurse draws blood from a 45-year-old woman. The nurse does not put the side rails up on the stretcher. As the nurse walks away to send the blood to the lab, the woman faints and falls from the stretcher. The patient sues the nurse. Both parties to the suit admit expert testimony and the emergency department's policy and procedure manual. The emergency room department manual states that side rails must be used for all children, elderly, and confused or unconscious patients. Expert testimony confirms that side rails are often necessary for children and the elderly because patients in these age groups fall from stretchers more frequently and are injured severely even from minor falls. The jury may determine that the nurse did not violate the standard of care in that situation because the nurse had no indication the patient was at risk for falling.

If the same facts are presented but the patient is an 80-year-old, the situation changes. Now the nurse does have some indication that the patient is at risk for falling and the standard of care changes for that situation. Most likely the nurse will be found to have breached the standard of care required for this situation.

The standard of care is not a cookbook of step-by-step ways to conduct oneself professionally in any given situation. It requires the nurse to be aware of any harm that may befall the patient and to take reasonable steps to prevent that harm. The standard of care comes from many sources (see **Part B**). The nurse is accountable to know the standard as developed through these multiple authoritative sources.

Nurse Practice Act

Each state has a Nurse Practice Act that defines the practice of nursing and determines whether nurses stay within their scope of practice. The scope of practice varies in each state. An agency's policies and procedures must not expand the scope of nursing practice.

Standards of Care in Specialties

Specialists are held to the standard of other similarly situated specialists. The conduct of a nursing specialist such as a pediatric nurse practitioner will be compared to that of other similarly situated pediatric nurse practitioners. When specialists have the responsibility of the same procedure, some states allow each specialty to be an expert on the standard of care for that procedure. For example, in a malpractice action against a pediatric nurse practitioner, a nurse midwife may explain to the jury the standard of care in neonatal resuscitation since both may perform that procedure under their state's NPA.

Majority versus Minority Views

There is a generally recognized course of treatment for each diagnosis within each specialty. The phrases "schools of thought," "best medical judgment," and "respectable minority" recognize that within each specialty there are alternative treatments for each diagnosis that are professionally acceptable to meet the standard of care.

6 Defenses to Negligence or Malpractice

Susan Westrick Killion, JD, MS, RN

Failure to prove elements of the claim

Voluntary release or waiver of claim
1. Signed release
2. Exculpatory clause that waives rights before they arise

Immunities
1. Institutional (e.g., charitable)
2. Governmental (e.g., federal employees)
3. Personal (e.g., Good Samaritan Act, shields ordinary but not reckless or gross negligence)

Defenses to Negligence or Malpractice Actions

Plaintiff's acts or conduct
1. Contributory negligence (may bar claim)
2. Comparative negligence (reduces or apportions damages)
3. Assumption of the risk

Procedural immunities
1. Failure to state a proper claim
2. Statute of limitations (in most states, claim is barred after 2–3 years; many exceptions, including concept of when reasonable to discover injury)

After a lawsuit is filed against a nurse, various defenses (see **Figure**) can be raised. These defenses may absolve the defendant completely or may limit the plaintiff's (or patient's) claim. They are based on various statutes or common-law doctrines, and more than one can be raised against a claim.

Failure to Prove Elements of Claim

In negligence or malpractice actions, 4 elements must be proved for a successful claim: (1) a duty to the plaintiff, (2) a breach of the duty or failure to act reasonably, (3) damage or resultant injury to the plaintiff because of this breach of duty, and (4) proximate (or legal) causation between the breach of duty and the resultant injury. Failure to prove even one of these elements will cause the plaintiff's claim to fail and thus would be a valid defense.

Voluntary Release or Waiver of Claim

In the process of settling a claim, a patient may sign a release absolving the defendant of all future claims or limiting claims based on the incident in question. Another means of voluntarily relinquishing rights is for a patient to have signed an exculpatory agreement or clause, serving as a release to future claims before they arise. The court may overrule these agreements if it feels that patients have been coerced or misinformed about their rights.

Immunities

An immunity from suit will act as a shield in case of a lawsuit. Examples of these are statutes or common-law doctrines that may apply to governmental or charitable-organization employees. However, many of these doctrines, especially charitable immunity, have been eroded over the years to allow legitimate claims to go forward. Most health care institutions are in reality profit-making organizations, even if part of their mission is charitable.

An example of federal immunity is the Federal Tort Claims Act (FTCA). Under this act the exclusive remedy for patients' claims while under the care of employees in governmental institutions is against the government and not the employees themselves. The government is substituted for the defendant and individual employees, including nurses, are protected. There are some exceptions to this rule. Also limited under the act is the right of active servicemen to bring claims against the government. The rationale for this is that they are receiving free medical care and disability pensions and that this is their exclusive remedy. However, civilian recipients of military medical care may sue the federal government, and military personnel may sue civilian medical caregivers.

Each state has its own statute called the Good Samaritan Act or Law, which provides for some form of personal immunity for acts or omission of medical care rendered by a volunteer who in good faith provides emergency medical assistance. Each state further defines what constitutes an "emergency," but it usually involves potential loss of life or limb so pressing that action must be taken. These acts encourage citizens and health care practitioners to assist in emergencies without fear of civil or criminal liability for their actions if a mistake is made. However, it is important to recognize that most often one is protected from ordinary negligence only and not from gross negligence or reckless behavior. Nurses rendering assistance are expected to follow accepted standards of nursing as guidelines. This doctrine applies when there is no nurse-patient relationship that would imply a duty of care under the circumstances (e.g., when a nurse is rendering care as a volunteer).

In almost all states there is no duty to render emergency assistance to strangers, but it could be argued that health professionals have an ethical duty to do so. In Vermont, in an exception to this rule, persons are required to provide reasonable emergency assistance as long as it poses no danger to themselves.

Plaintiff's Negligence or Conduct

Contributory Negligence
Another valid defense that can bar or limit the patient's claim of negligence against a nurse is the plaintiff's conduct, which can be viewed by the court as *contributory negligence* and in some jurisdictions is a complete bar to recovery of damages. The idea behind this is that the patient contributed to his or her own injury by not acting as a reasonably prudent person in the circumstances, and thus should not profit. Examples include patients' not following instructions, not following warnings about side effects from medications, providing false information that led to improper treatment, and failure to return for appointments for follow-up.

Nurses must carefully document patients' failure to follow instructions or to keep appointments.

Comparative Negligence
Some jurisdictions have not held to the strict standards of contributory negligence but have adopted a more flexible approach that incorporates *comparative negligence*. Using this doctrine the court would apportion the percentage of the injury from the plaintiff's own negligence to reduce any damage award. This puts responsibility on both persons to act reasonably under the circumstances. In some jurisdictions this rule is modified so that when the patient's negligence exceeds that of the defendant, the defendant's recovery of damages is barred altogether.

Assumption of the Risk
This defense incorporates the idea that the patient voluntarily assumes the risk of treatment and therefore has no claim against any resultant outcome that he or she specifically agreed to. It is similar conceptually to the informed-consent doctrine. It should be pointed out that the patient never assumes the risk of *negligent* treatment by a health professional, so in this situation, the defense may be of limited use if actual negligence can be shown.

Procedural Defenses

Failure to State a Proper Claim
Failure to state a claim upon which relief can be granted may incorporate various flaws in the plaintiff's action (e.g., failure to show that a nurse-patient relationship existed, claim does not allege or prove negligence but rather some other type of claim against the nurse).

Statute of Limitations
Most states have enacted statutes of limitations that limit the time in which a plaintiff may file an action for negligence or malpractice. Many of these are limited to a 2- or 3-year period. The actual time it takes for the case to come to trial may be several years, but the claim must be filed within the statutory period.

Various exceptions to the statute of limitations have evolved and vary from state to state. A generally accepted one is that the time limit may be extended to when the patient would reasonably have known of the injury (e.g., a patient had radiation treatment that caused fertility problems 10 years later). Nurses need to be aware of this when considering malpractice insurance needs, since claims may arise many years later.

Some states have a *statute of repose,* which sets absolute time limits for claims to be made. These cover the "should have known" concept and may apply to cases involving diagnoses of cancer.

Another way of working around the statute of limitations is for the patient to claim the action as ordinary negligence, rather than malpractice, since the time limit may be longer. Also the claim may be asserted as a contract claim that may not be affected by the statute.

7 Prevention of Malpractice— Part I
Katherine McCormack Dempski, JD, BSN, RN

A

Common Areas of Nursing Malpractice

- **Inadequate assessment of the patient** — failure to monitor and assess a change in a patient's condition and report the change to the patient's physician
- **Medication errors** — transcription errors, administration errors
- **Inadequate training for assignment** — accepting and performing an assignment that the nurse is not competent to perform and failing to recognize own limitations
- **Patient falls** — leaving patient "at risk for falls" unattended
- **Faulty equipment**
- **Inadequate communication** — failing to notify the physician of changes in patient's condition, failing to adequately document in the patient's medical record, failing to advise nursing supervisor of situations where patient injury may occur, such as inadequate physician response
- **Failure to follow proper policy and procedure**

B

To avoid malpractice claims, nurses need to

- Keep current with the state's Nurse Practice Act.
- Be familiar with facilities' policies and procedures.
- Understand the appropriate standards of nursing care.
- Document all nursing care accurately and thoroughly.

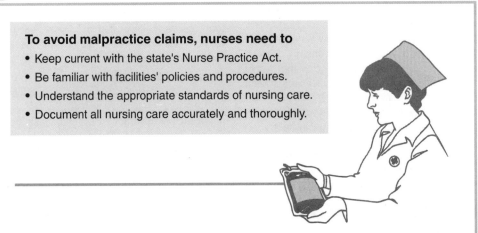

A nurse is negligent when the nursing care fails to meet the appropriate standard of care. Nurses named as defendants in a malpractice claim face potential financial loss and adverse psychological effect. Nurses should be aware of situations that are potential liability problems (see **Part A**) and take steps to avoid them (see **Part B**).

Physician's Orders

When orders are illegible, unclear, incomplete, against agency policy, may cause harm to the patient or are beyond the nurse's training, the nurse must discuss the orders with the physician. Illegible, unclear, and incomplete orders should be clarified and no assumptions should ever be made. Nurses have a duty to clarify medication orders and not to administer medications that may harm the patient whether by interaction with other medications or by incorrect dose. When questioning a medication order, nurses should use the many resources available such as the pharmacist, a reliable drug reference, supervisors, physicians, and if necessary, a physician's supervisor or colleague.

Nurses have a duty to be the patient's advocate and to know self-limitations. When questioning or not following physician's orders, the nurse should discuss the concerns with the physician and the nursing supervisor. Following the agency's chain of command policy is necessary in this difficult situation. A collaborative team effort will offer the best resolution to legal and ethical concerns.

Independent Duty

Nurses have an independent legal duty to the patient to make an accurate and thorough nursing assessment. The nurse must exercise this independent duty to investigate and inspect the patient's status and go up the chain of command when the nurse reasonably believes that the patient may suffer harm by following orders. Nurses have been held liable under this independent duty when they knew (or should have known) that the physician's diagnosis did not match up with the assessment and patient complaints and the patient suffered harm from the nurse's inaction.

Delegation of Tasks

Delegation is the transfer of responsibility for performing an activity while retaining accountability. Nurses delegate tasks to unlicensed assistive personnel (UAP) daily and should be familiar with the UAP's training and competency level. Delegating a task outside the UAP's level of competency or improper delegation increases the risk of professional liability. An *improper delegation*

is the delegation of a licensed activity as defined in the state's NPA. To prevent liability in this area, the nurse should be aware of the NPA and the ANA position statement or delegating tasks to UAP.

Medication and Transcription Errors

Administrating medication incorrectly is one of the most common areas of nursing negligence. This includes giving an incorrect dose, using the incorrect route, and improperly administering an injection. Improper placement of a decimal point can turn a dose into 10 times the ordered amount, and the nurse can be held liable for the error once the drug is administered.

Most transcription errors occur due to assumptions made by nurses when they are unable to read illegible handwriting. Frequent errors occur when transferring the order to the medication administration records. Most institutions have computerized methods that remove this step from the process, thereby decreasing some human error. When nonprofessionals transcribe orders, legal liability remains with the nurse.

Professional Responsibility and Limitations

Nursing negligence occurs frequently when a nurse takes on an unfamiliar nursing procedure or assignment. The standard of care does not change for an inexperienced nurse. Professionalism requires knowing one's limitations and taking steps to avoid patient harm. The nurse should follow agency policy for going up the chain of command for assignment change or utilize available resources such as experienced nurses or supervisors for guidance with unfamiliar procedures. When a nursing error is made, it is the professional responsibility of the nurse to use skill and expertise to intervene and minimize the harm done to the patient.

Prevention of Malpractice—Part II

Katherine McCormack Dempski, JD, BSN, RN

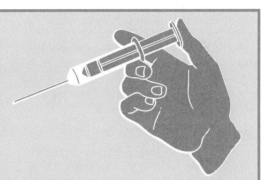

A Equipment Liability

- Failure to reasonably detect malfunction
- Failure to follow manufacturer instructions
- Failure to follow agency policy on maintenance
- Failure to detect harm
- Failure to properly use
- Failure to respond to alarms

Communication with Patients

Many negligence cases against health care providers have some element of poor communication between the provider and the patient. Patients who feel that the health care providers were attentive, caring, concerned, and truthful are highly unlikely to visit a malpractice attorney's office claiming injury due to negligence.

Proper Use of Equipment

The standard of care requires nurses to identify areas of risk of injury to their patient and take steps to avoid the harm. This includes the proper use of medical equipment (including restraints) (see **Part A**). Manufacturer's instructions must be followed, and once malfunctioning equipment is identified, the appropriate authority should be notified to have it removed for maintenance.

Performing Nursing Procedures

Nurses have a duty to perform nursing procedures correctly. Surgeons were once considered responsible for all negligent acts occurring during surgery (known as "captain of the ship" policy). Surgical nurses now have their own liability for incorrect sponge and needle counts. Nurses who are independent contractors to an agency also carry their own liability. Accordingly, agencies are not held responsible under the corporate liability theory for the contracting nurse's negligence.

Difficult Patients

Difficult patients who are more likely to sue are typically uncooperative, immature, dependent, and hostile to the medical staff. Unfortunately it is this difficult personality that makes most health care providers turn away, act aloof, or react in a hostile manner. Providing nursing care to this type of patient is unnerving. However, to avoid potential harm (and a malpractice suit) it is in everyone's best interest to continually provide the standard of care despite personality conflicts. This may require the nurse to assist the patient in identifying the source of the mistrustful and hostile feelings toward the health care staff. Providing consistent, polite, and attentive patient care and explaining all nursing procedures may help diffuse the hostility.

Documentation is a key factor in diffusing potential liability claims. Document the patient's concerns and complaints and how those concerns are being addressed, without labeling the patient or complaining about the patient's behavior. Documentation should reflect the nurse's role as patient advocate and that policies and procedures are being followed. An incident report or other internal review document is the more proper vehicle for documenting staff safety concerns or inappropriate behavior.

Risk Management

Risk management departments are responsible for improving quality of medical care by identifying potential risks and injuries to patients, staff, and visitors. Risk management teams consist of members from various departments and are coordinated through a trained risk management expert. Risk management teams collect information on and evaluate patient complaints, poor medical outcomes, and safety hazards. The data are collected from patient complaint forms, incident reports, utilization review reports, and other internal reporting systems. Risk management teams may also offer staff safety education to improve medical care and are a valuable resource on medical-legal issues.

Continuing Education

Continuing education to update assessment skills is the most valued tool a nurse has in preventing nursing negligence. Maintaining appropriate credentialing and reading professional journals keeps nurses informed on standard of care updates. Agency policies and procedures must be updated to reflect the current standard of care. Nurses who are members of the policy and procedure committee or a professional journal club are taking an active stand in updating their skills and preventing nursing malpractice.

9 Nurses as Witnesses

Roberta G. Geller, JD, BS, RN

Testimony Guidelines for Nurse Witnesses

1. Don't guess.
2. If you don't know the answer, say so.
3. If you don't remember, say so.
4. Be sure you understand the question.
5. Ask for clarification of the question as necessary.
6. Take your time; think before you answer.

PLUS

Fact Witnesses	Expert Witnesses	Witness to Documents
7. Prepare nursing notes in a timely manner. 8. Don't sign another nurse's notes. 9. Testify only to firsthand knowledge.	7. Review records before agreeing to be an expert witness. 8. Be certain the case is in your area of expertise. 9. Be thorough.	7. Assess capacity of the patient. 8. Don't sign if you believe the patient does not understand. 9. Check with your employer first.

Fact Witnesses

The nurse's role as a fact witness is to testify, in verbal or written form, about facts he or she has personally observed. A fact may be an action performed, an event, or an occurrence and can include the patient's condition, actions of others, the patient's environment, nursing practices, or documentation practices. The nurse may be a witness for either the plaintiff (the party bringing the lawsuit) or the defendant (the party being sued). In most instances, the testimony will be rendered at a deposition or at trial. A deposition is a question-and-answer session wherein one party to a lawsuit acquires information known only to the other party. Questions are first asked by the attorney for the party attempting to gather information. The witness answers the questions after taking an oath to tell the truth. Once the attorney asking the questions is finished, the other attorney may ask questions that relate to the questions and answers already addressed. Then, the first attorney may ask additional questions, and so on.

A court reporter is present and creates a stenographic record of all of the spoken words. Occasionally the deposition is videotaped.

The process of rendering testimony as a fact witness at trial is similar to that of a deposition. It will take place in a courtroom or hearing room before a judicial authority, usually a judge but possibly a magistrate or hearing officer. It may also take place in front of a jury.

Expert Witnesses

An expert witness is one who has superior knowledge of a subject by virtue of education and experience. Certainly a nurse, through nursing education and specialized experience in nursing, is well-qualified to serve as an expert witness at a deposition or trial. However, the focus of the testimony is not on the nurse's direct observations but on nursing care issues. The nurse may be called as an expert to opine as to the care that is the subject of the lawsuit or to testify to a standard of care.

Hence, qualifications and credentials will be at issue prior to the court's recognizing the nurse as an expert witness. The attorneys representing all parties may agree or "stipulate" to the nurse's qualifications. If they do not so stipulate, the attorney wishing to present the nurse as an expert witness will have to prove to the court that the nurse is qualified. The attorney may do so through submission to the court of the nurse's resume or curriculum vitae or other such written material.

The nurse will have the opportunity to review the records prior to participation as an expert witness. When reviewing them, the nurse should keep in mind his or her role in to the case (e.g., as an expert for the plaintiff or for the defendant or impartial). If the nurse is an expert witness for either party, questions directly relating to the specific case will be asked. It is expected that the opposing party will offer expert testimony that differs from the nurse's opinion. Therefore, the nurse must be familiar with the specific records relative to the case and prepared to substantiate any opinions.

If the nurse is testifying as to a standard of care, he or she will be asked general questions about any area of expertise (e.g., critical care, home care, obstetrics). Once this expertise is established, hypothetical questions will likely be asked. A hypothetical question is one that describes the issues similar to the case without identification of any specific person. The questioner will then inquire as to whether the care described in the hypothetical question deviated from the standard of care. The nurse will opine as to whether or not there was a deviation from the standard of care and must be able to substantiate any opinion in reliance on education and specialized experience.

It is imperative that the nurse be aware of any conflicts of interest that may arise out of serving as an expert witness. A conflict of interest is a situation in which there is a clash between professional, financial, or ethical interests of the witness. Such conflicts of interest will have a negative impact on the nurse's credibility because they create, at best, the appearance of a bias if not an actual bias. As soon as a potential conflict of interest becomes apparent to the nurse, it should be brought to the attention of the party that has retained his or her services.

Witness to Documents

Because of the nurse's proximity to patients, he or she may be asked to serve as a witness to legal documents. Some examples include but are not limited to a last will and testament, deed, living will, power of attorney, or appointment of health care agent. Although patients or family members may request the nurse to sign these documents as a witness, it is best not to do so since it may create ethical conflicts later.

The legal requirements for the execution (signing) of legal documents vary from state to state. Nonetheless, a nurse who is a witness to the execution attests to the capacity and adult age of the person signing, that the person is acting voluntarily, authenticity of the signature, and that he or she saw the other witness sign the document. The nurse could be called to testify at a later hearing if problems occur regarding circumstances of the signing.

The patient's capacity to sign a legal document refers to the ability to understand the nature and effect of the act. Determining the patient's capacity to sign a legal document does not involve extensive expert evaluation but rather observation and assessment. To assist the witnesses, the attorney conducting the execution will ask the patient a series of questions about the document and the patient's understanding, agreement, and willingness to sign it. The patient should be able to name the document and state that he or she read it and agrees with the contents. If the patient's condition prevents him or her from reading or speaking, the attorney may ask a series of yes or no questions and the patient may respond through body language. Common sense prevails in accordance with the patient's condition.

The nurse's familiarity with the patient affords the nurse a unique role as a witness to the execution of legal documents. If the nurse knows that confusion or medications may affect the patient's capacity, he or she must inform the attorney before the document is signed. If the nurse is not satisfied that the patient understands and agrees with the document, the nurse should not sign as a witness.

Nurses should check with their employers prior to serving as a witness to legal documents. Some employers have policies regarding this issue, and it is in nurses' best interest to comply with any such policy. The policy may require that employees not sign legal documents as a witness to avoid any ethical conflicts.

10 Professional Liability Insurance

Susan Westrick Killion, JD, MS, RN

A Checklist/Features

- Ask to see your employer's policy.
- Examine your own policy.
- Determine policy coverage and limits.
- Check provisions related to settlement, exclusions, indemnification, and limitations of coverage.
- Determine type of policy (claims made or occurrence).
- Keep coverage in effect after you leave job if covered by a claims made policy, or obtain a tail policy.
- Note rights and obligations of insured and insurer.
- Notify insurer of name or address changes, any change in job status or responsibilities, or any potential claims against you.

Claims Made Policy   vs   Occurrence Policy

Must be in effect when the claim is made.

Effective if the policy was in effect at time the incident occurred (applies to previous incidents even if claim is made years later).

B Individual Coverage   vs   Employer Coverage

- Usually covers volunteer work as RN.
- Covers state board action against your license.
- Covers representation by your own attorney.
- Consider if in high-risk areas of practice.

- Covers actions only if in the scope of employment.
- May not cover intentional torts.
- Represented by employer's insurance company or hospital attorney.

Nurses are at risk for liability if a malpractice claim against them is successful. One way to shift the risk of this liability is to buy professional malpractice insurance so that the insurer pays the claim. Malpractice attorneys increasingly name individual practitioners in lawsuits as well as the agencies for which they work. Many employers tell their employees they are covered for such claims by the employer's insurance. This may be true under most circumstances, but there are risks and disadvantages involved in relying solely on the policy of the employer. Some institutions are self-insured, and nurses need to find out the implications of this for their individual malpractice coverage. Nurses are accountable to know the terms, conditions, and exclusions of either their own or the employer's policy (see **Part A**).

Types of Policies

The insurance agreement sets out the terms of the policy and specifies the rights and responsibilities of the nurse (or agency) as the *insured* and the insurance company as the *insurer*. The agreement is a contract governed by contract law and by many special regulations determined by state and federal laws. Two basic types of policies are available:

1. Claims made. The policy must be in effect when the claim is made. If a claim is made years later and the policy is no longer in effect, the policy will not cover the claim. A tail policy may be purchased to cover a gap in coverage when one changes jobs or retires.
2. Occurrence. As long as the policy was in effect when the incident occurred, even if the claim is made years later, the policy will still cover the claim. This preferred type of coverage is broader but is usually more expensive.

Policy Provisions and Coverage

Each policy should be examined individually to determine its features. Every policy will state the *limits of coverage* (e.g., $1 million coverage/incident or $3 million coverage maximum/year). *Excess judgments* are any amount of damages that are above the policy limits. These become the responsibility of the nurse and are payable from personal assets. This can include the claimant's right to future wages.

Limitations and exclusions should be noted carefully. Professional liability insurance policies do not cover criminal acts, acts that are outside the scope of practice, or acts in settings other than those stated in the policy. Agency policies will not likely cover the nurse's conduct if it rises to the level of creating an extreme risk for the patient, such as an extreme overdose, as this is considered reckless behavior. Volunteer activities would not be covered unless specifically mentioned in the contract. Likewise a nurse's actions outside the scope of the state NPA would not be covered.

Because employer policies are usually limited to malpractice claims or professional negligence, acts of ordinary negligence or actions by a state board of nursing against a nurse's license are not covered. Nurse's individual malpractice policies increasingly cover some of these areas not covered by employer policies, especially state board actions, and this is one advantage of having an individual policy (see **Part B**). The nurse's individual policy most likely would cover attorney's fees even if the nurse is wrongly accused of misconduct by the state board. Punitive damage awards are usually excluded from coverage, since the purpose of these damages is to punish the wrongdoer.

Most insurance policies give the insurer the right to *settlement* of a claim or lawsuit without the consent of the insured. In some cases if the insurer refuses a reasonable settlement offer, it may be liable for the judgment even if above the policy limits. Sometimes nurses do not want to settle a claim because then they will not be allowed to present their side of the alleged negligent incident. However, the cost of litigation is very high and it is often in the best interest of all parties to settle the claim or lawsuit.

Responsibilities of the Insured

The insured agrees to cooperate with the insurer in processing all claims. (1) The insurer must receive timely notice of any claim against the nurse. In fact, it is best to notify the insurer of any *potential* claim or untoward incident so that if an investigation is required it can be done in a timely manner. (2) The nurse must provide the insurer of any change of address, name, or work status. (3) The insured must pay the premiums when due to ensure continuance of the policy. (4) The nurse must cooperate with the insurer in handling the claim and must be truthful in all dealings.

Rights of the Insured

The insured has the right to have claims processed in a timely and competent manner. The insurer has the duty to defend the claim and provides an attorney who works for the insurance company.

Reasons for Individual Liability Insurance

Many nursing organizations recommend that nurses carry individual professional liability policies to ensure protection of the public, who have the right to recover damages when claims are valid. Nurses are increasingly named in lawsuits as plaintiffs' attorneys seek damages from all who are involved. The doctrine of *respondeat superior*, which makes the institution responsible for the acts of employees, will not automatically relieve named defendants (nurses) when liability is found. In addition, although not often used, the employer can exercise the right to *indemnification* against the nurse, especially if the employer's interest is adverse to the nurse's. Indemnification means that the employer can try to recover the damages it was responsible for on behalf of the employee.

Nurses with individual policies will be provided an attorney representing their interests, not the employer's, and their defense costs will be covered.

Whether or not to have an individual professional liability policy or rely on an employer's policy is an individual decision. Nurses need to consider their employment situation and potential risk of lawsuits, personal financial situation, and professional ethical concerns. When there is overlap in coverage with institutional and individual policies, the insurance companies determine which policy, or whether both policies, will cover. Since individual policies are available at reasonable rates and there are many advantages to having individual coverage, it is prudent to follow this course of action.

11 Refusing an Assignment/ Patient Abandonment

Susan Westrick Killion, JD, MS, RN

Conditions to Allow Refusal of an Assignment

1. Nurse lacks the knowledge or skill to give competent care.
2. Nursing actions outside the scope of the NPA are expected.
3. Health of the nurse (or her fetus) is directly threatened by the nature of the assignment.
4. Nurse has not been oriented properly to the unit and safety is jeopardized.

Steps to Follow When Refusing an Assignment

1. Express specific reasons for refusal to a supervisor.
2. Explore alternatives such as reassignment, buddy system, or sharing tasks with another staff member.
3. Document specifics of the incident in personal notes, including who was notified.
4. Be willing to adhere to properly implemented floating or crosstraining policies.
5. Make sure that other staff are available to care for patient to avoid charge of patient abandonment.

Acceptance of Assignment with Reservation or under Protest

1. Fill out any forms for this purpose.
2. Clearly document the facts of the incident on agency records and personal notes.

Refusing a patient assignment presents a dilemma for the nurse. Many nurses do not want to disrupt patient care or the work environment but in some instances have an ethical and legal duty to refuse an assignment. Abandonment occurs when the nurse refuses to care for the patient and no one else is available to do so; it involves negligence. Avoiding charges of patient abandonment is a prime consideration, and the nurse needs to be on solid ground when circumstances warrant such refusal (see **Figure**).

Legal Framework

Negligence theory provides guidance in terms of professional responsibilities to patients. Nurses have a duty to provide reasonably prudent care to patients in same or similar circumstances. If a nurse refuses a patient assignment, and a later charge of negligence or professional malpractice is brought, the impact of the refusal will be considered. If harm to the patient results, a charge of negligent abandonment may be sustained. Conversely, if a nurse accepts an assignment for which he or she is unprepared and harm results, the same outcome of negligence may be found.

The nurse must also be aware of the scope of practice as defined in the state's NPA when deciding whether to accept or refuse an assignment. If the assignment includes undertaking tasks that are outside its scope, then there is a legal duty to refuse the assignment. Nurses can be subject to disciplinary procedures by the state board of nursing for any violations of the act.

Another pertinent frame of reference is the ANA (American Nurses Association, 1985) *Code for Nurses*, which requires nurses to use informed judgment when deciding to accept a patient assignment or when making assignments to others. Nurses are expected to use individual competence and qualifications in seeking consultation or for accepting responsibilities. They also must provide care to patients regardless of their social or economic status or their health problems. Professional codes of ethics may be used in malpractice cases to help establish the standard of care that should have been followed in a particular situation.

Factors to Consider in Accepting or Refusing an Assignment

1. **Knowledge and skill.** Nurses who are unfamiliar with a particular patient's nursing care needs have an ethical duty not to care for that patient. This is based on concerns for patient safety and the need for all patients to receive competent care. An inexperienced nurse caring for a complex client can jeopardize the patient and consideration should be made to change the assignment or provide support by a more experienced nurse. Any care that involves tasks outside the scope of the NPA should be considered a valid basis for refusal.
2. **Health of the nurse.** According to standards set by the ANA, a nurse is expected to provide care to any patient who needs care when doing so presents no more than a minimal risk to the nurse. For example, a nurse who is pregnant can refuse to care for a patient if doing so poses a direct threat to the fetus. However, when there is no direct threat and the health care worker can be protected through universal precautions, refusal to care for patients (e.g., with AIDS) has not been upheld. In individual cases it could be established that a particular patient is uncooperative and therefore does pose a direct threat to the nurse's safety.
3. **Orientation to unit.** Lack of orientation to a unit can present issues of patient safety. For example, not knowing where emergency equipment is kept can be hazardous and not being familiar with routines of the unit can impact on quality of care and safety.
4. **Availability of other staff.** If another staff member is available to provide care, this may be the best solution. However, if the unit is understaffed, the only alternative may be for the nurse to provide the care to the patient. If problems occur later, the court will likely view the situation in the context of what was reasonable under the circumstances.
5. **Modification of assignment.** It may be possible to share the patient with another nurse or to provide only the part of the care that the nurse is competent to provide. For example, a nurse who is floated to a coronary care unit from a general unit may only be able to handle some nursing interventions, but not the specialized intervention related to assessing cardiac monitors. A buddy system may be another way to share an assignment.

Acceptance of Assignment with Reservation or under Protest

A nurse may need to accept an assignment even though there are valid reasons for not doing so. The nurse may risk being fired or other action by the employer. An important step in this situation is for the nurse to specifically state to the supervisor why the assignment should not be accepted. A statement such as "I have never worked with patients receiving chemotherapy" provides clear information about the basis for refusal. The nurse should document the incident in his or her personal notes, including facts about the conditions of accepting the assignment with reservation, who was notified, and any alternative solutions the nurse offered, such as trading assignments with another staff member.

The nurse needs to put the organization on clear notice of the situation (e.g., understaffing), to shift the liability to the corporation (corporate liability) in case a negligence action is brought later. It is the responsibility of nursing management and the agency or corporation to ensure that adequate numbers of qualified staff are available to care for patients.

Some state nurses' organizations provide a form that can be filled out and filed with the supervisor. The form usually has check-off boxes to indicate the specific basis for refusing the assignment, such as not being oriented. The nurse should keep copies of all written memos or forms submitted to supervisors.

Avoiding Charges of Patient Abandonment

By accepting an unreasonable assignment, the nurse risks responsibility for any negative consequences. Whether this is fair or not is an unsettled question, and the nurse must decide what to do, while weighing the risks and benefits.

In all cases the nurse needs to consider patient abandonment. It is proper to refuse patient assignments for valid reasons, but the nurse must be sure the patient is not abandoned. The nurse cannot refuse an assignment for moral or religious reasons if there is no one else to care for the patient. Doing so is considered patient abandonment and would constitute negligence on the part of the nurse. To prevent potential problems, a nurse should not work in areas where conflicts between personal beliefs and patient care occur frequently.

Crosstraining and Floating

Employers generally have the right to expect nurses to "float" to similar types of units as long as they have proper training and support. The recent trend to crosstrain employees for other jobs reduces the need to refuse assignments due to lack of training or skill. A nurse may risk being fired for unreasonably refusing to float to other units or for severely criticizing an employer's policies for crosstraining. In an era of downsizing, nurses will face issues of refusing or accepting patient assignments on a more frequent basis.

12 Delegation to Unlicensed Assistive Personnel

Susan Westrick Killion, JD, MS, RN

A *Delegation*—transferring to a competent individual the authority to perform a selected nursing task in a selected situation

Accountability—being responsible and answerable for the actions or inactions of self or others in the context of the delegation process

Unlicensed assistive personnel (UAP)—any unlicensed personnel, regardless of title, to whom nursing tasks are delegated (e.g., patient care aides, attendants, or associates; nurse technicians; orderlies; assistants; multitrained or crosstrained personnel; nurse extenders; nurse aides)

Supervision—the provision of guidance or direction, evaluation, and follow-up by a licensed nurse for completion of a nursing task delegated to UAP

B

To delegate	Not to delegate

Knowledge

State statute or NPA	Delegation prohibited by NPA, board
State board rulings	ruling, or other regulatory agency
Institutional policies	Task not in job description of UAP
Job description of UAP	No documented competency for UAP of task

Assessment

Patient's individual needs	Patient's condition requires licensed
Competency of UAP for task	person to complete task
	UAP not competent to perform task

Communication

Clear as to time frame	Unclear, incomplete information
Clear as to immediacy of information needed	
Clear as to prioritization for multiple tasks	

Supervision

Provided for UAP, including instruction	Nurse not able to provide supervision of
Evaluation of patient outcomes by the nurse	UAP or to assess patient outcomes of task

Task can be safely delegated to UAP (each component must be present for delegation to occur) | **Task cannot be safely delegated to UAP (task cannot be delegated if any criterion is present)**

As the licensed caregiver, the nurse is responsible and accountable for the quality of care that patients receive. The nurse may delegate or assign tasks to an unlicensed caregiver, but accountability in terms of outcomes for the patient is retained by the nurse. A UAP is acting *for* the nurse in implementing selected patient care activities but is not acting *in place of* the nurse. The professional judgment and decision-making by the nurse can never be delegated. See the definitions in **Part A**.

Legal Framework for Delegation

The first frame of reference to ensure proper delegation (see **Part B**) is the statute or NPA that defines the scope of practice for nurses in a particular state. These statutes generally follow the model set forth by the ANA, which defines the practice of nursing by a professional nurse as the process of diagnosing human responses to actual or potential health problems, including supportive and restorative care, health counseling and teaching, case finding and referral, and collaborating in the implementation of the total health care regimen. The definition set forth in the statute limits what the nurse can delegate by defining what is nursing practice itself.

Other authoritative references include any state board rulings on the use of UAP and position papers from the National Council of State Boards of Nursing (NCSBN) or the ANA. Although these are not legal references, they have the authority of law and can be viewed as sources for determining the standard within the profession. The standards related to delegation would be reviewed if a case of malpractice against a nurse involved a question of improper delegation.

Guidelines/Situations for Delegation

- Delegable task. The nurse first should determine if the task is properly delegable. For example, giving medications or interpreting clinical data cannot be delegated because these are licensed functions. However, it is generally agreed that routine tasks (e.g., taking vital signs) or personal care activities (e.g., bathing) for stable patients with predictable outcomes can be assigned to UAP.
- Patient's needs. The nurse is responsible for individual patient assessment and determination of nursing care needs. Therefore, even though an intervention such as giving a bath may be routine, the nurse may need to complete this task for certain patients if further assessment or health teaching is needed. The nurse should refuse to delegate any task that would jeopardize patient safety.
- Competency of UAP. Job descriptions for UAP should clearly specify their responsibilities. UAP should have a record of documented competencies to perform tasks and should have participated in a formalized educational program that provided instruction. However, it is the duty of the nurse to ensure that UAP are competent in particular situations (e.g., they may not be able to measure blood pressure properly even though there is documentation that they can). It is the nurse's responsibility to determine ability and provide proper instruction for UAP or complete the task himself or herself. The nurse must provide supervision for UAP and serve as a resource. The sole criterion for determining who should complete a task in a particular situation is patient safety, as determined by the nurse.
- Communication. Clear directions must be given to UAP so that the task can be completed properly. For example, the nurse should not say, "I need a finger stick done on Mr. Jones." A better instruction would indicate the immediate need for a blood glucose measurement and to report the value to the nurse immediately, who will determine if insulin is needed. It is suggested that the nurse obtain "minireports" throughout the shift, to clarify data obtained and to provide any supervision necessary for UAP.
- Evaluation. As part of the nurse's duty to supervise UAP, the nurse is responsible for evaluating their performance. This is an opportunity to provide positive and negative feedback as well as supervised practice of a skill if needed. The ability to set priorities for completion of tasks is an essential skill needed by UAP and often requires guidance by the nurse.

Liability Issues in Delegation

Improper Delegation and Nurse Liability
The nurse can be liable for improper delegation in several circumstances. One example is when a task that should not be delegated (e.g., medication administration) is assigned to UAP. Another example is when the nurse delegates a task to UAP who are not competent to perform the task. While nurses can generally rely on documented competencies of UAP, there may be information that the nurse knows or should have known to indicate UAP are not competent in a particular situation. Another example of improper delegation occurs when the nurse does not provide the required supervision for UAP. The nurse should always be available for questions or further instruction.

Proper Delegation without Nurse Liability
If the nurse has delegated properly, UAP can be individually liable for their actions. One example is when UAP do not inform the nurse of an inability to perform a task or when UAP perform a task incorrectly, even after instruction and supervision. UAP who perform tasks that are beyond those delegated or are outside their competencies are liable for their own actions and for mistakes or adverse patient outcomes as a result of their actions. The liability of UAP is generally shifted to the institution, as the employer.

Staffing Issues
Inadequate staffing is not a rationale for delegating tasks. In such an instance the nurse needs to document his or her refusal to delegate a task as based on concern for patient safety and its effect on patient care. This should be forwarded to a supervisor who has the power to correct the staffing. By taking these steps, the nurse is shifting the liability to the institution for any untoward outcomes resulting from the situation.

Proper Delegation
Proper delegation involves (1) the right task, (2) the right circumstances, (3) the right person, (4) the right direction/communication, and (5) the right supervision. In all situations, the nurse's professional judgment determines what can be delegated safely to UAP.

1. A health care institution markets itself as a comprehensive care center able to coordinate and meet the community's health care needs. A patient goes to the emergency department where the nurses are employees but the physicians are independent contractors. The patient exhibits signs of an impending cerebral vascular accident (CVA) (slurred speech, drooping facial expression, and one-sided weakness) with a congested cough and wheezing. He is discharged with the diagnosis of pneumonia. Which of the following may he bring a civil action against?

(A) The nurses individually for failing to recognize and communicate the symptoms to the physician

(B) The physicians, as independent contractors, for failure to diagnose and treat the CVA

(C) The hospital under corporate liability for the action of the nurses as employees and the physicians as independent contractors

(D) All of the above

2. When incorporating concepts of law and ethics in practice, the nurse must consider that:

(A) Ethical codes do not have the force of law and will not be looked at by courts for guidance

(B) Legal duties are often minimal and ethical codes may require conduct beyond legal accountability

(C) Fulfilling legal duties will prevent any ethical conflicts

(D) Patient's wishes will always supersede ethical or legal codes

3. Which of the following would typically *not* be included in a state's Nurse Practice Act (NPA)?

(A) Scope of practice guidelines

(B) Definition of what constitutes practice outside the scope of nursing (e.g., the practice of medicine)

(C) Definitions of what constitutes unprofessional conduct

(D) Requirements for maintaining licensure

4. In states with mandatory licensure for RNs:

(A) Anyone who works as a nurse for compensation must be registered with the state as an RN

(B) Anyone can work as a nurse for compensation but cannot use the title RN unless registered with the state as an RN

(C) Not only are nurses required to be registered but also they must be certified

(D) A nursing license from a neighboring state would be recognized as valid in the state in which the nurse is practicing

5. A nurse administers potassium chloride to a patient by intravenous (IV) push, although the physician's order reads for it to be given by IV piggyback. The patient has a cardiac arrest and dies. What type of actions might the nurse become involved in as a result of this error?

(A) Criminal action

(B) Civil malpractice action

(C) Administrative law action (disciplinary action)

(D) All of the above

6. The state board of nursing *cannot* take which of the following actions against a nurse?

(A) Suspension of the nurse's license for a period of time

(B) Censure of a nurse

(C) Placing a nurse on probation

(D) Imprisonment

7. The nurse administers pentobarbital to a patient when phenobarbital was ordered. There was no injury to the patient; however, the nursing supervisor reported the incident to the state board of nursing. The nurse is notified of the charges brought against her and a disciplinary hearing is held. What is the role of the state board of nursing?

(A) To protect the public

(B) To uphold standards of nursing practice

(C) To investigate all complaints to determine if disciplinary action is appropriate

(D) All of the above

8. Standards of care are:

(A) The optimal degree of professional skill

(B) Used to show gross negligence and incompetence

(C) Used to determine what is negligent performance

(D) None of the above

9. Professional negligence occurs when a nurse:

(A) Provides nursing care that results in an adverse outcome

(B) Fails to provide the optimal level of nursing care

(C) Fails to respond as a reasonable prudent nurse

(D) Exercises an error in judgment

10. A home care nurse working for a proprietary agency instructed a patient to change his dressing every day and to observe the wound for signs of infection. When the nurse returned 2 weeks later, the original dressing was still in place. The wound showed signs of infection, and the patient required antibiotic therapy. The wound became worse and resulted in tissue damage. In a malpractice action against the nurse 1 year later, the patient claimed negligent supervision of the wound. A defense that would *most likely* be available for the defendant nurse to raise would be:

(A) Assumption of the risk

(B) Comparative or contributory negligence

(C) Charitable immunity

(D) Statute of limitations

11. A home care nurse visits a patient who had surgery 3 weeks ago. As part of the patient's care plan, he was instructed to perform range of motion exercises. However, he has not done so, and it is now 3 weeks later when the nurse visits. The patient is complaining that he is having difficulty walking and continues to have problems with his recovery for several months. If a lawsuit is later filed claiming malpractice against the nurse and physician:

(A) The patient is entitled to a recovery because his informed consent amounted to a contract for services that was not successfully fulfilled.

(B) A defense that could be raised is contributory negligence.

(C) The patient will not recover since he assumed the risks of failure when he signed the surgical consent form.

(D) The nurse cannot be sued because she works for an agency.

12. In most states, the Good Samaritan Act provides immunity from civil liability to:

(A) Volunteers providing emergency medical care when there is no legal duty to assist

(B) Professionals providing emergency medical care in emergency department or acute care settings

(C) Nonmedical volunteers for ordinary negligence and professional medical volunteers for gross (extraordinary) negligence

(D) None of the above

13. When providing care to patients, the nurse increases the risk of liability when:

(A) Not carrying out an incomplete physician's order

(B) Administering predrawn and labeled injections prepared by the pharmacy

(C) Notifying a physician's supervisor when an order may be harmful to a patient

(D) Doing none of the above

14. A nurse is making rounds on the surgical floor when Ms. Clark, who just had a hysterectomy, says, to him, "You people are wretched humans, you get pleasure out of using me as a pin cushion." The nurse should:

(A) Identify her as a difficult patient and resolve to only enter her room when a nursing procedure needs to be done

(B) Defend himself by explaining the necessity of needle sticks for lab procedures and pain medications

(C) Offer her special attention, offer to work with her for a solution, and visit her when no nursing procedure needs to be done

(D) Ask another nurse to switch assignments because he has a personality conflict with the patient and does not want to antagonize her further

15. A nurse is a fact witness in a personal injury lawsuit. The attorney representing the plaintiff asks the nurse a question at a deposition about the plaintiff's injuries, but the nurse isn't sure if the attorney is asking about the state of the plaintiff's injuries on admission or on discharge to her nursing unit. The nurse should:

(A) Give as much information as possible to cover both possibilities

(B) Decide to answer about the state of the injuries upon admission

(C) Ask the attorney to be more specific

(D) Decide to answer about the state of the injuries upon discharge

(E) None of the above

16. A nurse is taking care of a patient who is "pleasantly demented." The patient is always smiling and agreeable to all suggestions but doesn't understand

events as they happen. The patient's family arrives to visit with an attorney and requests that the nurse witness the patient's signing of a deed to her home so that the daughter will own the property for estate planning purposes. The nurse should:

(A) Check with her employer to determine if there is a policy about nurse's witnessing documents

(B) Inform the attorney that the patient, although smiling and agreeable, doesn't understand things as they happen

(C) Refuse to witness the document

(D) Prepare written documentation of the events in the chart as soon as possible

(E) All of the above

17. A malpractice claim is brought against a nurse in the year 2000. The case involves an incident that occurred at a previous job in 1996. The nurse will be covered for this incident:

(A) Only if the nurse is still working for the previous employer (employer's policy will cover)

(B) If he or she was covered by an individual or employer occurrence policy at the time of the incident

(C) If he or she was covered by a claims made policy in 1996

(D) By her new employer's policy as long as it is an occurrence policy

18. The employer's malpractice insurance will cover the nurse's actions if the negligent act is:

(A) Of an extremely reckless nature, such as to endanger a patient through outrageous conduct

(B) Outside the scope of the NPA

(C) Within the employee's job description

(D) One that occurred when the nurse was off duty but constituted performing volunteer nursing duties

19. A nurse is asked to work a double shift on a unit he is unfamiliar with. The nurse should do all of the following except:

(A) Determine whether he can safely provide care for the population of patients

(B) Ask to be oriented to the unit

(C) Request that a nurse who is familiar with the unit work with him

(D) Refuse the patient assignment and file a complaint with the union

20. A nurse caring for several patients becomes ill while on duty and decides she cannot continue to work that day. To avoid a later claim against her for patient abandonment, she should:

(A) Tell her supervisor that she is leaving

(B) Inform both her coworkers and the supervisor that she needs to leave the work area due to illness

(C) Go to a physician to get a note to validate her illness

(D) Not worry about letting anyone know, since her shift will be over in an hour anyhow

21. The nurse is assigned to a group of patients on the evening shift. A UAP is working with the nurse. Which of the following interventions can be assigned to the UAP?

(A) Administer an antibiotic cream to a patient's arm after the UAP gives the patient a bath

(B) Complete a health history and admission assessment on a patient since the patient is not in acute distress

(C) Take vital signs on a patient who has had surgery 4 hours earlier

(D) Monitor and adjust the patient's IV line after the nurse instructs the UAP how to perform this task properly

22. A patient assigned to a nurse fell while in the bathroom. The nurse had instructed the UAP to assist the patient with walking on an as-needed basis. Assuming that the patient should have been assisted and was not, who is legally liable for the patient's fall?

(A) The nurse since he or she is in charge of the UAP

(B) The UAP since direction was given by the nurse

(C) Neither the nurse nor the UAP since each was acting properly

(D) Both the nurse and the UAP could be liable since each had an independent duty to the patient

1. The answer is D.

The nurses and physicians are liable for their part of the malpractice. The hospital is liable under corporate liability for the negligent acts of its employees (vicarious liability) and for the negligent hiring and retention of the negligent independent contractors (the physicians). The hospital will be held liable for any negligent emergency department policy and procedures that were followed in the treatment of this patient if those policies caused the patient's injury.

2. The answer is B.

Ethical codes often go beyond legal requirements, which may only require a minimal standard of conduct. Answer A is incorrect because ethical codes are sometimes viewed by courts as evidence of the standard of care required in certain cases. Answer C is incorrect because ethical conflicts can still exist even if legal duties are implemented. For example, the nurse legally may be required to protect confidential information provided by a patient but know that revealing it to another person may protect him or her. Answer D is incorrect because the law supersedes patients' wishes, and ethical codes may do so in some cases (i.e., suicide).

3. The answer is B.

The state statute or NPA does not define what is outside the scope of practice for nursing. Anything not defined in the statute as nursing is considered outside the scope of practice for nurses. Other practice statutes, such as for physicians, would need to be consulted for specifics as to what constitutes practice as a physician.

4. The answer is A.

Mandatory licensure means that both the title and the functions of the nurse are protected in these states. All states have this type of licensure. Answer B defines a situation of permissive licensure. Answer C speaks to certification, which is a voluntary credential or in some cases may be required for advanced practice. Answer D refers to the idea behind multistate licensure, which has not yet been accepted by all states.

5. The answer is D.

The state might bring negligent homicide charges against the nurse, subjecting the nurse to a criminal proceeding. The patient's family may bring a malpractice claim against the nurse, and the state board may bring disciplinary charges against the nurse.

6. The answer is D.

The state board of nursing does not have the power to imprison a nurse. That can only occur when criminal charges are successful against a nurse, and this would not be handled by the state board but would be adjudicated by a criminal court.

7. The answer is D.

The state board of nursing is empowered by the NPA to administer, establish, and enforce standards of nursing practice.

8. The answer is C.

Standards of care are used as evidence of negligent professional performance. They are not the optimal level of performance nor do they define gross (or reckless) or even incompetent conduct.

9. The answer is C.

Negligence is the failure to meet the definition of the standard of care. An error in nursing judgment or not providing extraordinary care does not necessarily violate the standard of care. Providing the reasonable degree of nursing care does not guarantee that a patient will not experience what is statistically an adverse result.

10. The answer is B.

The defense of either contributory or comparative negligence would most likely be available to the nurse because the patient did not follow the instructions and thus did not act reasonably under the circumstances. He contributed to his own injury, which in some states would bar recovery of damages or in others would limit recovery of damages, assuming there was any negligence found against the nurse. Answer A is incorrect because the patient does not assume the risk of negligent treatment. Answer C is not correct because the agency is not a charitable entity, and this exception has been eliminated in most jurisdictions. Answer D is incorrect because the statute of limitation usually is 2–3 years.

11. The answer is B.

The patient did not perform the exercises that were recommended and thus contributed to his own problems. This contributory negligence can be raised as a defense to any claim of negligence or malpractice. In some states this could be called comparative negligence. Answer A is incorrect because informed consent does not waive a valid claim for negligence and does not become a contract. Answer C is not correct because the patient does not assume the risk of negligence or malpractice. Answer D is incorrect because the nurse can be sued individually, although the agency as the employer would likely be sued as well.

12. The answer is A.

The act applies to all volunteers (medical or nonmedical) to encourage assistance in emergencies when there is no legal duty to assist. B is incorrect because this does not apply to medical personnel when there is a health care provider–patient relationship. When a person comes into the emergency department, there is a patient relationship. C is incorrect because the act provides immunity for ordinary and gross negligence for nonmedical volunteers. Medical volunteers enjoy immunity for ordinary negligence but are held to a higher standard than nonmedical volunteers and are expected to perform without gross negligence under the circumstances. For example, nonmedical volunteers may not be expected to maintain an airway in an unconscious accident victim but medical volunteers would.

13. The answer is B.

Administering any medication drawn up by someone other than the nurse carries an increase in liability. The nurse giving the medication is the last line of defense to prevent negligence when a dose is incorrect. Although pharmacists are a good source for information on medications and doses, they have been known to make up incorrect amounts. Always verify the amount. In this case, call the pharmacy and check whether the amount is correct and consult a reliable drug handbook to determine the doses in which the drug is available. A and C are appropriate actions.

14. The answer is C.

This nurse needs to build a trusting nurse-patient relationship. Offering the patient attentiveness and visits without making her feel like a "pin cushion" may foster the nurse-patient relationship. The nurse should utilize supervisors and more experienced nurses if necessary and make it a team effort. Patients who have a satisfactory relationship with their nurse are less likely to sue should they be injured. A, B, and D will foster a distrustful relationship with the patient.

15. The answer is C.

The nurse should not answer a question she doesn't fully understand or one that is unclear. To do so presents inaccurate information. If she is asked the same or similar question at the trial but gives a different answer because she was confused at the deposition, her credibility will be diminished. It will appear as though she's changing her answers and is an unreliable witness. A, B, and D are incorrect for the same reasons.

16. The answer is E.

A, B, C, and D are all appropriate actions for the nurse to take. The nurse should check with his or her employer to see if the nurse will violate policy if he or she agrees to witness signing of the document. Because the nurse knows the patient and her condition, the nurse should tell the attorney that although the patient appears to agree and understand, her condition makes that very unlikely. Because the nurse cannot in good faith believe the patient has the capacity to understand the nature and effect of signing the deed, the nurse should not bear witness to the signing. Written documentation should be completed as close to the time of the events as possible, to accurately record them.

17. The answer is B.

The nurse will be covered for this incident if there is current coverage by his or her own occurrence policy. This type of policy covers back to when the incident occurred. Answer C is incorrect because the claim must be made when the claims made insurance policy is in effect. Answer A is incorrect because the nurse does not have to be presently working for the employer for the insurance to cover. Answer D is incorrect because a new employer's policy will not cover incidents from a previous job.

18. The answer is C.

The nurse's actions generally are covered if they fall within the nurse's job description and scope of duties. Answer A is incorrect because these actions are so extreme that the policy does not cover them. When acting in such an extremely dangerous manner, the employee is deemed to be acting on his or her own behalf and not that of the employer. Answer B is incorrect because acts covered for malpractice must be within the scope of the NPA, since the contract is covering for nursing actions. Answer D is incorrect because volunteer acts are not covered by the employer unless specifically stated.

19. The answer is D.

The nurse would risk being fired for insubordination for refusing the assignment and filing a complaint without more of a basis to do so. A nurse refusing an assignment needs to be on solid ground for doing so. Along with being familiar with the terms of employment on this issue, the nurse needs to have a reasonable basis for refusal. Answers A, B, and C list valid assessments and steps to take before deciding whether to accept the assignment. If these are not in place, the nurse could refuse the assignment. In no case should the nurse accept the assignment if the criterion in A is not met (i.e., nurse must be able to safely care for the patients).

20. **The answer is B.**

The nurse needs to inform both the supervisor and her coworkers of the situation so that adequate coverage for her patients will be provided. Answer A is not adequate because unless coworkers know of the situation, patients can be placed at risk. There was an action against a nurse by a state board of nursing for patient abandonment based on these facts. The nurse stated that she felt "so horrible" that she left without informing her coworkers, but she had informed her supervisor. This was not enough to avoid the charge of patient abandonment since she did not ensure coverage of her patients by coworkers. Answer C is not correct since validating the illness is not the issue. Answer D is not correct because she is placing patients at risk even though it may be only a short time until the next shift.

21. **The answer is C.**

A UAP generally can be assigned routine tasks on a stable patient. The answer does not indicate that the patient has any special needs requiring nursing intervention. Answer A is incorrect because the UAP cannot administer medications. Answers B and D include actions that require nursing judgment and decision-making, so they cannot be delegated to the UAP.

22. **The answer is D.**

Both the nurse and the UAP have independent duties to the patient to carry out care interventions. The nurse does remain accountable for the outcome of the intervention (i.e., the patient's fall), but the UAP could also be liable for not following proper instructions. If the UAP was trained to assist such patients and did not carry out the proper intervention, then the UAP would also be liable. It is also possible that the nurse's directions may not have been clear to the UAP, and the nurse could be liable for the improper delegation. The nurse is not automatically liable for all the UAP's actions. The particular facts and circumstances of the fall and the delegation to the UAP would need to be considered.

PART II
Liability in Patient Care

13 Patients' Rights and Responsibilities

Cynthia Keenan, JD, BA, RN

A   Nurse's Role in Protecting the Rights of Patients
- To provide services with respect for human dignity and the uniqueness of the patient unrestricted by considerations of social or economic status, personal attributes, or the nature of health problems
- To safegaurd the patient's right to privacy by judiciously protecting information of a confidential nature
- To safegaurd the patient and the public when health care and safety sre affected by the incompetent, unethical, or illegal practice of any person
- To educate and inform the patient of his or her rights and to help facilitate maintenance and adherence to those rights

B   Patients' Rights per Code for Nurses with Interpretive Statements
- To determine what will be done with their own person
- To be given accurate information, and all the information necessary for making informed judgements
- To be assisted with weighing the benefits and burdens of options in their treatment
- To accept, refuse, or terminate treatment without coercion
- To be given necessary emotional support

C   Patients' Rights per American Hospital Association
- To know the name of the physician or person responsible for their care
- To refuse treatment
- To expect a reasonable response, within the capacity of the hospital, to the patient's requests
- To be advised of any plan of human experimentation
- To expect a reasonable continuity of care while hospitalized and upon discharge
- To examine and receive an explanation of services charged regardless of source of payment
- To know the rules and regulations of the hospital that apply to their conduct as a patient

Over the years, several organizations have enumerated various patients' rights, the most prominent of which have come from the ANA, American Hospital Association (AHA), and the American Medical Association. For a nurse to fully implement the professional and moral obligations to patients, a knowledge of patients' moral and legal rights is necessary. Without this knowledge, the nurse cannot successfully fulfill the mandate of the code, which is to protect and support those rights.

Sources of Patients' Rights

Since the 1970s, society and the legal system have worked to provide the basis for what we now know as patients' rights. Beginning with the right to informed consent, other important issues evolved: the right to privacy (Roe v Wade) and the right to refuse medical treatment (Karen Ann Quinlan case) are 2 of the more renowned and established rights.

The Patient Self-determination Act (PSDA) of 1990 also provided the legal means by which patients could, by law, obtain more control over their health care, treatment, and decisions pertaining to both. The act requires all providers receiving Medicaid funds to provide individuals with written information regarding their rights to make decisions about their medical care. Medical providers are also required to inform patients about their rights to establish advance directives at the time of admission.

In addition, in 1997, the Advisory Commission on Consumer Protection and Quality in Health Care Industry, issued a proposal for a national bill of patients' rights. Four categories were enumerated: the right to make medical decisions based on full information, the right to confidentiality, the right to emergency care, and the right to be treated with respect.

The Nurse's Role and Duty in Protecting Patients' Rights

The *Code for Nurses with Interpretative Statements* sets forth the nurse's moral and professional obligation to patients, based on a value belief system (see **Part A**). The nurse needs to take into account the inherent rights of patients. The nurse has a responsibility to protect the patient's ability to manage his or her own health care and treatment. This philosophy of self-determination fosters and supports the patient's need for autonomy to the greatest extent possible. The ANA *Code for Nurses* requires that nurses treat and provide services to their patients with respect for the human dignity and uniqueness of each one, by recognizing each patient's rights.

In conjunction with the mandate to protect and facilitate the delivery of medical care based on these rights, the nurse also has an obligation to the health profession to see that the patient is not acting in a manner that would thwart treatment or exacerbate a medical condition.

Patients' Rights—Nurse's *Code of Ethics* with *Interpretative Statements*

ANA supports the patient's right to self-determination. In its *Code for Nurses with Interpretative Statements,* the ANA incorporates the rights of patients into its mandate that requires a respect for human dignity and the uniqueness of each patient without prejudice. (See **Part B**).

Patients' Rights—American Hospital Association

In response to the legal precedent regarding the right to informed consent and privacy, the AHA has set forth a patients' bill of rights. In doing so, the AHA recognizes the potential that implementing such rights has for greater satisfaction of care between the patient and providers, which will inherently increase and promote healing. Although these rights specifically note the hospital's responsibility in adhering to them, by virtue of nurses' employment within the hospital environment, their knowledge of these rights is essential in order to fully implement their ethical duty as set forth in the code.

Consistent with the ANA code, the AHA bill of rights refers to the manner of care, right of privacy, and right to be informed of any and all treatment options, and alternatives. In addition, the AHA sets forth patients' rights (see **Part C**). Clearly, although all of these rights do not directly relate to hands-on patient care, they most certainly apply to the overall care patients receive from nurses. For example, in order for patients to receive reasonable continuity of care, they need to know where they are to go and when and what physician they will be seeing. This should follow through for discharge planning as well.

If patients are not aware of their right to refuse treatment, they may silently submit to a procedure or treatment plan that they do not entirely understand or feel comfortable undergoing. It is the nurse's obligation to ensure that patients have received enough information to understand the need for the procedure, the mechanics of the procedure itself, and the outcome if in fact the procedure is not informed. Without this information, patients' rights are violated, and the nurse has abandoned the moral obligation under the code.

Patients' Responsibilities—American Medical Association

In order for a mutually respectful relationship between medical provider and patient to function optimally, both parties need to take responsibility to work toward a common goal: the attainment and maintenance of the patient's good health. In spite of the fact that patients have legally protected rights by virtue of their role as patients, they also have responsibilities to themselves and their medical providers. The American Medical Association has incorporated into its guidelines criteria for patients' responsibilities. The nurse whose duty is to protect and preserve the patient's health cannot do so without the spirit of cooperation.

14 Confidential Communication– Part I
Susan Westrick Killion, JD, MS, RN

A Disclosure Permitted

- With consent by patient, may be a signed waiver

- When information is necessary for other caregivers to care for patient

- If statutes require disclosure, e.g., child abuse reporting law

- If common law right exists to protect the public interest, e.g., safety of blood supply

- If duty to warn an identifiable victim in great danger warrants disclosure

- If court proceedings require disclosure

B Disclosure Not Permitted

- When nurse-patient communication is protected under a privileged communication statute or common law

- To relatives, spouse, or friends unless consent given by patient

- When information is requested by unidentified caller

C Consequences of Disclosure Without Permission

- Exposure to civil suits for breach of confidentiality or invasion of privacy

- Disciplinary action by state board of nursing

- Job loss since employer would have cause for discharge

Confidential communication involves any information a nurse obtains about a patient in the context of the nurse-patient relationship. When patients seek health care, they have a legitimate expectation that information about them will be kept confidential. By ensuring confidentiality, health care workers promote the desirable policy of full disclosure of information by patients. This full disclosure is necessary to treat patients adequately. Maintaining confidentiality of information also protects health care workers from legal and ethical challenges to unauthorized release of information.

Legal and Ethical Framework

Professional codes of ethics for nurses provide the ethical basis to keep patient confidences. Explicit language in the ANA *Code for Nurses* prohibits such disclosure. Privacy rights are grounded in the U.S. Constitution and have been made explicit in many federal and state statutes. Various patients' bills of rights speak to the issue of confidentiality of patient information. Standards set by the Joint Commission on Accreditation of Healthcare Organizations (JCAHO) and agency policies and standards all contain expectations of maintaining patient privacy. In addition, patients are protected from breach of confidentiality and assurance to the right of privacy under tort or negligence law.

Disclosure Permitted

There are several exceptions to the general rule of nondisclosure of confidential information (see **Part A**):

- *Patient permission to release information.* The patient may give verbal or written permission to release information. The written waiver states that the patient waives the right to keep the information confidential but should be specific as to what information can be released and to whom. Agencies usually have printed forms to be used, and a copy should always be placed in the patient's health care record.
- *Other health care workers or agencies.* Relevant information can be shared with other caregivers or agencies who have a legitimate right to know the information. Caution should be exercised in disclosing only the information necessary for care.
- *Statutory or other legal duty to report.* Some types of information are required to be reported to public health agencies or other authoritative bodies (e.g., a statutory duty to report gunshot wounds or suspected child or elder abuse and mandatory reporting of some communicable diseases). In-

formation can be released to insurers or other agencies such as workers' compensation boards after claims are filed. If there is any question as to disclosure, the nurse should check agency policies or with a supervisor before any information is released.

- *Common law or public interest.* There have been extreme situations where the court has supported release of confidential patient information when it is in the public interest or is required for the safety of other patients (e.g., disclosing names of blood donors when the safety of the blood supply has been endangered). In other cases, regulations or laws permit disclosure of contagious diseases when a contact person's health is in danger. Nurses need to exercise caution in using this exception and be aware of specific exceptions permitted for the patient's situation; e.g., one cannot assume that a spouse has an automatic right to know information about his or her spouse. Even though patients should be encouraged to reveal information that puts others at risk, they may have a right to withhold sensitive information (e.g., about sexually transmitted diseases). This situation presents an ethical dilemma for the nurse, and the physician or supervisor may need to be consulted. The common law has protected at-risk individuals when their direct safety is threatened.
- *Duty to warn.* In some very narrow circumstances nurses may have a professional duty to disclose confidential information to protect an identifiable victim. Nurses should document repeated serious threats against another, but their duty could extend beyond documentation. They may have a legal and ethical duty either to report this to appropriate authorities or in some exceptional cases, to warn the intended victim.

15 Confidential Communication–Part II

Susan Westrick Killion, JD, MS, RN

A   Disclosure Permitted

- With consent by patient, may be a signed waiver

- When information is necessary for other caregivers to care for patient

- If statutes require disclosure, e.g., child abuse reporting law

- If common law right exists to protect the public interest, e.g., safety of blood supply

- If duty to warn an identifiable victim in great danger warrants disclosure

- If court proceedings require disclosure

B   Disclosure Not Permitted

- When nurse-patient communication is protected under a privileged communication statute or common law

- To relatives, spouse, or friends unless consent given by patient

- When information is requested by unidentified caller

C   Consequences of Disclosure Without Permission

- Exposure to civil suits for breach of confidentiality or invasion of privacy

- Disciplinary action by state board of nursing

- Job loss since employer would have cause for discharge

Disclosure Not Permitted (see Part B)

- **Privileged communication.** Some jurisdictions have statutes that provide patients the right of privileged communication with certain health care workers, which sometimes includes nurses. Confidential information learned in the context of the nurse-patient relationship may be protected against disclosure in legal proceedings. This legal privilege belongs to the patient and usually is exercised if the patient has the expectation of privacy in the circumstances. Since not all jurisdictions include nurses in the group of confidential caregivers, one needs to follow specific state statutes where the nurse is practicing; an attorney will advise the nurse regarding this should the situation arise. The information does not necessarily refer to just medical information but could be anything revealed during care, even criminal activity or dishonesty.

- **Release to relatives or friends, or in telephone conversations.** The nurse needs to follow the general rule of nondisclosure of confidential information in almost all situations. Only general information about the patient's condition can be given out. Information should not be released to relatives, spouses, visitors, or others without explicit permission from the patient. One should not inadvertently tell another patient in the room of another patient's diagnosis. As a general rule no information should be given out over the telephone as the nurse does not know to whom he or she is talking. The nurse should tell the caller to contact the patient's family directly.

Consequences of Disclosure of Confidential Information (see Part C)

- *Exposure to civil suits.* For unauthorized release of information, a nurse may be held liable to a patient in a tort action for breach of confidentiality. A *tort* is a civil wrong resulting from breach of a legal duty to another that may be intentional or negligent (nonintentional). The nurse's employer may also be held vicariously liable or liable under a theory of corporate liability.

    Another tort that can be the basis of liability is *invasion of privacy*. This tort protects persons from public disclosure of private facts and has been the basis for liability for release of medical information. Disclosure of an especially sensitive medical fact (e.g., a diagnosis of AIDS) could lead to an award of punitive damages against the defendant. This tort can include publication of photographs of the patient released without his or her permission.

- *Disciplinary action by the state board of nursing.* Violation of ethical codes or negligence in performing ordinary duties can be the basis of a disciplinary proceeding against a nurse. It is well-recognized that patient information should be kept confidential and there is an expectation of privacy in nurse-patient interactions.

- *Job loss.* A nurse could be discharged from his or her job as a result of a proven breach of confidentiality related to the care of patients.

Confidentiality in an Era of Information Technology

Caregivers need to be especially vigilant to protect patients' privacy and confidentiality rights in an era of expanded information technology. If it is necessary to send patient information by facsimile (FAX) to another caregiver or agency, the cover sheet, and each page should be stamped "Confidential." This shifts the burden to the receiver to maintain the fax communication as confidential.

Many institutions have computers in the hallways for the convenience of staff. The nurse needs to be careful that while documenting care, private patient data is not visible to passersby. Patient care lists on clipboards and notebooks should not be left carelessly in patient rooms or within view of others. Nurses need to be constantly watchful for unintended disclosure of private information in all areas of practice.

16 Competency and Guardianship

Susan Westrick Killion, JD, MS, RN

A

Competency (sometimes used interchangeably with capacity) — able to understand the consequences of decisions and make judgments based on rational understanding; not judged to be incompetent by a court of law

Legal incompetence — lacking the capacity to make rational decisions, as declared by a court of law (usually state probate court) through formal proceedings

Guardian (or conservator) — a person who acquires legal responsibility for another (the ward) through the legal process of guardianship; exception: parents considered to be the natural guardians of their minor children, and no court proceedings required

Guardian ad litem — an impartial person appointed by the court to assure that the rights of the incompetent individual are protected during a legal proceeding; a guardian for the purpose of litigation

---

B   Guardianship Process

Presumption of competency
↓
Behavior indicates lack of decision-making capacity
↓
Petition filed with probate court to determine competency
↓
Appointments
• Guardian ad litem
• Legal counsel
• Medical/psychological testing
↓
Hearing: evidence presented about person's ability to handle affairs and to understand consequences of decisions
↓
Negotiation: for less-restrictive alternative, e.g., appointing a power of attorney

C   Outcomes of Hearing
→ Petition dismissed
→ Limited guardianship
→ Plenary (complete) guardianship
→ Outcome appealed
→ Restoration hearing held later if circumstances change (removes guardianship)

D   Practice Pointers
• Make notation in the chart if patient has a guardian.
• Work with guardian in the best interest of the patient.
• Report any conflicts or abuse of power by the guardian to proper authorities.

Any nursing care must be consented to, and in order to give the requisite consent, a person must be competent. Most patients give verbal or implied consent when the nurse implements usual patient care activities. However, there are situations when the patient is temporarily incapacitated to give consent (e.g., an illness creating a loss of consciousness or dementia). In these situations consent is often presumed, unless there is evidence (e.g., an advance directive) that a patient would not want the type of care he or she is receiving. In other situations there is a legal determination that a person is incompetent and a guardian is appointed to act for that individual. See the definitions in **Part A**.

Presumption of Competence

In all states, adults >18 years old are presumed to be competent to make decisions about their medical care. This overriding presumption of competency serves to guide interactions with patients in health care settings but can be overcome by presenting proof to the court that the person lacks the capacity to make decisions. Those who are questioning the competency of the individual have the burden to present clear and convincing proof that the person lacks this capacity.

Determining Competency

For patients who temporarily lack a decision-making capacity (e.g., heavily sedated or with a high fever), it is proper to render usual nursing care. However, if the patient might not want the particular care or the family questions the care given to the patient, it is best to document this objectively in the health care record and bring it to the attention of the physician. An example is when a patient is receiving chemotherapy, but the family does not agree. When a patient is temporarily or permanently incapacitated, the court may appoint a temporary guardian to help determine what is best for the patient. Nurses should use caution when there is a potential conflict between the family members and the patient's best interest. Nurses have a duty to act in the best interest of the patient and to fulfill their role as a patient advocate.

Guardianship Process/Determination of Competency

The determination of a patient's competence centers on the person's decision-making capacity and not merely on his or her medical diagnosis. **Part B** outlines the guardianship process and **Part C** shows the possible outcomes of the hearing.

If incapacity is determined, a guardian is appointed. The guardian is often a family member, but if none is available, the court may appoint a close friend or an impartial individual. The court determines the type of guardianship, plenary or limited. If plenary (or complete) guardianship is awarded, the guardian has control over all the individual's (now referred to as a *ward*) affairs. A limited guardianship is less restrictive and may be applied only to the individual's financial affairs or medical decisions. The court could also appoint a temporary guardian for a period of emergency or sudden or prolonged illness.

For all patients with guardians, clear notations on the health care record should identify the type of guardianship, name of the legal guardian for the patient, and how to reach the guardian by phone or mail, as this person can give consent for all medical and health care issues. The guardian continues the role until the ward is not incapacitated, perhaps for the rest of the ward's life. A hearing can be held to petition to remove the guardianship if circumstances warrant a change.

Guardianship proceedings are *not* initiated lightly, and one is not appointed unless a real need is determined by clear and convincing evidence; serious consequences result from a determination of incompetency. It intrudes on a person's autonomy and diminishes his or her privacy. The goal of guardianship is to protect the individual and protect his or her assets. However, the guardian could potentially abuse the responsibility. If the nurse observes abuse of the situation, the nurse cannot ignore his or her role as a patient advocate (see **Part D**).

Situations Where Guardians May Be Present

- Minors. Parents are the natural guardians of children <18 years old. If the parents are divorced, the custodial parent is the legal guardian unless the court determines otherwise. Some minors are considered emancipated if they are married or living apart from their parents and may be able to make their own decisions.
- Elders. Elder patients frequently have guardians. These elders may be in extended care facilities or in the home. Concerns about an elder's decision-making capacity should be brought to the attention of either family members or agency personnel such as supervisors or social workers. The nurse should document objectively on the patient's record the assessment data important to this concern and what referrals were made. If an abusive situation is involved, proper authorities, such as elder protection services, need to be notified.
- Psychiatric patients. Because a patient has a psychiatric illness or is involuntarily committed to a psychiatric facility does not mean the person lacks decision-making capacity. These patients can still refuse treatment and make their own decisions unless certain circumstances arise. The question for the court becomes one of whether the person is capable of understanding refusal or consent to a procedure and the consequences of that decision.
- End-of-life decisions. Although the court may appoint a guardian for a person who is unable to make end-of-life decisions, it is increasingly common for persons to execute written documents called advance directives that delegate to others this responsibility: a durable power of attorney, which delegates to a named person the authority to make certain decisions if the patient later becomes incompetent; a durable power of attorney for health care, which would apply only to health care decisions as determined by state statutes; and a living will, which allows the patient's wishes to be carried out, usually in situations of terminal illness or vegetative state. Other times the court may direct a guardian to use substituted judgment in the best interest of the ward, consistent with the ward's values and preferences.

Implementing Procedures Related to Competency and Guardianship

In all cases the nurse acts in the best interest of the patient and is aware of the duty to work with any guardian on the patient's behalf. If a health care provider encounters a patient who lacks decision-making capacity and there has been no legal determination, guidance should be sought through policies and procedures in the agency. If these are lacking, a supervisor or administrator should be notified for direction. Some state statutes indicate who would give consent in these situations, and agency policies need to be consistent with them.

17 Informed Consent-Part I

Katherine McCormack Dempski, JD, BSN, RN

Informed Consent	
Information:	description of procedure risks and benefits of procedure reasonable alternatives and their risks and benefits
How much information:	material risks and benefits reasonable person would want to know before undergoing or refusing procedure (majority view) or material risks and benefits reasonable physician would consider (minority view)
Assessment of patient competence:	communicates understanding of procedures and information given

Historically, lack of consent to medical treatment entitled a patient to sue for battery. *Battery* is the unlawful or unauthorized touching of another. Informed consent is now recognized as a professional standard of conduct, and negligence is the basis for liability.

Elements of Informed Consent

A patient gives informed consent when 3 elements are met:

1. Information. The patient should be informed of the risks and benefits associated with the treatment,

the risks and benefits involved in refusing treatment (including that refusing a procedure does not mean that all other medical care will be withdrawn), the probability of a successful outcome, alternatives to the procedure, and the credentials of the one performing the procedure. It would be difficult to make the patient aware of every conceivable risk and benefit to a procedure or treatment. Therefore, the patient should be informed of all the "material risks and benefits" of the procedure a reasonable person would want to know when deciding to undergo or refuse the treatment.

2. Voluntary consent. For consent to be voluntary, the patient must not be under any influence or coercion. Nurses are often responsible for administering medications prior to procedures and should verify that informed consent was obtained before medicating, as a sedated patient cannot give voluntary consent (and may lack the competence to do so).

   A patient's voluntary consent to treatment can be expressed either in writing (by a signature) or verbally (and documented by the person obtaining the consent). Voluntary consent also can be implied by a patient's actions, e.g., when a person holds up an arm for a needle stick. On the other hand, silence by a person does not constitute consent to treatment in a situation where a reasonable person would speak up before receiving the treatment.

3. Competence. A patient must be competent to give consent to a medical provider. Competent patients can communicate choices, understand relevant information concerning treatment, and appreciate the situation as it applies to them. A nurse can assess a patient's ability to communicate choices by asking the patient to respond to the information given on the procedure. As the patient responds, the nurse may assess any defects in the patient's attention span or memory that may detract from the ability to make an informed decision. The whole process may simply have overwhelmed the patient, but this would need to be addressed also.

Obtaining Consent

The physician performing the medical or surgical procedure is responsible for obtaining informed consent (see **Part A**). Advanced-practice nurses are responsible for obtaining informed consent prior to performing any risky or invasive procedure that falls within their scope of practice. The patient's consent is usually evidenced by the patient's signature on a consent form. Individual state statutes may require that consent be in writing. Agency policies should reflect any specific state requirements, and anyone responsible with obtaining informed consent must be aware of these requirements.

Nurses at the bedside are responsible for explaining all nursing procedures to the patient. The patient's consent is implied when the procedure is explained and the patient allows the nurse to begin nursing care. Procedures that are not invasive or risky do not require informed consent. Of course, what is risky and invasive needs to be defined and the nurse should be aware of the agency's policy on informed consent.

A nurse should never be delegated the responsibility of obtaining informed consent for a medical or surgical procedure being performed by a physician. Even when the nurse is aware of the risks involved in a medical procedure, the nurse may not be aware of the risks specific to that patient or know the exact procedure the physician has planned. The nurse who obtains informed consent under these conditions runs the risks of misleading the patient and all the legal liability that follows.

Witnessing Consent

The nurse's role in the informed-consent process usually involves witnessing the consent, i.e., observing the patient consent to the procedure by signing the consent form. In some cases a court may ask the witnessing nurse to identify the signature or explain the circumstance under which the consent was obtained, or ask the nurse if the consent was given voluntarily.

Witnessing consent at the bedside often means that the patient will ask the nurse some questions regarding the procedure or outcomes. The nurse should answer questions regarding the nursing care involved in the procedure. Questions regarding medical care should be referred to the physician so that the nurse does not mislead the patient. The nurse should document the patient's concerns and how it was addressed.

Lack of Consent: The Nurse's Responsibility

The nurse should always notify the physician prior to a procedure if a consent form is not in the medical record. Nurses may be liable for professional negligence or battery when they know or should have known (by checking the medical record) that a physician did not obtain informed consent and the nurse did nothing about it. The nurse would be expected to follow the agency policy for this situation, including notifying the physician involved and the nurse's supervisor. The physician's supervisor may need to be notified as well.

Informed Consent–Part II

Katherine McCormack Dempski, JD, BSN, RN

Exceptions to Informed Consent

Emergency	1. Patient unable to consent 2. Serious bodily injury or death may result 3. No one available with legal authority to consent 4. Reasonable person would consent 5. No known reason why this specific patient would refuse (e.g., Jehovah Witness)
Therapeutic privilege	Medical reason to withhold process from patient (very specific criteria, check agency policy)
Patient waiver	Personal choice to not know medical risks and benefits

---

Minors

In most states, 18 years is the age of majority. The general rule is that a parent or legal guardian must give consent for medical treatment of a minor. However, there are statutory exceptions to this. Many states allow minors to consent to medical testing and treatment of sexually transmitted diseases, human immunodeficiency virus (HIV) infection, mental health, substance abuse, and pregnancy. Emancipated minors may also consent to their own medical treatment. The American Academy of Pediatricians recommend that competent children over 13 be part of the consent process.

Emergency Exception to Informed Consent

Health care providers have implied consent to render medical care in an emergency. The 5 requirements for this emergency exception to apply are:

(1) the health care provider must reasonably believe that delay in treatment waiting for the patient's consent would result in serious bodily injury or death;
(2) the patient is unconscious or otherwise incapable of giving consent;
(3) no one available has the legal authority to act as the patient's guardian, agent, or the next of kin;
(4) a reasonable person would consent under the circumstances; and
(5) the health care provider has no reason to believe that this particular patient would refuse treatment. For example, the health care provider may have to reconsider a blood transfusion if it were known that the patient has certain religious beliefs against such treatment even in an emergency situation.

Incompetent Patients

Incapacity to consent may come from a temporary condition such as sedation or unconsciousness or be more long term such as a mental illness. A patient's incompetence to consent to a medical procedure must be determined by a physician according to the health care agency's bylaws and applicable state law. Consent to treat incompetent patients must come from someone with legal authority to do so. This can be the next of kin in an emergency. Each state designates the order of authority for the next of kin (e.g., parents may consent for an unmarried adult child, a spouse may consent for a spouse).

Limitations to Informed Consent

Informed consent is not unlimited, and health care providers can be liable for extending consent to further treatment not explained and consented to by the patient. During a surgical procedure the surgeon would be expected to treat any emergency situation that arose unless the patient informs the surgeon otherwise. The best informed consent covers an emergency situation without being overly broad and thus not valid.

Special Informed Consent

Many states now have HIV statutes that require a health care provider to give specific information to the patient when obtaining informed consent such as counseling and confidentiality. Specific documentation is required, therefore health care providers must be aware of these state statutes.

Specific federal laws outline informed consent requirements in experimental treatments. It is a detailed consent form and the patient must be allowed to withdraw from the experiment at any time.

Religion

Competent adults may refuse medical treatment (even life saving treatment) for religious reasons without medical or legal interference. Courts may become involved (by appointing a temporary legal guardian for healthcare decisions) when a minor may suffer serious bodily harm or death.

Refusal of Treatment

Susan B. Ramsey, JD, BSN

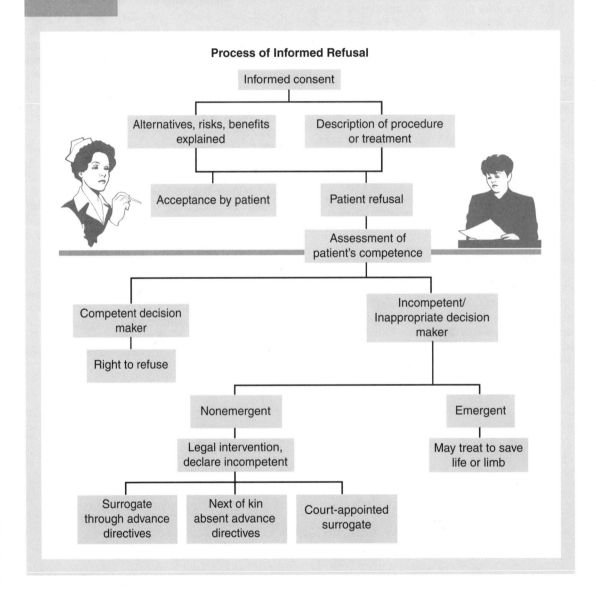

Process of Informed Refusal

Informed consent

Alternatives, risks, benefits explained

Description of procedure or treatment

Acceptance by patient

Patient refusal

Assessment of patient's competence

Competent decision maker

Right to refuse

Incompetent/ Inappropriate decision maker

Nonemergent

Legal intervention, declare incompetent

Emergent

May treat to save life or limb

Surrogate through advance directives

Next of kin absent advance directives

Court-appointed surrogate

Nurses and patients often misunderstand a patient's legal decision-making power. Patients have control over what is done to their bodies and minds as long as they have not been judged incompetent. A person is presumed competent until proved otherwise. However, nurses must be aware that even though a patient has the right to refuse medical care, this refusal must be an "informed refusal." Often the nurse bears the burden of ensuring the patient has received the appropriate teaching.

Right to Refuse Treatment——Generally

In 1990, the U.S. Supreme Court, in the case of *Cruzan v Director, Missouri Department of Health*, recognized that individuals have a constitutionally protected liberty interest in refusing unwanted medical treatment.

Patient Self-Determination Act

As a result of the *Cruzan* case, Congress passed the federal PSDA of 1990. This law mandated that every hospital, nursing home, health care agency, and health maintenance organization (HMO) receiving Medicare and Medicaid funds must provide adult patients with a statement of rights under state statutory law to make health choices, including the right to refuse treatment and to execute an advance directive.

Patients' Bill of Rights

Following the enactment of the PSDA, individual states (if they had not already done so) created or modified their own patients' bill of rights. Nurses should review the pertinent bill of rights available at the health care institution or by state law.

Informed Consent

Informed consent is the process by which a fully informed patient participates in choices about his or her health care. The essential parts of this decision-making process include discussions about (1) the nature of the medical decision or procedure; (2) reasonable alternatives to the recommended intervention; (3) the relevant risks, benefits, and uncertainties related to each alternative; (4) assessment of patient understanding; and (5) the acceptance of the intervention by the patient (see **Figure**).

For the consent (or refusal) to be valid, the patient must be competent to make the decision and the consent (or refusal) must be voluntary. It is important that the patient understand the health care provider's reasoning process for the recommendation. The discussions should be carried out in lay terms.

Assessment of Patient's Competence

In most cases, it is clear whether a patient is able to comprehend the information and is therefore considered competent. However, in some situations, it is not so clear. Patients in a health care setting are often extremely anxious and fearful. This should not be confused with a person's ability to make reasonable decisions. There are a number of different legal standards in which a person's legal competence could be judged. However, generally an assessment should be made of the patient's ability to (1) understand the situation (i.e., does the patient know where he or she is and why he or she is in the hospital); (2) understand the risks associated with the procedure; and (3) communicate a decision based on that understanding.

When a patient's competence is unclear, a psychiatric consultation may be helpful. Again, just because a patient refuses treatment does not in and of itself mean the patient is incompetent. Treatment refusal may be a sign that the health care provider should pursue further the patient's beliefs and understanding about the decision, as well as his or her own.

If the patient is demonstrated to be incapacitated or incompetent to make health care decisions, a surrogate decision-maker must speak for the patient. Specific procedures defined by each state's law must be followed to appoint a surrogate decision-maker. If no appropriate decision-maker is available, the physician should act in the best interest of the patient until a decision-maker is located or appointed. With respect to minors, the decision-maker is presumed to be the parent or guardian. The protocol or procedure in obtaining informed consent for a child should follow the direction of obtaining consent from an adult. However, there are instances in which the health care provider may act against the parents' choice and act in what may be considered in the best interest of the child.

Informed Refusal

Although the patient has the right to refuse medical treatment, the nurse's duty to the patient does not end at documenting "patient refuses." The nurse has a legal duty to ensure that the patient's decision to refuse treatment is an informed one. Patient teaching on the risks of refusing treatment is an essential element to the patient's right to refuse. A nurse who documents in the medical record "patient refuses treatment" has not completed the duty owed to the patient. Documentation must reflect the teaching presented to the patient and that the patient refuses with an understanding of the risks.

In *Hackathorn v Lester Cox Memorial Center,* a nurse was liable to a patient for the burns received from a heating pad despite the nurse's attempts to assess his back. The patient was admitted for a herniated disk. The nurse documented that she asked the patient to "roll over" so she could assess his back for heating pad burns. He refused several times. When the pad was removed, he had several serious burns requiring treatment, and it caused a delay in surgery for the herniated disk. The nurse claimed contributory negligence by the patient for his own injuries (based on his refusing the nursing assessment). The court found that the nurse did not complete her duty by informing the patient of the risk of heating pad burns and the need for periodic assessment. Furthermore, the nurse could not prove (through documentation) that the patient was even capable of rolling over for a back assessment upon her request. Therefore, the patient's refusal was not "informed" and did not contribute to his own injuries. The nurse should have documented that the patient was educated on the benefits of complying and was physically capable of complying with the nurse's request yet refused with knowledge of the risks for burns.

20 Pain Control

Barbara Dunham, JD, RN and
Katherine McCormack Dempski, JD, BSN, RN

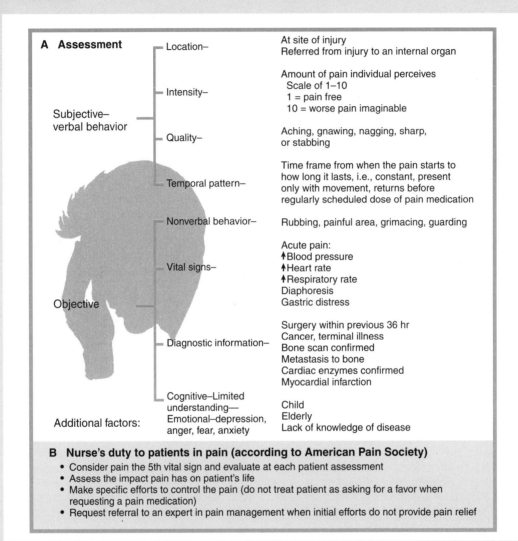

A Assessment

Subjective–verbal behavior

- Location– At site of injury / Referred from injury to an internal organ

- Intensity– Amount of pain individual perceives / Scale of 1–10 / 1 = pain free / 10 = worse pain imaginable

- Quality– Aching, gnawing, nagging, sharp, or stabbing

- Temporal pattern– Time frame from when the pain starts to how long it lasts, i.e., constant, present only with movement, returns before regularly scheduled dose of pain medication

- Nonverbal behavior– Rubbing, painful area, grimacing, guarding

Objective

- Vital signs– Acute pain: / ↑Blood pressure / ↑Heart rate / ↑Respiratory rate / Diaphoresis / Gastric distress

- Diagnostic information– Surgery within previous 36 hr / Cancer, terminal illness / Bone scan confirmed / Metastasis to bone / Cardiac enzymes confirmed / Myocardial infarction

Additional factors:

- Cognitive–Limited understanding— / Emotional–depression, anger, fear, anxiety / Child / Elderly / Lack of knowledge of disease

B Nurse's duty to patients in pain (according to American Pain Society)

- Consider pain the 5th vital sign and evaluate at each patient assessment
- Assess the impact pain has on patient's life
- Make specific efforts to control the pain (do not treat patient as asking for a favor when requesting a pain medication)
- Request referral to an expert in pain management when initial efforts do not provide pain relief

Sources for Standards

The nurse's duty to provide appropriate pain management for patients is derived from several sources. Professional standards include the ANA position statement on pain management as part of the nurse's role in end-of-life decisions and the U.S. Department of Health and Human Services Agency for Health Care Policy and Research (AHCPR) guidelines for clinical practice for pain management. In 1992 the AHCPR released guidelines for both acute pain management and cancer pain management. The American Pain Society also has position statements on treatment at the end of life and pain assessment as a 5th vital sign. These authoritative references would likely be cited by courts in establishing what would be the proper standard of care in these situations.

Additionally some states have passed legislation in the form of statutes called pain relief acts. These acts generally specify that neither disciplinary nor state criminal prosecution shall be brought against health care providers for the therapeutic treatment of intractable pain.

Pain Defined

Pain is one of the most compelling reasons why people seek medical care. Pain is a protective mechanism that alerts the person to potentially harmful stimuli.

There are three types of pain: (1) *Acute pain* occurs immediately after an injury and continues until the healing is completed. If acute pain is not managed effectively, it can progress to a chronic state. (2) *Chronic pain* lasts for a prolonged period of time, usually for >6 months and is often associated with depression. (3) *Malignant pain* can be described as intractable and is often associated with cancer.

Assessment

A nurse is responsible for assessing subjective and objective data (see **Part A**). A physical assessment including a review of the patient's vital signs is essential. The nurse should also assess the emotional response to pain and the results of diagnostic tests that confirm painful events, such as a bone scan that confirms metastasis of cancer to the bone.

Treatment

The most common approach of pain management is the use of analgesic medication. The physician orders analgesics; however, the nurse is responsible for administering the drugs, evaluating their effectiveness, and notifying the physician if the relief of pain is inadequate. In a hospital setting, the nurse

- Determines if and when an analgesic is given, as most analgesics are ordered as an as-needed basis (prn);
- Selects the appropriate analgesic when more than 1 is prescribed;

- Knows the drug's potency, absorption, and pharmacokinetics;
- Evaluates the effectiveness of the medication;
- Observes for side effects; and
- Reports to the physician when a change in medication is needed.

In the nonhospital setting, the nurse is responsible for advising the patient about analgesic use.

Postoperative Pain

Postoperative pain is treated according to specific guidelines. Narcotics should be given around the clock for the first 36 hours, *not* prn. Analgesics should be given before or as soon as pain returns and before activity, such as ambulation or incentive spirometer use.

Liability Issues

Some people believe that administering large doses of morphine constitutes assisted suicide or euthanasia. It is the position of the ANA that relieving pain, even if it hastens death in a terminally ill person, is the ethical and moral obligation of the professional nurse; it is not euthanasia or assisted suicide. This position must be consistent with the patient's wishes.

Nurses need to continually update and implement current standards of care. Agency policies need to be consistent with these so that the nurse's legal duty to provide pain relief for patients can be fulfilled. Documenting pain assessment as "generalized" or "severe" and describing pain relief as "good," "better," or "fair" is inadequate and fails to show that the standard of care was met. Holding back pain medication in the belief that the patient is addicted without proper assessment, evaluation, and medical diagnosis is considered "inhuman treatment" and leaves the nurse professionally liable. The nurse has a shared responsibility and independent duty to provide appropriate pain management for patients, and the patient must be part of the decision-making process (see **Part B**).

21 Patient Teaching and Health Counseling
Susan Westrick Killion, JD, MS, RN

A   Patient Teaching

- Assess patient need (include cultural, ethnic, literacy).
- Include teaching aids — written instructions.
- Provide documentation.

Discharge Instructions

- Include who was taught in documentation.
- Written instruction is recommended.
- Include person's name and phone number to call if questions arise later when at home.

Emergency Department

- Written instruction is recommended.
- Ensure that patient and/or family receives information.

Inpatient Settings

- Require patient to demonstrate skills.

B   Minimizing Risks of Liability

- Completely document content, skills, and materials provided.
- Document if patient refuses teaching.
- Use standard teaching protocols.
- Evaluate teaching; ensure that patient receives and understands teaching.

The nurse's role in patient teaching and health counseling is receiving greater emphasis in practice, owing to changes in the health care environment (e.g., shorter stays for patients in institutions, more patients being treated in outpatient settings, increased numbers of patients in home care settings, increasingly chronic and complex health care conditions). These factors, along with greater emphasis on preventative care and health counseling, contribute to the need for nurses to be highly skilled and accountable in patient teaching.

Legal and Ethical Framework

Legal, institutional, and professional standards formulate the basis for the nurse's duty to teach patients. Most state laws that define nursing practice include specific language addressing the area of patient education or health counseling. Even if not specifically stated, this duty is implied in language stating that nurses carry out plans of care for patients and treat their responses to health care problems. National standards such as the ANA standards of practice and JCAHO require that patient education be included and documented in individual plans of care. The ANA standards require that teaching-learning principles be included in these activities. In addition, providing ethnic and culturally sensitive care requires incorporating these aspects into patient teaching. Patients' bills of rights include the right to health care information, and nurses share responsibility for ensuring this right. Many nurses will find that their job descriptions include duties related to patient teaching and health counseling. Teaching hospitals usually incorporate teaching as part of their mission statement, and this may include patient teaching as well.

Principles of Patient Teaching

The first step to consider in patient teaching is to assess the teaching needs of the patient, or the teaching that is required in a particular situation (e.g., teaching related to a diagnostic or surgical procedure) (see **Part A**). The nurse should assess what the patient knows and begin from there. The nurse needs to consider language barriers, literacy, ethnic and cultural background, and age and emotional status of the patient; otherwise, teaching and learning can be impaired, placing the patient at risk.

For complex procedures that need to be taught (e.g., injection techniques), handouts, visual aid s, and actual equipment should be used. The patient should demonstrate the learned procedure so the nurse can evaluate the effectiveness of the teaching. The taught content and skills should be documented in the appropriate health records. Using these principles ensures that the nurse is meeting the standard of care as required for the situation.

Teaching in Various Settings and Circumstances

Discharge Instructions
Patients are required to receive discharge instructions as part of their discharge planning from various health care institutions. These instructions are often in writing, with a copy retained for the health care record. In some situations, these instructions need to be given to a family member or other health care providers instead of the patient. If a patient is not provided with a copy of discharge instructions and harm results because of it, liability may result. It is most often the nurse who has the duty to provide the discharge instructions and to collaborate with the physician and other health team members for specific instructions.

Emergency Departments
When patients are discharged from the emergency department, specific instructions should be given to patients and caregivers. *Written* discharge instructions are a part of the standard of care for many conditions when patients are discharged from the emergency department and need to be incorporated into practice. Documentation should include that the patient or caregiver *receives* the information.

Inpatient Setting
Even relatively simple patient procedures need careful teaching, as exemplified by *Chamberlain v Deaconess Hospital, Inc.*, 324 N.W.2d 172 (Ind. Ct. App. 1975), a case deciding whether a patient was properly instructed on how to collect a 24-hour urine sample.

Health Counseling and Advice
The question of whether a nurse engaged in inappropriate teaching for a patient who requested information on an alternative treatment was raised in *Tuma v Board of Nursing, 100 Idaho 74, 593 p.2d 711 (1979)*. A patient receiving chemotherapy requested the nurse to return in the evening to discuss Laetrile treatments. The patient's physician heard about this from a family member and the hospital made a complaint about the nurse to the state board of nursing. After a hearing, her license was suspended for 6 months. She appealed this decision to the state supreme court, which overturned the suspension, reasoning that there was not adequate warning that this behavior would result in violating the statute for unprofessional conduct, and thus the statute was vague as applied to these facts. The issues discussed in the case raise valid concerns about how far patient teaching can go, if it is viewed as interfering with the physician-patient relationship as was alleged in this case.

Medications
Teaching patients about side effects and precautions while taking certain medications is a shared duty with other health professionals. Nurses in advanced practice with prescriptive authority need to be especially vigilant in this area. Physicians have been held liable in numerous cases where patients were not adequately warned of side effects and injury resulted. Liability can also extend to foreseeable third parties, such as those injured while patients under the influence of medications are operating a motor vehicle.

Minimizing Risks of Liability from Patient Teaching

Complete documentation related to patient teaching can help avoid claims that teaching was not done (see **Part B**). Written materials should supplement teaching, and copies of these should be in patient records or easily accessible if a question arises. Family members or other caregivers should be included in the teaching, with the patient's permission. When a patient refuses to accept teaching, a note to this effect should be recorded. This documentation becomes important if the patient later makes a claim of negligence. "Contributory negligence" on the part of the patient will reduce or bar his recovery for damages.

Standard teaching protocols should be available for common conditions, and these should be reviewed and updated periodically. Continuing education classes on teaching strategies incorporating cultural and literacy concepts can be especially helpful for nurses.

Focusing on the evaluation aspect of teaching can help ensure that the standard of care is met. Taking time to evaluate whether the patient and family *understand* the teaching is the best way to ensure this. In areas such as 1-day surgery where there is limited contact with the patient, there should always be someone who can be contacted if questions later arise related to the discharge instructions. In fact, it is good practice for nurses to make follow-up phone calls to patients to evaluate their status after discharge.

22 Medication Administration– Part I
Susan Westrick Killion, JD, MS, RN

A Medication Administration

Follow standard of care for safe administration

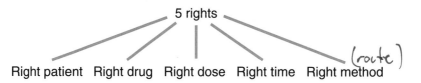

5 rights

Right patient   Right drug   Right dose   Right time   Right method *(route)*

Failure to follow 5 rights = Medication error = Possible patient injury

Malpractice action (civil action; nurse may be liable for damages)

Disciplinary action by state board (license suspension, revocation, censure)

Criminal action or charges for serious errors resulting in death or serious injury (nurse may be fined, possible confinement)

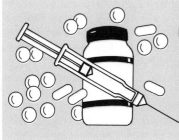

B Prevention of Errors

1. Individual accountability
2. Risk management analysis for system failures
3. Corrective steps in system
4. Individual education

Nurses are responsible for administering almost all medications to patients. Negligence in the area of medication administration has become one of the greatest areas of liability for nurses and their employers, sometimes resulting in multimillion dollar awards. Many times these errors result from failure to follow the basic rules of safe administration. Other reasons for the rise in errors include the vast numbers of medications a nurse is responsible for, the increasing complexity of drug administration methods, multiple medication dosing for individual patients, failure to update knowledge of drugs and their implications, and increased nurse-patient ratios.

Liability Issues

Negligence

Traditionally the area of negligence or malpractice law has governed a nurse's actions in medication administration (see **Part A**). This means that a nurse has a duty to follow correctly written physicians' orders (or advanced-practice nurses' orders if permitted by state statute) for drug administration to patients. This duty includes implementation of the *5 rights* of drug administration: *right* patient, *right* drug, *right* dosage, *right* time, and *right* method. Failure to follow any of these steps can result in a successful malpractice claim against a nurse. However, not all medication errors result in liability and a finding of professional negligence or malpractice. The plaintiff (or patient) who brings the action still must prove (1) a duty, (2) a breach of the duty, (3) proximate causation between the breach of the duty and the injury, and (4) injury to the patient. Many medication errors do not result in injury to the patient and would not support a civil action for negligence.

Criminal Charges

A recent Colorado case involving negligent administration of a drug to an infant underscores the reality that criminal charges can be brought against nurses in situations involving medication errors. This tragic case in which the error resulted in the death of an infant involved multiple individual and system failures. The events occurred in 1996 when a physician prescribed "penicillin G benzathine, 150,000 U, IM," but had not written the order clearly. The pharmacist misread the order and prepared 2 syringes with a dose of 1,500,000 U (having read the "U" to be an extra "0"). Since the volume of the drug was in 2.5 mL, the nurses determined that 5 separate injections would need to be administered. Not wanting to subject the infant to this, the nurses consulted with a neonatal nurse practitioner (NNP) who decided the drug could be given IV. They checked drug reference books but did not find the information to be clear and made incorrect assumptions about the name of the drug and its administration. This particular drug was to be given IM only. The NNP then changed the route of administration for the order, and the drug was given by IV push by herself and another advanced-practice nurse. After part of the medication was administered, the infant became unresponsive, resuscitation efforts were unsuccessful, and the infant died. It was determined that the infant died as a result of the drug (a 10-fold overdose) being injected IV, which caused a massive pulmonary embolism. After these events and following disciplinary action by the Colorado state board of nursing, the district attorney indicted the nurses for "criminally negligent homicide." This was the first time criminal charges had been filed against nurses for a medication error.

The outcome of the case (in 1998) was that 2 of the nurses (the nurses who actually administered the drug) plead guilty and accepted plea bargains rather than face a possible guilty verdict by a jury and potential permanent loss of their licenses. These nurses received a 2-year deferred sentence, probation, and an order for community service that includes education of student nurses about their errors in this case. They can return to court after the 2-year period and request that their cases be dismissed. The third nurse who was not directly involved in the administration stood trial and was acquitted of these charges by the jury.

The fact that the nurses were charged in this manner has been the subject of heated public and professional debate, but the case serves as a signal to professionals as to the potential consequences of errors in their professional roles. The district attorney who brought the charges contends that the case was not about a simple medication error, but rather a case of nurses changing the route of administration ordered by the physician, thus providing a "gross deviation from the standard of care" that unjustifiably placed the patient at extreme risk of danger.

The response of the nursing community has largely centered around the need to treat this type of error as a system failure and address it as a risk management issue. Commentators have also stated that disciplining these nurses should have remained with the state board of nursing, which is the agency delegated to regulate the profession and to protect the public.

23 Medication Administration–Part II

Susan Westrick Killion, JD, MS, RN

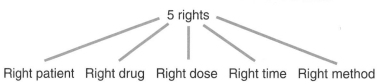

A Medication Administration

Follow standard of care for safe administration

5 rights

Right patient   Right drug   Right dose   Right time   Right method

Failure to follow 5 rights = Medication error = Possible patient injury

Malpractice action
(civil action; nurse may
be liable for damages)

Disciplinary action
by state board
(license suspension,
revocation, censure)

Criminal action or
charges for serious
errors resulting in death
or serious injury (nurse
may be fined, possible
confinement)

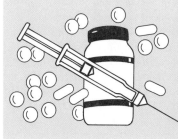

B Prevention of Errors

1. Individual accountability
2. Risk management analysis for system failures
3. Corrective steps in system
4. Individual education

Disciplinary Action by the State Board of Nursing

The state board of nursing would normally be involved if a medication error resulted in a serious injury or death of a patient. Sometimes the state board will require a nurse to complete a continuing education course or will restrict his or her practice in some other way. Any of the sanctions available to the state board could be used, including revoking the license, which would mean the nurse could no longer work as an RN.

Risk Management Considerations

Nurses remain individually accountable for their own errors even if someone else started the chain of events. For example, if a medication is ordered incorrectly, it is up to the nurse to clarify the order. Since it is the nurse who will administer the drug to the patient, he or she becomes the last checkpoint for the patient's safety.

It is important for nurses to acknowledge mistakes and to document them accordingly on incident reports and patient records. A nurse should never falsify any patient record, but doing so as related to medication errors (especially with narcotics) will usually violate the NPA. Nurses must follow all institutional protocols, but they may be required to go beyond protocols to provide for patient safety.

When incidents related to medication errors are tracked, trends and patterns can be identified. This will help to positively identify system errors that can be dealt with effectively by the agency or institution. Many medicolegal experts agree that when egregious errors occur, it almost always involves system failure in >1 department and level of the organization.

Another outcome of tracking errors is to identify certain medications with a high risk of injury to patients and to pay particular attention to these. Some of the medications that have resulted in significant patient injury and high awards for damages following litigation are insulin, potassium chloride, digoxin and other potent cardiac drugs, chemotherapeutic agents, narcotics, and anesthetics. It is recommended that extra checkpoints be included when administering these drugs, such as having 2 nurses check dosage and administration methods.

National studies and programs are tracking data related to medication errors and estimate that nearly one-half of these errors are preventable. Reasons for errors have included poor product labeling, inadequately trained staff, understaffing, poor communication, and system failure. In light of these considerations, nurses must be vigilant in their practice in fulfilling their responsibility to patients in terms of safe administration of medications.

24 Clients with AIDS and HIV Testing

Katherine McCormack Dempski, JD, BSN, RN

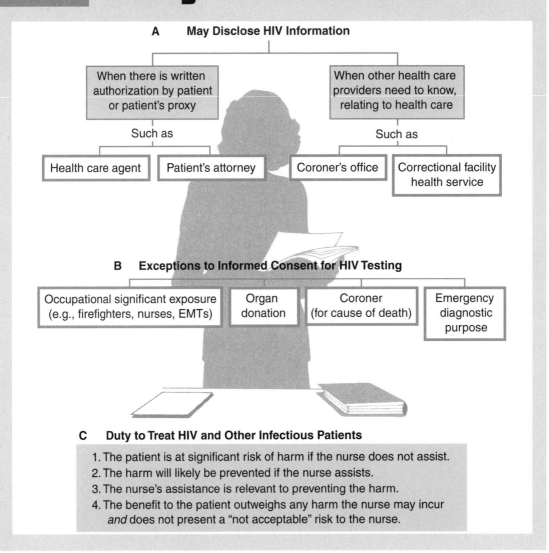

A   May Disclose HIV Information

When there is written authorization by patient or patient's proxy

Such as

- Health care agent
- Patient's attorney

When other health care providers need to know, relating to health care

Such as

- Coroner's office
- Correctional facility health service

B   Exceptions to Informed Consent for HIV Testing

| Occupational significant exposure (e.g., firefighters, nurses, EMTs) | Organ donation | Coroner (for cause of death) | Emergency diagnostic purpose |

C   Duty to Treat HIV and Other Infectious Patients

1. The patient is at significant risk of harm if the nurse does not assist.
2. The harm will likely be prevented if the nurse assists.
3. The nurse's assistance is relevant to preventing the harm.
4. The benefit to the patient outweighs any harm the nurse may incur *and* does not present a "not acceptable" risk to the nurse.

To encourage widespread testing, federal and state statutes have evolved to ensure confidentiality surrounding the testing process and diagnosis of HIV and AIDS. The federal statute sets the minimum amount of confidentiality that must be in place for each state. Each state has its own rules governing the confidentiality surrounding AIDS and HIV testing.

Confidentiality

In general, health care providers who obtain HIV information must keep that information confidential. There

are usually a few exceptions to the rule of strict confidentiality (see **Part A**). Whenever disclosure is made, it must include a written statement warning the individual receiving the information that it is confidential and protected by law. A violation of the confidentiality law makes the individual liable in a private cause of action by the patient.

Warning Known Partners

Specific rules govern warning third parties of a patient's HIV status. Physicians and nurses have a duty to their patients to keep HIV information confidential. This is an ethical duty and in most states a legal duty defined by statute. Most statutes do not authorize nurses to pass this information to known partners. However, the ANA has a position statement on warning known third parties at risk. The ANA supports the ethical responsibility of disclosing HIV information to an identified partner at risk by the nurse's patient when certain conditions apply. The nurse must be the primary care provider, the patient must have received counseling on the benefits of warning partners, and the nurse must reasonably believe the patient will not warn the partner. Any nurse in the position of disclosing HIV information to warn a third party should consult an attorney familiar with both the state statute defining the legal duty and professional organizations' position statements defining any ethical duty. When the two are at odds, the nurse will need to know how to reconcile them.

Informed Consent for HIV Testing

Health care providers may not order HIV testing without written or oral consent documented in the medical record. Each state will have its own HIV informed consent statute with which health care providers need to be familiar. HIV informed consent is very specific and goes beyond the informed consent required for surgical procedures. First, the person obtaining the informed consent must explain the purpose of the test and the benefits of early diagnosis and treatment. The patient must be informed of the confidentiality in the testing process and that HIV testing is not a prerequisite to medical treatment. The patient must also be aware that recording HIV information in the medical records when it relates to medical treatment is permissible and that disclosure to known individuals at risk may be statutorily required. Documentation must show that all of the above criteria were met. To avoid liability, health care providers ordering the test must make a good faith effort to comply with all requirements and convey that informed consent was given.

Counseling is an important element in all HIV informed-consent statutes. Counseling must be offered on discrimination, emotional issues, prevention of transmission, and the possible need of notifying others at risk. Documentation of all counseling provided is an essential element of the informed-consent statutes. Laboratories running the test need to verify that informed consent is in the record before running the test. The results must go directly to the health care provider ordering the test to protect confidentiality.

Exceptions to Informed Consent

There are specific exceptions to obtaining informed consent for HIV testing (see **Part B**). In urgent care situations when the patient is unconscious or otherwise unable to consent and no one authorized to consent is available, testing may be done if needed for immediate diagnostic purposes. Testing may be done when health care providers or other occupations (firefighters or emergency medical technicians) have a significant exposure in the course of their occupational duty and the patient refuses testing. This means that nurses who have a needle stick injury should be able to have the patient tested even if he or she refuses. Agency policies need to be followed strictly in reporting the injury. The deceased may be tested if the diagnosis is necessary for the cause of death. Testing may also be done prior to organ donation. In each situation the specific statute and agency policies must be followed carefully.

Americans with Disabilities Act

The ignorance and fear surrounding the AIDS virus leaves HIV-positive individuals vulnerable to discrimination. Federal courts have recognized HIV as a disability because the stigma attached to it interferes with one's ability to perform "activities of daily living." Therefore, HIV has become a protected disability under the Americans with Disabilities Act (ADA).

An HIV-positive patient made a successful discrimination claim against his surgeon for an unnecessary 2-day delay in surgery while the operating team waited for HIV "safe suits" to arrive. The federal court ruled that the delay was unreasonable because the Centers for Disease Control and Prevention (CDC) guidelines for universal precautions do not require safe suits and therefore the patient was treated differently from others based on his HIV status.

Duty to Treat HIV Patients

Both the American Medical Association and ANA have issued ethical statements on the duty to care for HIV-infected patients. Both agree that it is professionally unethical to deny medical and nursing treatment to a patient based solely on the patient's HIV status. This includes denying care to a patient who refuses to undergo HIV testing. HIV patients may be transferred to another health care provider or facility that is better equipped to provide care to the patient, but the transfer must be to benefit the patient's care rather than the personal preference of the health care provider. However, the ANA recognized that nurses are not legally or ethically required to put personal health at risk. For example, an immunosuppressed nurse is justified in requesting to not care for infectious patients just as a pregnant nurse should not care for a patient with cytomegalovirus (which is harmful to the fetus). Guidelines issued by professional organizations are often used to show the standard of care in these situations and should be followed. See **Part C**.

25 Abusive Situations

Susan B. Ramsey, JD, BSN

Reporting Process

Suspected abuse/neglect of:
Child or vulnerable adult (physical/mental condition
   limiting self care OR elderly, age defined in statute)

Report to:
   Child Protective Services
   Adult Protective Services

   Long-term care ombudsman (usually when an
   agency or health care provider is involved)

   State licensing board (when health care provider
   is involved)

   Law enforcement (if required under statute)

When:
   Written or verbal report within 24 hours of incident

Nurses are often at the entry point for patients faced with family violence. *Family violence* is defined as inappropriate and damaging interpersonal harm among individuals with interpersonal relations regardless of their actual biological or legal relationships. Such harm includes child physical abuse and neglect; child sexual abuse; domestic partner abuse; and elder mistreatment, abuse, and exploitation.

Child Abuse

There are 4 general types of abuse: (1) physical abuse, (2) sexual abuse, (3) emotional abuse, and (4) neglect. Neglect is the common form of child maltreatment. It is only in the past 20 years that all states have mandated child abuse reporting laws. Unfortunately, abuse cases are thought to be severely underreported. According to the National Child Abuse and Neglect

Data System (NCANDS) and the National Incidence Study of Child Abuse and Neglect, both of which are sponsored by the U.S. Department of Health and Human Services, in 1996 approximately 3 million children were involved in some form of reported abuse.

It is critical that nurses, as well as other health care providers, be able to identify children in abusive situations. A discrepancy between the physical findings and the explanations of how an incident occurred is a valid reason for a nurse to suspect abuse. A classic example is evidence of healed fractures that have no plausible explanation. The effects of child abuse on younger children can include aggressive behavior, social withdrawal, depression, lying, stealing, thumb sucking, as well as behaviors that are inappropriate for the child's age. Older children and adolescents are more likely to be involved in substance abuse, exhibit problems at school, engage in risky behavior (engaging in risky sexual encounters, high-speed driving, etc.), or suicidal behavior.

Mandated reporting laws require that suspected abuse of a child be communicated to the appropriate authorities. Each state has specified social services or law enforcement agencies to which an incident of suspected child abuse must be reported. In addition to health care professionals, a number of other professionals are considered "mandated reporters." It is important to note that the usual confidential nature of medical treatment usually is waived in the child abuse situation. Therefore, health professionals are expected to report suspected child abuse even if their knowledge comes from the patient. Moreover, most states have provisions that protect individual health care professions (including nursing) from legal liability as long as the reporting was done in good faith. Finally, many states have laws that expose a health care provider to legal action, criminal and/or civil, for failing to report suspected abuse to the appropriate authorities.

Elder Abuse

Elder abuse refers to (1) neglect; (2) abuse, both physical and psychological; (3) financial exploitation; and (3) neglect by self or caregiver. The most easily recognizable abuse is physical abuse. Recognition, assessment, and treatment of abuse in the elderly are complicated by a number of factors. An abused elder may be fearful of the abuser, be ashamed to acknowledge dependency on the abuser (especially his or her own adult children), or be loyal to the abuser. Again, it is important for the nurse to recognize signs of an abusive situation. When a health care provider suspects that an elderly patient is a victim of physical abuse, there are often clues to assist

in assessment of the situation. Explanations inconsistent with noted injuries and delay in seeking treatment of the injuries are examples of signs and symptoms of abuse. The behavior of the family members or caretakers also can suggest a pattern of abuse. For example, behaviors include excessively detailed accounts of the injuries, undue concern with the cost of treatment, and refusing to let the elderly person be interviewed or treated without their presence. Interventions for abused elders should focus on maintaining safety and evaluating the patient's capacity to protect himself or herself. Some elders may lack the mental capacity to make informed choices about their situation. Therefore, it may be necessary for the nurse who recognizes elder abuse to seek a court order for conservatorship or guardianship.

Some states have mandatory reporting statutes for healthcare providers who have a reasonable belief (legitimate basis for suspecting abuse) that a vulnerable adult (physical or mental impairment limiting self-care or an adult older than the age set by the statute, such as 60). Immunity is provided for (such as a civil libel suit) when the report is done in good faith. A nurse who intentionally or negligently (by missing the signs a nursing assessment would provide) fails to report abuse may face a criminal charge under the statute and disciplinary action by the licensing board. The statute will specify the reporting process (see **Part A**). In addition, the agency may have a specific policy to follow and require specific documentation.

Partner Abuse

In the time it takes to read this chapter, 4 women will have been victims of domestic violence. Again the "signs and symptoms" of partner abuse can be clouded by the patient's fear in disclosing information that he or she has been a victim of abuse by a partner. In many abusive situations, the battered partners will try to remedy the situation themselves by trying to change their behavior. For example, "I shouldn't argue so much, he gets so angry."

Nursing assessment and interventions include asking the right questions and referrals to appropriate social service or law enforcement agencies. Unless the abused partner is a "vulnerable adult" there is no mandatory reporting requirement. However, the emotional impact a violent environment has on children is well documented. In situations in which there may be child abuse, mandated reporting laws, which require reporting, may assist in providing the vehicle for family treatment and removal of the abusive family member.

26 Reproductive Services

Katherine McCormack Dempski, JD, BSN, RN

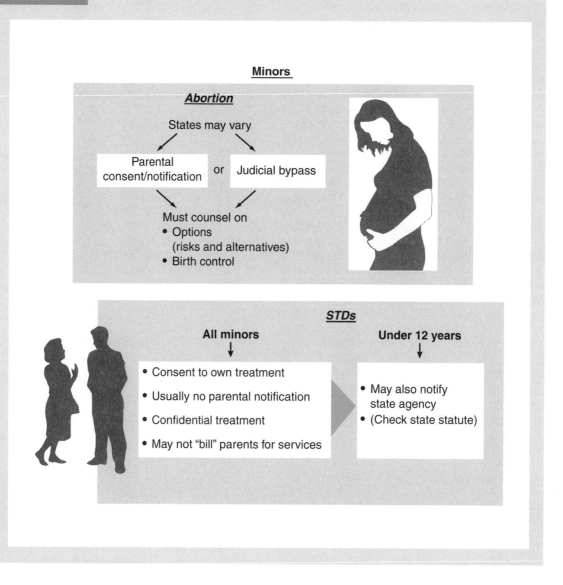

Minors

Abortion

States may vary

Parental consent/notification   or   Judicial bypass

Must counsel on
- Options
  (risks and alternatives)
- Birth control

STDs

All minors

- Consent to own treatment
- Usually no parental notification
- Confidential treatment
- May not "bill" parents for services

Under 12 years

- May also notify state agency
- (Check state statute)

Abortion

The ANA position statement on abortion recognizes that patients have a right to privacy and a right to make informed heath care decisions based on full disclosure of information. Nurses have an obligation to inform the patient of all health care choices that are legal. Abortion prior to fetal viability is a legal health care choice. Health care providers are able to objec-

tively discuss this choice but are not required to participate in a procedure that is ethically disagreeable to them.

Adults

A woman's right to privacy includes her decision to continue with or terminate a pregnancy up to the point of fetal viability. Once the point of fetal viability is reached (somewhere in the second trimester), the state has some interest in preserving life and can put some limits on abortion. However, these limitations cannot cause an undue burden on the woman. *Undue burden* has not been completely defined and has been determined on a case-by-case analysis. The court has upheld a restriction on federal and state funding for abortions but struck down provisions requiring a woman to obtain her husband's written consent. Husbands may not compel a wife to complete or terminate a pregnancy.

The court has also struck down a state provision requiring physicians to follow a specified informed-consent form prior to completing abortions. The court found it too intrusive on the physician-patient relationship since the consent form disregarded the physician's judgment on what was relevant to each individual's case. Recently, the court upheld a statute requiring physicians to test fetal viability when the pregnancy is around the 20th week. Technology has changed in the 20 years since the *Roe v Wade* decision, enabling younger fetuses to survive longer. Some states have a medical emergency exception that permits dispensing with the informed-consent requirement when the physician makes a good faith conclusion that medical complications of pregnancy necessitate a therapeutic abortion. This exception sometimes includes serious mental health issues. Each state specifically enumerates what constitutes a medical emergency (such as loss of life or major bodily function).

Minors

Each state has statutes governing abortions on minors (see **Figure**). Nurses practicing in areas providing abortion to minors must be concerned with parental notification and counseling. There are variations in each state on whether a minor may receive an abortion without parental consent. The U.S. Supreme Court answered the question of whether the right to privacy included a minor's right to an abortion in *Planned Parenthood v Danforth* and *Bellotti v Baird*. An unemancipated minor's right to reproductive choice is not equal with that of an adult, even in the early stages of pregnancy. No state provision may categorically deny a minor the right to an abortion, and parents may not have absolute veto power over the minor's decision. Although states and parents may not exercise absolute veto power over a minor's reproductive choice, a minor has no absolute right to exercise that choice without authorization from a parent, guardian, or judge. Therefore, states may involve parents by requiring parental notification without giving parents the power of consent. States must be consistent in ensuring that third parties do not have absolute power over another's decision to terminate a pregnancy. Constitutionally, states may require parental consent but the state must also include an alternative to parental consent. This alternative has become known as a *bypass provision.* The bypass provision grants courts the power to deter-

mine if a minor is mature enough to consent to an abortion without parental consent or notification. This alternative recognizes that parental consent is not always in the best interest of the minor. Abusive or strained relationships may only worsen when parental consent or notification is required.

All minors must be counseled on options such as adoption and keeping the baby. The minor must sign a form stating she was not coerced and she understands the risks and alternatives. Birth control options also must be discussed. States also may require the health care providers to counsel minors on available clinics for birth control services as part of abortion informed consent.

Minors and Treatment for Sexually Transmitted Diseases

Minors have the highest sexually transmitted disease (STD) rate of any age group, yet they seek treatment the least because they fear parental notification by health care providers. Health care providers in the position of treating minors must be aware of the specific state legislation on minors. Most health care providers treating minors for STDs are concerned with parental consent even though litigation against providers in their area is uncommon. State statutes will enumerate the age of minority for consenting to reproductive services, which include testing for HIV and STDs. Some states may require that the state public health or family advocate services be notified that a minor under a certain age (usually 12 years) is seeking reproductive services. This is not the same as parental notification.

Once a minor is diagnosed and treated for an STD, the confidentiality statutes require that all information related to the treatment be given only to the young patient. Communicable disease reporting and public health notification requirements are the exception to this. Confidential treatment includes the billing process. The minor is responsible to pay for services and the parents may not be billed (see **Figure**).

Health care providers must obtain the minor's informed consent to treatment and determine whether the minor understands the nature, risks, and benefits of the procedure as well as any alternative treatments.

Fertility Clinics

Fertility clinics engaging in artificial insemination and in vitro fertilization have an ethical and legal duty to screen semen donors for diseases that may harm the woman and the fetus such as HIV, cytomegalovirus (CMV), hepatitis, and herpes. Personal information on donor family history and genetic diseases also should be provided just as it is for adoption proceedings. Clinic personnel have a professional duty to handle all specimens with due care. Therefore, documenting the custodial chain of command for each specimen is an important legal concern of clinic staff.

27 Handicapped or Critically Ill Newborns

Katherine McCormack
Dempski, JD, BSN, RN

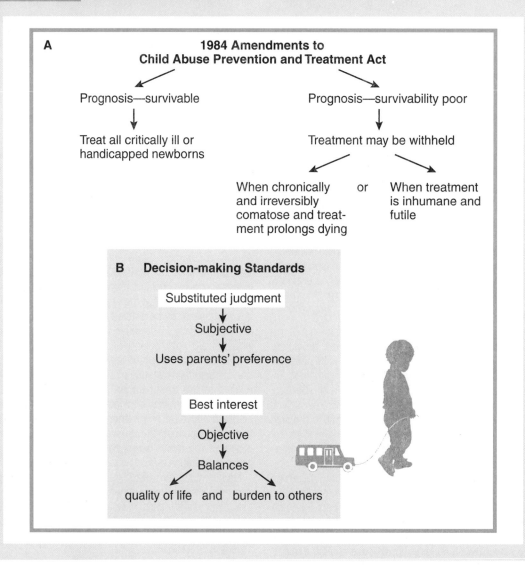

A   **1984 Amendments to Child Abuse Prevention and Treatment Act**

Prognosis—survivable

Treat all critically ill or handicapped newborns

Prognosis—survivability poor

Treatment may be withheld

When chronically and irreversibly comatose and treatment prolongs dying   or   When treatment is inhumane and futile

B   **Decision-making Standards**

Substituted judgment
Subjective
Uses parents' preference

Best interest
Objective
Balances
quality of life   and   burden to others

Medical, legal, and ethical dilemmas often arise in the treatment and care of premature and handicapped newborns. No clear guidelines dictate the initial delivery care of extremely premature or severely handicapped newborns. Health care providers must determine how aggressively they will treat or if they should treat at all. This decision is complicated because viability is often not immediately appreciated. Because of this initial uncertainty, physicians seek to buy time by providing aggressive treatment while determining viability. The issue is further complicated by the harmful and sometimes fatal side effects of the aggressive treatment performed to save the infant. Although health care providers may not wish to provide futile or harmful treatment, they are aware that delaying treatment may harm an otherwise viable infant.

Federal Regulation: Child Abuse Prevention and Treatment Act

In 1984 Congress passed the Child Abuse Amendments to the preexisting Child Abuse Prevention and Treatment Act (CAPTA) to prevent "medical neglect" of handicapped newborns by "withholding medically indicated treatment from disabled infants with life-threatening conditions." For purposes of the amendments, also known as the "Baby Doe" regulations, "medically indicated treatment" is treatment likely to correct life-threatening conditions. There are limited exceptions to the treatment requirement based on the infant's ability to survive (see **Part A**). The legal and ethical debate continues over the medical interpretation and applicability of these regulations.

Interpretations of the Child Abuse Amendments

The amendments and guidelines require that medical treatment be based on the infant's survivability and not the quality of life. The regulations are difficult to apply in certain cases. For example, the standard for "chronically and irreversibly comatose" is not always clear to medical providers. The exception to treatment requiring that intervention be both futile and inhumane is also confusing to health care providers. The regulation seems to require inhumane treatment unless it is also futile and futile treatment unless it is also inhumane.

State Child Protective Agencies

State child protective agencies are empowered to enforce the regulations. Guidelines accompanying the regulations require that child protective services take action when parents refuse consent for treatment recommended as an overall plan, even when such treatment would not itself improve all life-threatening conditions.

Decision-Making Process

The courts deciding difficult handicapped and critically ill newborn cases look to the CAPTA regulations and other legal standards (see **Part B**).

Substituted Judgment

Courts use the "substituted judgment" standard when an incompetent patient is unable to make his or her own medical decisions. This standard is a subjective approach where the courts gather evidence from various sources concerning the patient's preference toward medical care. The court then substitutes its judgment for that of the patient. Although the substituted judgment standard in its purest form is impossible to apply to infants who never made their medical preference known, courts have used the parents' preference as evidence.

Best Interest

Courts use the "best interest" standard when an incompetent patient's preference to medical care is not known. This objective standard uses a surrogate decision-maker to determine the patient's best interest. Courts and physicians often use this standard when making a treatment decision for infants. The best interest standard balances the benefits, burdens, and risks of treatment. This standard differs from the others because it considers "quality of life" and the burden of treatment on others. In a quality-of-life analysis, one's personal worth or social use is not considered, but pain, suffering, and enjoyment of life are. "Burden of treatment" on others includes the emotional and financial impact treatment will have on the infant's parents. Emotional and financial burdens often lead to the dissolution of the marriage. Siblings of handicapped newborns are also at risk for emotional crisis. Hospitals funding the long-term medical care of handicapped newborns are financially burdened.

State Interests

It is well-established that competent individuals have a right to refuse medical treatment. However, this right is sometimes balanced against the state's significant interest in preserving life, which includes suicide prevention and the protection of third parties (such as an unborn viable fetus). The state's interest in preserving life rarely takes into consideration the infant's quality of life. The state's interest often assumes that all treatment will be beneficial unless the infant is not likely to survive.

Pediatrics Ethical Standard

The American Academy of Pediatrics' (AAP) position statement on critically ill infants and children states that parents and physicians should make reasoned decisions together through informed parental consent. Benefits and burdens of treatment should be considered. The AAP acknowledges that legal and ethical standards may require the intervention of child protective services when parents and physicians disagree and their differences cannot be resolved through an ethics committee.

Judicial Review

The judicial response time in sorting through the complex medical issues of critically ill infants is slow. Furthermore, the public record policy of judicial proceedings ensures no privacy for the families and physicians involved. Therefore, it would seem that judicial involvement in critically ill newborn cases would be kept to a minimal. However, courts are increasingly expressing the view that judicial involvement is the best avenue for resolution.

28 Restraints

Katherine McCormack Dempski, JD, BSN, RN

A Agency Restraint Policy Outline

- Physician's order and frequency for renewal
- Emergency use guidelines
- Alternatives to restraints
- Informed-consent process to follow
- Indications for restraint use
- Frequency of restraint release
- Family involvement process
- Method to verify patient's wishes on restraints
- Frequency of staff monitoring
- Staff assistance with patient's activities of daily living
- Criteria for discontinuing the restraint

C Staff Education

- Review of risk factors for falls
- Training on using alternative measures to restraining
- Training on the proper application of restraints (including reviewing each manufacturer's warnings and procedure steps and checking labels for size limits)
- Teaching that restraints are "prescriptions" and must have a physician's order (or that of another health care provider licensed in the state to order restraints)
- Teaching that restraint use requires more intervention by staff for monitoring and assisting with activities
- Teaching of the legal liability involved in restraint use
- Review of agency's policy and procedure on restraint use

B Documentation

Prior to Restraint Use
- Assessment of risk factors
- Alternatives taken
- Patient behavior prior to restraints (patient dangerous to self or others)
- Patient teaching
- Patient view on restraints (by advance directives)
- Family involvement and view on alternatives to restraint use

After Restraint Use
- Medical indication for use
- Alternatives that had failed
- Physician's order
- Family notified and how, as well as family response
- Time and date applied and type of restraint used
- Frequency of staff monitoring and patient condition each time
- Assessment of limb or body part restrained prior to application and each time staff monitors
- Condition of skin before, during, or after restraint applied
- Informed consent process (who is present, teaching content, patient's response)

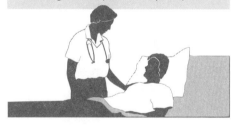

The current medical trend is for a restraint-free environment. Restraint-related injuries include death from strangulation, skin tears, abrasions, and loss of circulation. Restraint use increases complications such as joint contractures, incontinence, pressure sores, decubitus ulcers, constipation, impaction, and orthostatic hypotension. The nurse has a duty to identify a patient at risk for falling and take steps to prevent the fall. Restraint use, however, has its own liability issues.

Physical restraints include any device or material attached to or adjacent to the patient that cannot be easily removed by the patient and that restricts freedom of movement or prevents access to the patient's own body (e.g., jackets, vests, leg and arm restraints, arm boards, hand mitts, lap cushions or lap trays, sheets tightly tucked in or wrapped across the patient). Placing a wheelchair against a barrier that prevents a patient from moving is a form of restraint. Side rails can be a form of restraint when used on a patient unable to put the side rail down to get out of bed. *Chemical* restraints are drugs that leave the patient lethargic and noncombative.

Indications

Under the federal Omnibus Reconciliation Act (OBRA), residents of long-term care facilities have the right to be free of restraints. The act states that restraints should only be used to ensure physical safety of the resident or that of another resident and only when there is a physician's written order (unless there is an emergency). The order should specify the duration for which the restraints are to be used and under what circumstances they can be applied.

In all facilities, restraints can only be applied when medically indicated for diagnostic and treatment purposes. Restraints should never be used for staff convenience, especially when there is a staff shortage. They must never be used for discipline.

In an emergency situation, nurses may use judgment regarding use of restraints. The physicians should be notified immediately. In most cases the family will need to be notified as well. The nurse should document the risk factors indicating restraint use. Restraints should be removed when there is no further medical indication for their use and as per physician's order.

Informed Consent

Nurses and physicians must educate the patient on the risks, benefits, and safety measures of restraint use so the patient can make an informed decision. In the case of a minor or incompetent patient, a legal guardian, legal surrogate, or health care agent may grant informed consent for restraint use. In long-term care settings it is always recommended to give the family notice when one is restraining a resident. Inform the family of the medical reason for the restraint and the risk factors identified. Always verify that a patient's advance directives do not state a desire to be restraint free.

Identifying Patients at Risk

Staff at long-term and acute care facilities should be aware of patients at risk for falls such as the elderly and young children as well as sedated or confused patients. The elderly and young children are often seriously injured when they fall. This same population is also at risk for injuries from restraints. Young children who are restrained during and following a surgical procedure must be monitored.

The surgery suite is a high-risk area for restraint-related injuries. Unconscious patients are unable to inform the staff that nerves are being compressed or circulation has been diminished. Numerous lawsuits have involved patients awaking from surgery only to discover they have been injured due to improper positioning from operating room restraints. The operating room records are often replete of information on staff's monitoring circulation and checking patient position during the procedure.

Agency Policy

The agency policy on restraints should reflect health care standards (see **Part A**). For example, the agency should use only FDA-approved restraints. Policies should also reflect the federal standards on restraints as well as the applicable state law on restraint use. Long-term care facilities should acknowledge the federal Nursing Home Reform Act statement on a restraint-free environment for residents. Under the act, nursing homes are required to promote their residents' quality of life.

Federal Regulation

FDA approval is required for all restraints. The FDA maintains a complaint file on restraint use that is accessible to the public under the Freedom of Information Act (FOIA). The FDA also publishes safety alert notices that warn of the hazards associated with certain restraint devices. Continued use of a restraint that is a known hazard could be considered a violation of the standard of care.

The FDA requires the manufacturers to label the restraints. Nurses should verify that the vests, jackets, and other torso-restraining devices are labeled for size, weight limits, and device orientation (such as front/back and top/bottom). Labels should also include cautionary information (such as flammable), application steps, and warnings for incorrect application.

The Safe Medical Devices Act (1990) obligates facilities using restraints to report to the FDA all restraint-related deaths or injuries within 10 working days.

Documentation

Documentation must support the medical indications for restraint use as related to diagnosis or treatment (see **Part B**). Documentation should reveal that the restraint was not used for staff convenience and should indicate the frequency of monitoring the patient and that the patient was assisted with activities of daily living such as dressing, feeding, and toileting. Documentation must show that the informed-consent process took place.

Staff Education

The most effective way to decrease patient injury from falls and liability is for agencies to have in place a complete staff education course on restraints and fall prevention (see **Part C**).

29 Emergency Psychiatric Admissions

Melinda S. Monson, JD, MSN, RN

A Preventing Liability
- Know and strictly follow the state law and the facility's policy.
- Always work in conjunction with a skilled interdisciplinary team that specializes in mental health assessment.
- Assess the patient in a safe and nonthreatening environment, with particular attention to the presence of weapons and the immediate opportunity for harm.
- Establish a checklist that readily identifies the criteria for involuntary admission.
- Precisely document all findings, conclusions, and bases for commitment.
- Encourage confidential peer review and case studies on all patients who have been civilly committed.

B Dangerous Individuals Are
- Suicidal or homicidal
- At risk of imposing serious bodily harm to self or others
- Unable to satisfy their own basic physical needs if allowed to remain at liberty

Categories of Patients Most Frequently Found to Be Dangerous
- Substance abusers
- Individuals who are noncompliant with medications
- Individuals with long histories of violent behavior

C Procedural Process
Clinical assessment (usually performed initially by the nurse, followed and confirmed by other members of the interdisciplinary team)
- Detailed patient history
- Mental status examination with emphasis on suicidal/homicidal and safety issues
- Physical evaluation pertaining to self-care, nutrition, and coping strategies

Careful documentation
- Subjective and objective data
- Detailed support for the decision to commit
- Comprehensive plan of treatment

Civil certificate
- Signed by physician
- Witnessed as required

Strict adherence to institution policy governing commitment
- Admission procedures
- Clinical and judicial review
- Time parameters
- Discharge procedures

Although most individuals who are mentally ill recognize and welcome the need for treatment, others, by virtue of their impaired judgment and sense of reality, may resist treatment. In many settings, the nurse is the frontline consultant who, in conjunction with an interdisciplinary team of mental health professionals, is charged with the duty of ensuring that an individual in psychiatric crisis receives proper treatment. At times, proper treatment includes involuntary admission, also known as *civil commitment*. To avoid legal liability, the nurse must exercise due diligence in assessing and identifying patients subject to emergency civil commitment (see **Part A**).

Patient Rights versus Risk of Harm

Under the federal constitution, all individuals have the right to free speech, liberty, privacy, and procedural due process. Likewise, societal values encourage individuals to maintain a sense of personal integrity by exercising these rights without fear of undue judgment or constraint. The manner by which these rights are to be protected within the health care settings is outlined in state statutes, case law, and patients' bills of rights. Of primary concern is the delicate balance that exists between the patient's right to refuse medical treatment and the need to protect the patient and others from harm. The balancing of the two is greater in the mental health setting where legislation frequently recognizes a heightened sense of patient vulnerability.

The concept of emergency psychiatric admissions is akin to that of general emergency treatment. Specifically, patient consent is usually not required when lifesaving measures are necessary. Although nonconsensual treatment of mentally ill patients is almost never legally permissible, it is allowed when the individual demonstrates a danger to self or others.

Clinical Criteria for Determining Danger

Danger is generally defined as a serious mental condition that has been present for 30 days. Unfortunately, predicting which patients are dangerous is an imperfect science. However, several criteria have been established to identify patients who are dangerous (see **Part B**). Approximately one-third of all psychiatric emergency service patients present with suicidal or homicidal ideation, or both. The difficulty in predicting whether or not an individual is dangerous occurs when the patient presents without any history of having attempted suicide or having performed an assaultive act. Nurses have a tendency to overpredict individuals whom they believe to be dangerous, which is significant when considering legal liability and whether proper weight was given to the issue of patient rights versus risk of harm. On the other hand, liability has been imposed when nurses have failed to identify a dangerous patient who warrants emergency admission.

Legal Basis

As noted, mental illness alone is not a sufficient legal basis for detaining a patient. Additionally, in *O'Connor v Donaldson* (1975), the U.S. Supreme Court held that a state cannot constitutionally confine a patient without providing the necessary treatment or rehabilitation to enable reintegration into society.

Civil commitment is permitted but not required under all state statutes. Although civil commitment statutes vary from state to state, most set forth the essential elements pertaining to the nature and extent of commitment including the length of time one may be detained, mandatory psychiatric and judicial review, and the procedure by which a patient may challenge the process.

Under no circumstances should civil commitment be automatically equated with incompetence, since civil commitment does not negate the presumption of competence. Rather, even patients who have been admitted involuntarily to psychiatric service enjoy an absolute right to refuse medical treatment including antipsychotics, unless or until deemed incompetent to make such decisions. Likewise, the nurse may not assume that involuntary admission results in the forfeiture of basic patient rights or allows for legally sanctioned imposition or expansion of treatment. Simply stated, civil commitment provides the patient a safe environment under which he or she may seek treatment. The typical process under which civil commitment evolves is shown in **Part C**.

Legal Causes of Action

Several legal causes of action are associated with civil commitment. Three may be brought directly by the patient who alleges he or she has been wrongfully committed, and the fourth is typically commenced by a third party (i.e., someone other than the patient or mental health care worker) for damages allegedly sustained when the patient should have been committed but was not.

False Imprisonment

Although this cause of action is most commonly associated with improper civil commitment, it is the most difficult to sustain. The reason is that the claim implies that the mental health professionals deliberately and maliciously held the patient by ignoring the statutory requirements for commitment or by failing to evaluate the patient prior to commitment. The patient must prove the following to recover damages:

1. In the absence of his or her consent, the patient has been willfully restrained, restricted, or confined as a result of the defendant's actions.
2. The defendant intended to restrain, restrict, or confine the patient.
3. The defendant failed to adhere to the statutory requirements governing civil commitment.
4. The defendant's actions caused the patient injury.

Wrongful Commitment

A cause of action for wrongful commitment is based on negligence as opposed to deliberate intent. To prove that he or she has been wrongfully committed, a patient must show that the mental health professional erroneously certified the patient for commitment by virtue of a negligent diagnosis. Thus, although the diagnosis was rendered in good faith and without malice, it was negligently determined.

Infliction of Emotional Distress

Although relatively uncommon on their own, causes of action sounding in infliction of emotional distress are frequently linked with claims of negligence. Most claims alleging causation between an act and an emotional injury require evidence that the alleged mental stress produced physical injury. However, courts in various states have loosened this requirement, and some have allowed recovery in the absence of actual physical injury. It is conceivable that a patient who has been falsely imprisoned or wrongfully committed may be awarded damages solely based on emotional distress.

Failure to Warn of Harm to Third Party

This cause of action allows a third party to recover for injuries related to a mental health provider's failure to commit a dangerous patient. The seminal case is *Tarasoff v Regents* (1976) whereby the defendant was held liable for failure to warn an identified victim that the patient was dangerous and intended to harm her. The underlying legal issue was whether the patient should have been civilly committed in light of his expressed violent ideations.

30 Organ and Tissue Donation and Transplantation
Maureen Townsend, JD, RN

Matching Donors and Recipients
The Organ Procurement and Transplantation Network (OPTN) and The Scientific Registry of Transplant Recipients

- Acceptable organ donors can range in age from newborn to senior citizens.
- Donors are people generally in good health who have died suddenly, often through accidents, and have been declared brain dead. In this condition, brain function has permanently ceased, but the heart and lungs continue to function with the use of artificial life supports.
- There are 66 organ procurement organizations across the country which provide procurement services to the 275 transplant centers nationwide.

1. Patient enters the system

A. Donor enters the system

| Transplant Center | → | Waiting List |

| Donor Hospital |

2. Transplant center evaluates patient, adds name to waiting list, and transmits request to OPTN.

B. Hospital and Organ Procurement Organization (OPO) evaluate donor, transmit organ availability to OPTN.

3. OPTN adds patient to its waiting list. When a suitable organ match is found, transplant center is notified.

C. OPO compares available organ with OPTN patient waiting list. When a suitable patient is found, Recovery Team is notified.

Organ Procurement and Transplantation Network*

4. Transplant Team receives organ, performs transplant. →

← D. Recovery Team removes organ. Organ is transported to recipient transplant center.

Transplant Data

Follow-up: 6 month, 12 month, then annually

Scientific Registry of Transplant Recipients*

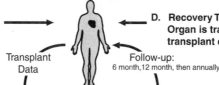

*Operated by the United Network for Organ Sharing (UNOS), Richmond, Va., under contract with the Health Resources & Services Administration, Bureau of Health Resources Development, Division of Organ Transplantation.

Legislation

Organ and tissue donation and transplantation are regulated by federal and state legislation. Current legislation in the United States prohibits the buying and selling of organs based on the belief that human organs and tissues are not products to be sold, but rather are humanitarian gifts. The following key acts affect donation:

1. The National Organ Transplant Act, passed in 1984, provides for the establishment of a task force on organ transplantation and an organ procurement and transplantation network and authorizes financial assistance for organ procurement organizations (OPOs).
2. The Omnibus Reconciliation Act of 1986 sets forth hospital protocols for organ procurement and standards for organ procurement agencies. Hospitals

participating in Medicare and Medicaid programs are required to establish written protocols to identify potential organ donors. The term *organ* means a human kidney, liver, heart, lung, pancreas, and any other human organ or tissue. Under these protocols, a health care facility must:

a. Ensure that families of potential organ and tissue donors are aware of their options to donate, or decline to donate, organs and/or tissues;
b. Encourage discretion and sensitivity with respect to the circumstances, views, and beliefs of the families of potential donors; and
c. Notify an OPO designated by the Secretary of Health and Human Services of potential organ donors.

Agency Protocols

Hospital policies and procedures must include criteria for identifying potential organ and tissue donors and a mechanism for notifying the family of each potential organ and tissue donor of the option to donate or to decline to donate organs or tissues. The protocols must indicate who notifies family members of their options and how such notification is handled. The protocol must provide for acceptance of a family's decision to decline the option to donate organs. Only staff members who have completed a training program designed to ensure discretion and sensitivity with respect to circumstances, views, and beliefs of the family are involved in the effort to identify potential donors and to make families of potential donors aware of their options. Additionally, hospitals must establish a training program consistent with these requirements in cooperation with the OPO to train and retrain staff members designated to notify the family of its options.

Donation Process

Organ donors usually die as a result of trauma, stroke, primary brain tumor, or cerebral anoxia (lack of oxygen to the brain). Homicide and suicide victims can donate organs with a medical examiner's permission. A person of any age may be a candidate for organ donation. Excluding criteria include transmissible disease (e.g., AIDS, hepatitis), sepsis, cancer (other than primary brain tumor or skin cancer), and organ-specific disease. Donors can be classified as a cadaveric organ donor—a person who died of an injury or illness that did not affect the major organs and who can be maintained on mechanical support; living related organ donor—a living person who donates a kidney (or a part of the liver or a lung) to an immediate blood relative; or living nonrelated organ donor—a nonblood relative or other person.

Tissue donors do not require intact circulation, but timing is still a critical factor and tissue donation surgery needs to take place within a maximum of 24 hours after death. A person who dies of cardiac (heart) failure is automatically disqualified from organ donation but may be a tissue donor. Even if an autopsy is required (e.g., for homicide and some accident victims), tissue donation is often possible. Organ donors can also donate tissue. Age limits vary for each type of tissue.

A health care team member or family member can alert the OPO of a potential organ or tissue donor. Prior to donation, donation coordinators begin donor evaluation by obtaining information about the time and cause of death, past medical history, and the immediate medical condition. Medical contraindications are ruled out and the family is approached, given the option of donation. The opportunity to donate is discussed with the family if the deceased has not consented previously. Consent for organ or tissue donation has to be given by the individual or by the legal next of kin.

Consent for Donation

Becoming an organ or tissue donor is as simple as filling out a Uniform Donor Card, signing it in the presence of 2 witnesses, and obtaining their signatures. It is important for the donor to notify family members of the wish to be a donor because donation will be discussed with them at the time of death. Sometimes the donor card is lost or not available, in which case the family will be asked to make the decision on the patient's behalf.

If there is no donor card, current policy in the United States requires that the donor or the next of kin give permission to proceed with organ and tissue donation (informed consent). In some states, "presumed consent" allows organs and tissues to be removed at the time of death without the permission of the donor or next of kin, as long as there has been no indication that donation is against the wishes of the donor. Legislation and policy have been written to protect the rights of the patients who have indicated, by signing a donor card, their desire to donate organs and tissue.

Procuring the Organ

When the organ donor has been evaluated completely and consent has been obtained, the donor will be taken to the operating room to have the organs removed. Matching of tissue donors with recipients is performed after the tissues are removed (see **Part A**). Unlike organs, which must be transplanted within hours, tissue can be stored for a longer time, up to several years for bone tissue. Because most cadaver tissue is processed, genetic matching is not required.

Donation Network

The Organ Procurement and Transplant Network (OPTN) maintains a computer system in Richmond, Virginia [also known as the United Network for Organ Sharing (UNOS)] that contains the names of individuals waiting for organs in this country. There are >150 transplant centers that share organs through this computerized organ-sharing system.

31 Discharge Against Medical Advice
Lynda L. Nemeth, JD, RN

A Discharge Against Medical Advice–Competent Adult
1. Offer services and treatment.
2. Explain risks and benefits for refusal of care.
3. Is this a competent adult?
4. Document item 2.
5. Attempt to have patient sign a waiver of treatment.
6. Continue to offer support, transportation, discharge instructions, supplies, and medications.
7. Document item 6.

B Discharge Against Medical Advice–Other Than Competent Adult
1. Offer services and treatment.
2. Explain risks and benefits for refusal of care.
3. Is this adult not competent, i.e., a minor, adult with questionable behavior, adult with evidence of alcohol or drugs?
4. Document item 3.
5. Seek surrogate for consent, i.e., parent, court-appointed conservator, health care agent.
6. If surrogate not available, seek guidance through risk management, social services, and administration.

C A Nursing Checklist for Patients Requesting to Leave Against Medical Advice

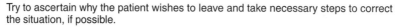 Try to ascertain why the patient wishes to leave and take necessary steps to correct the situation, if possible.

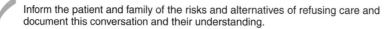 Inform the patient and family of the risks and alternatives of refusing care and document this conversation and their understanding.

 Depending on the situation, notify the appropriate members of the health care staff–the physician, the nursing supervisor, social services, and if necessary, risk management, security, or the police.

If all efforts to convince a patient to stay and receive necessary care have failed, provide the patient with a waiver to sign which states that the patient has been advised of the risks, benefits, and alternatives of refusing treatment and the potential consequence of such refusal. If the patient refuses to sign the waiver, document on the form that the information was given to the patient, provide the date, and sign your name after your comments and place in the patient's medical record.

Patients leaving an environment where medical care is available and either refusing initial treatment or continuing treatment cause concern from a medical, legal, and ethical viewpoint. Issues surrounding the rights of the patient, the accountability and liability of the provider, and the various settings where discharge against medical advice (AMA) may occur frequently cause uncertainty on the part of medical and nursing staff alike.

Patients' Rights

Under both common law and various constitutional rights, competent adults have the right to make decisions regarding their medical care and any invasions into the privacy of their body. *Competency* is defined as having the ability to understand the nature and effects of one's acts.

Nurses' Role

Nurses have a duty to act as the patient advocate. While it is a physician's responsibility to explain the risks, benefits, and alternatives to patients to enable them to make an informed decision or to give informed consent, the nurse may be the key player in getting patients to consider the alternatives or consequences of accepting or refusing care.

The nurse should document all efforts to provide the patient with the information necessary to make a decision to accept or refuse care. Documentation should be objective and include the date, time, who spoke with the patient, what the patient was told, comments made by the patient, and the final disposition. The nurse should also document names, telephone numbers, and referrals given to the patient on discharge as well as a description or listing of any preprinted instructions or verbal instructions on discharge.

A waiver, or refusal-of-care form, should be presented to the patient for signature and inclusion in the record. A refusal to sign the form should be noted on the document, which the person who proffered the information should sign. Continuing efforts to help the patient who refuses care or chooses discharge against medical advice should also be documented. For patients who do not fall into the designation of competent adult, attempts should be made to seek a surrogate decision-maker such as a parent, court-appointed conservator, or health care agent, while maintaining the patient in a safe environment.

Provider Liability

Various legal consequences should be considered when patients choose discharge against medical advice. If there is any question of the competency of the patient and the patient leaves, sustains an injury from failure to provide medical care, and sues, an action could be brought against the provider for abandonment or negligence.

The nurse has a duty to take appropriate action when there is a question of patient competency. The question should be raised with the examining physician and a psychiatric evaluation performed, if necessary, prior to allowing the patient to leave. The nurse as well as the provider could be held liable if a patient is allowed to leave against medical advice and there was any question as to the patient's ability to make a decision in his or her best interest.

If the assessing physician disregards the nurse's question of competency, the nurse should notify the supervisor of the concern and follow the chain of command. All efforts to protect the patient from future harm based on decisions made when the patient was incapacitated should be documented in chronological order, as should any follow-up efforts to check on the patient's safety after discharge.

The nurse might be in the dilemma of trying to balance the duty to protect the confidentiality of the patient against the duty to warn others of potential harm by the patient (to self or others). At times the nurse may have to make a decision to notify the police to either detain the patient, help find the patient who left without treatment, or notify relatives or friends if the patient verbalized threats against them. The nurse should be familiar with the employer's policy on police notification and involve the appropriate supervisory personnel in the decision to notify the authorities. Any decisions that would lead to a breach of confidentiality should be discussed and approved by the physician and appropriate management personnel.

Conversely, if a competent adult chooses discharge against medical advice and attempts are made to detain the patient, a legal action could be brought against the provider for assault, battery, or both and for false imprisonment.

Emergency Medical Treatment and Labor Act

Nurses should be cognizant of the Emergency Medical Treatment and Labor Act (EMTLA). The federal government enacted this "antidumping" law in 1986, and after several years of amendments, the Health Care Financing Administration (HCFA) adopted new regulations that expanded its scope in 1994. Under EMTLA, emergency department physicians and nursing staff are required to perform an appropriate medical screening examination and stabilize the patient prior to transfer if an emergency medical condition is identified. Patients may not be discharged or transferred unless they *refuse* treatment or request a transfer. Nurses working in an emergency department should be familiar with the federal mandates, hospital's policies, procedures, and forms to comply with this law in case a patient refuses a medical screening examination and stabilization or transfer. Nurses should ensure that documentation is appropriate and that the patient has a full understanding of the risks and alternatives of accepting or refusing care.

Nurses in the hospital emergency department may encounter particular problems when a pregnant patient has an actual or potential emergency medical condition, refuses care, and attempts to leave against medical advice. The risks to the unborn child must be weighed in relation to the rights of the mother to refuse care. In these instances, the nurse must immediately involve the supervisor, social services, and potentially outside agencies, such as the department of children and families, to protect the life of the unborn child.

Predictors

People who have a previous history of leaving against medical advice are more likely than not to repeat this behavior. Patients who do not have a primary care physician and those who have to wait an extended period for clinic appointments or emergency department visits have a higher incidence of choosing to leave without being seen. Other factors are religious beliefs and personal or financial obligations.

1. A Medicaid patient has confided in the nurse that he took an illegal drug prior to being admitted because he was nervous about the elective standard procedure he is to undergo. He is not acting inappropriately, but the nurse is concerned about the effects of the drug when mixed with the anesthetic. The patient's nurse first should:

(A) Keep the information quiet, for the sake of protecting his privacy

(B) Recognize that Medicaid patients have little or no understanding of the ramifications of such actions, and ignore it

(C) Tell the charge nurse and attending physician

(D) Speak with the patient about his fears and concerns

2. A man in a white lab coat is seen perusing a patient's charts. Although the nurse assumes he is a physician or on staff at the hospital, the nurse has never seen him before. The nurse should:

(A) Ignore him because the nurse is too busy to stop and ask him who he is

(B) Look for some kind of identification on his person that would indicate a connection to the hospital

(C) Identify himself or herself as the patient's nurse and ask him his name

(D) Ask other staff members if they have ever seen him before and if someone recognizes him, let it go

3. The nurse has just learned some information of a sensitive nature from a patient. To fulfill an ethical duty to the patient and maintain confidentiality, the nurse should:

(A) Determine if the information has any bearing on the patient's health care needs before it is charted

(B) Document the information in the health care record before it is forgotten

(C) Maintain the confidentiality of the information and not chart or report it regardless of what it is about

(D) Communicate the information only if the nurse feels it is in the best interest of the patient

4. The nurse should be vigilant in protecting private patient information. Which of the following indicates the nurse is following proper legal and ethical duties in this regard?

(A) Visitors are informed of the patient's progress if they are close relatives

(B) Spouses are automatically informed of their spouse's medical procedures if reproductive information is involved

(C) Work papers with patient-identifying information are kept behind the desk where only staff are allowed

(D) A newspaper reporter calls for information on a patient and the nurse reveals only favorable information of the patient's status

5. A nurse is caring for a patient who is heavily sedated. The patient previously told the nurse that he does not want chemotherapy. However, the family now wants to begin treatment. The best course of action for the nurse is to:

(A) Start the chemotherapy, since the physician has provided orders for it

(B) Refuse to begin the chemotherapy, since the patient now lacks the capacity to consent to therapy and has given clear notice that he does not want it

(C) Request the social worker to initiate guardianship proceedings since the family cannot give valid consent without a court order

(D) Consult the hospital ethics committee

6. A home care nurse notices that an elderly patient is having trouble managing her affairs. There is evidence that she is not eating properly and does not follow through on taking medications. There are no immediate family members to monitor her. The nurse should:

(A) Consider this a problem for the social worker and make a referral before her next appointment, which is scheduled next month

(B) Continue to observe the patient but take no further action until after a few more visits

(C) Document the observations in the health care record, initiate a social worker referral, and make some temporary arrangements (with the patient's permission) for assistance through the agency

(D) Initiate guardianship proceedings since the elder is not competent to care for herself

7. Informed consent is obtained prior to:

(A) All nursing procedures that involve touching the patient

(B) Only surgical procedures

(C) Invasive medical procedures that involve risks

(D) All emergency treatment

8. Informed consent requires which 3 elements?

(A) Confidential communications, patient competence and consent standard

(B) Information, patient competence, and voluntary consent

(C) Voluntary consent, patient competence, and patient's signature

(D) Voluntary consent, information, and patient's signature

9. A 78-year-old widow presents to the emergency department after a reported fall down the stairs at her home. She appears slightly confused and frail. She is complaining of back and hip pain. The physicians have recommended hip surgery. She tells the nurse how her late husband died on the operating room table several years ago, and she has sworn never to have surgery. The nurse should:

(A) Contact the legal department immediately

(B) Tell the patient she is being silly and she needs to have the surgery or she will never walk again

(C) Discuss your concerns with the charge nurse or the social worker or both

(D) Assess the patient's understanding and ability to comprehend the information further before taking any other action

10. A 27-year-old woman with strong religious beliefs against blood transfusions presented to the emergency department following a severe motor vehicle accident. Given the large lacerations and significant blood loss, the physicians wish to order several blood transfusions. She refuses, indicating that according to her religious beliefs she may not receive blood transfusions. The medical staff believes that if she does not receive blood transfusions in the next several hours, she will go into shock and possibly die. The nurse should:

(A) Call the risk management department immediately

(B) Seek intervention or consultation with the patient's spiritual adviser

(C) Assess whether the patient appears fully competent and aware

(D) Do all of the above

11. The nurse is caring for a 40-year-old woman who underwent a colon resection under general anesthesia

12 hours earlier. Upon arrival to her room, she is holding her abdomen, is not moving in bed, and is clenching her teeth. She complains of pain that has been present in the incisional area for the last hour. She is also complaining of nausea. She requested pain medication earlier. However, it was approximately 30 minutes too early for her as-needed dose of meperidine (Demerol), 75 mg intramuscularly every 4 hours. Her vital signs are as follows: temperature by mouth 100°F, blood pressure 140/90 mm Hg, respiratory rate 20, and heart rate 100 beats/min. All of these values are increased over her last set of vital signs. What does the nurse do first?

(A) Administer the meperidine

(B) Ask the patient additional questions about her pain to determine the nature, source, and intensity of the pain

(C) Notify the physician for an increase in the dosage of meperidine

(D) Medicate the patient for nausea

12. A home care nurse is caring for a 62-year-old man who is terminally ill with lung cancer, with metastases to the kidneys and cervical spine. Upon the nurse's arrival to his home, the bedridden patient is semiconscious and moaning. His blood pressure is 104/66 mm Hg; heart rate, 88 beats/min; and respiratory rate, 10. His wife and son are present and express concern about his pain and the ineffectiveness of the previous dose. The nurse checks the physician's orders and notes an order for morphine sulfate, 5 mg subcutaneously every 4 hours as needed. The nurse checks the medication records and notes the patient's last dose was administered approximately 4 hours earlier. The nurse knows from the medical records that the patient does not want to be in pain but is concerned about the respiratory depression associated with the administration of morphine sulfate and the respiratory rate of 10. Under the ANA's position on the administration of opioids to terminally ill patients in pain, an appropriate intervention would be to:

(A) Withhold the medication because of the diminished respiratory rate

(B) Offer alternative comfort measures

(C) Reassure the family that this pain is expected

(D) Administer morphine sulfate now

13. To ensure that the standard of care is met when the nurse is providing discharge instructions, the nurse should do all of the following except:

(A) Provide written instructions

(B) Assess the patient's literacy level

(C) Request the patient to demonstrate any skill needed for home care (such as dressing change)

(D) Take no further action if the patient refuses to participate in discharge teaching

14. A patient requests the nurse to teach him about an experimental drug that is not available at the hospital where he is receiving treatment. In fact, his physician does not approve of this treatment, but the nurse has some knowledge of it. Before the nurse decides how much teaching would be appropriate in the situation, she should consider that:

(A) She can teach the patient anything and refer him for treatment elsewhere

(B) No matter what the patient wants to know and how it is affecting his present treatment, it will not interfere with his present relationship with his physician

(C) She should not inform the physician about this or make a note in the chart since it may be contrary to the present treatment

(D) It may be best to explain to the patient that if he chooses this alternate therapy, the physician needs to be informed so the physician can consider this in light of his present treatment

15. A colleague who is busy asks a nurse to help administer her medications. The nurse is not familiar with one of the IV drugs to be given. The most *reasonable* action for the nurse to take is to:

(A) Give the medication following steps she has used with other IV drugs

(B) Refuse to give the medication because she is unfamiliar with it, and take no further action

(C) Look up the medication in authoritative drug references or check with a pharmacist regarding administration

(D) Consult with another nurse about how to administer the drug

16. A nurse has given the wrong medication to a patient. The nurse should do all of the following *except:*

(A) Chart the medication in the patient's medical record

(B) Take no action if there is no apparent patient injury

(C) Fill out an incident report

(D) Monitor the patient and document observations and assessment data

17. Nurses may disclose a patient's HIV information:

(A) When a known sexual partner is also a patient of the nurse

(B) To a family member who requests the information

(C) Never

(D) To other health care providers for the purpose of medical treatment when the information is in the medical record

18. The purpose of the HIV statutes related to public health and safety is to:

(A) Provide confidentiality

(B) Encourage early detection and treatment and prevent further transmission

(C) Disclose information to protect third parties

(D) Make HIV a protected disability

19. A 78-year-old widow presents to the emergency department after a reported fall down the stairs at her home. She is disoriented and frail, and her clothing appears somewhat disheveled and wrinkled. She is complaining of back and neck pain. Upon removing her clothing, the nurse notices several bruised areas on her arms. She is unable to tell what happened. Her adult son, however, is quick to point out how clumsy his mother is and how she won't change her clothing from day to day. He also will not leave the examining room while the nurse attempts to assist her in putting on a hospital gown. The nurse should:

(A) Contact protective services immediately

(B) Order the adult son to leave the room

(C) Discuss concerns with the charge nurse or the social worker

(D) Ask the patient directly if her son has harmed her

20. A 6-year-old first grader presented to the school nurse for the 10th time with a headache at 11 AM. The child does not have a temperature or chills but appears to be a bit shaky. Orange juice and crackers usually relieve the headache and the shakiness. The child is not very talkative about her home life and is evasive when asked about breakfast each time she is in the nurse's office. This time she has several large welts on her arm as well. When asked about the welts, she says she was "very bad." The nurse should:

(A) Contact the parents by letter

(B) Call the police

(C) Send her back to class after the juice and crackers

(D) Speak to the principal about reporting concerns to the local child protective agency and if the principal wants to wait, follow her advice

(E) Speak to the principal and if she doesn't want to contact the child protective agencies, do so anyway because the nurse is that concerned

21. An 11-year-old seeking STD treatment and birth control goes to the nurse practitioner in a family health clinic. The nurse knows that in most states the nurse:

(A) Must notify the girl's parents but this can be done after she is treated because the nurse doesn't need their consent for treatment

(B) Must notify her parents and get their consent prior to treating her

(C) May have to notify the state family services agency because she is under 12

(D) Can treat her without parental consent and charge her parents for services rendered

22. A surgical nurse who is religiously opposed to abortion for any reason is assigned to the operating room where an abortion is scheduled to save the mother's life. The nurse may:

(A) Not refuse an assignment for moral reasons

(B) Refuse an assignment for moral reasons but not under these facts because the goal of the abortion is to save the mother's life

(C) Refuse the assignment by notifying the supervisor and immediately leave the room to show the refusal

(D) Notify the supervisor and stay in the room until adequate relief is provided

23. A young woman arrives at the hospital in labor 26 weeks' gestation. She has had no prenatal care and is an IV drug user who is well known by the emergency department as being HIV positive. The baby girl is born with no spontaneous respiration and weighs less than 1,000 grams. She is intubated and head computed tomography reveals areas of intracranial bleed, most likely from an anoxic episode while in utero. Which of the following persons or resources is in the position to be the primary decision-maker for this infant's medical decisions?

(A) The mother is the primary decision-maker—it is presumed that as a parent she will act in her child's best interest

(B) The primary care provider has the medical expertise to determine the infant's prognosis and how aggressively the infant should be treated based on that prognosis

(C) The ethics committee should decide because it acts as a nonemotional facilitator with consultation from various experts who are not directly involved in the infant's care and have no personal gain

(D) All of the above

24. The Indiana case that influenced Congress to pass the 1984 Child Abuse Amendments involved a Down syndrome infant with a life-threatening physical ailment that had a 90% chance of being corrected. The parents refused treatment and the court upheld their right to do so. Which of the following was the legal standard used by the court to make this decision?

(A) Judicial review

(B) Substituted judgment

(C) Best interest

(D) State interest

25. The first line of defense in preventing falls is to:

(A) Properly restrain the patient

(B) Use side rails

(C) Assess the patient's risk factors

(D) Provide continuous monitoring

26. Proper use of restraints is indicated when:

(A) The family requests that the patient be restrained

(B) It is medically necessary for diagnostic or treatment purposes

(C) The patient is at risk and the staff is shorthanded and cannot provide monitoring

(D) The patient is noncompliant with a bed rest order

27. When predicting whether a patient is dangerous, all of the following factors should be considered except:

(A) Suicidal or homicidal ideation

(B) The risk of imposing bodily harm

(C) Whether the patient is taking antipsychotic medications

(D) Whether the patient can satisfactorily care for his or her own basic needs

28. Civil commitment or involuntary emergency admission is:

(A) Mandated by all states

(B) Analogous with a determination of incompetency

(C) A means by which treatment can be imposed even in the absence of patient consent

(D) A method of protecting the patient and others during psychiatric crisis

29. Hospital protocols for organ procurement (required for hospitals that participate in Medicare and Medicaid programs) must incorporate all of the following *except:*

(A) Notifying family members of their options to donate or to decline donation

(B) Use of only trained hospital personnel to work with families to discuss these options

(C) Use of patients who have donor cards without consideration of other potential donors

(D) Criteria for identifying potential organ and tissue donors

30. To ensure that their wishes are carried out at the time of consideration of organ donation, the nurse should inform patients or potential donors that:

(A) Persons should have made out a donor card and carry it with them at all times

(B) Family members should be informed of the patient's wishes

(C) Registration with an organ donation agency must have taken place in order for donation to occur

(D) Both A and B

31. A pregnant patient is admitted to the emergency department for a fever and respiratory illness. After being screened and examined, the physician finds that the patient is stable, but recommends inpatient treatment with IV antibiotics. The patient refuses this plan and wants to be discharged against medical advice (AMA). The nurse determines that:

(A) The patient cannot be discharged AMA because she is pregnant.

(B) The Emergency Medical Treatment and Labor Act (EMTLA) prevents her from leaving because the hospital can institute treatment, even in a nonemergency situation.

(C) Since the patient has been determined to be stable, she can most likely be discharged as long as there is an alternate treatment plan that does not present harm to the fetus.

(D) The patient should be allowed to leave as soon as the risks of nontreatment are explained to her, without considering the risks to the fetus.

32. A patient tells the nurse that she is leaving against medical advice despite the fact that she is seriously ill and in need of treatment. An acceptable action to take when someone chooses discharge against medical advice is to:

(A) Threaten to call security if the patient tries to leave the facility

(B) Put the patient in 4-point restraints

(C) Medicate the patient so he or she is unable to leave without assistance

(D) In a nonthreatening manner, explain the risks and alternatives of refusal of treatment; ask the patient to sign a release; offer assistance in discharge, transport, and medications/supplies; and give the patient written discharge instructions and names and numbers to call if the condition worsens

PART II: ANSWERS

1. **The answer is D.**

Although telling the charge nurse and attending physician is warranted, speaking with the patient *first* to obtain an understanding of his concerns may facilitate a means to educate and inform the patient of his rights. A direct explanation of the procedure and the possible drug interaction gives him some of the information he needs to make a choice about whether to proceed or not. One cannot protect a patient's privacy if the possibility of medical complications is present. The patient needs to know that as well.

2. **The answer is C.**

As a professional, the nurse cannot be timid or cavalier about protecting a patient's confidentiality. Although another staff member may have seen the man before, that does not ensure that he has a right to read a patient's chart or has a role in the patient's care. The nurse should confront the stranger, in the spirit of trust and cooperation, and ask enough questions to resolve concerns about his status.

3. **The answer is A.**

The nurse needs to first determine if the information is relevant and necessary to patient care. Patients may confide private information related to financial difficulties, marital infidelity, or other information that has no bearing on medical treatment. Answer B is not correct because the information may not necessarily need to be documented in the medical record. Answers C and

D are not correct because the nurse may need to reveal the information to an official agency as required by law or regulation, and it may not necessarily be in the best interest of the patient to do so. Sometimes confidential information must be revealed because it will protect others.

4. The answer is C.

Keeping work papers behind the desk keeps them from public view and protects the patient's right to privacy. Answer A is incorrect because permission must be received from the patient before information is disclosed to any relatives. Answer B is incorrect because even though it is tempting to give spouses this information, it may be something that the patient wishes to keep confidential. Answer D is incorrect because any information, even if favorable, cannot be revealed without the patient's permission.

5. The answer is B.

The nurse should not begin the treatment when there is a conflict with the patient's expressed wishes when he was competent. Answer A is incorrect because there is a question of patient consent, so the order should not be initiated. Answers C and D are not necessary until other interventions have been implemented. These actions are used as a last resort.

6. The answer is C.

The nurse needs to document properly the observations, but action should be taken as well. The support of a home health aide may be all that is needed, and the least restrictive alternative to the patient's autonomy should be sought. Answer A is incorrect because this problem should be dealt with in an interdisciplinary manner. Answer B does not include an intervention that would protect the patient's health and welfare. Answer D is incorrect because it is too drastic and makes assumptions that are beyond the facts presented.

7. The answer is C.

All invasive medical procedures that carry risk require informed consent. B is incorrect; although surgical procedures are invasive and usually carry some risk, there are also medical procedures that require consent. A and D are incorrect because informed consent is necessary before all invasive procedures that carry a risk. Not all emergency treatment is invasive and risky, and touching a patient requires consent (usually implied by the patient's action) but not informed consent.

8. The answer is B.

It states all 3 of the elements. A is incorrect because confidential communication is always a necessary re-

quirement of patient care but not a specific element of informed consent. C and D are incorrect. While consent, patient competence, and information are all elements of informed consent, the patient's signature is not necessary in some states as long as there is documentation on the informed consent in the medical record.

9. The answer is D.

Patients can refuse any type of medical intervention if they are competent to do so. Being slightly disoriented and frail does not necessarily assume incompetence. Certainly the patient's fears of surgery are based on her own experience with the loss of a life partner. While answer C may also be appropriate, a further assessment of her understanding is warranted before any other action is taken.

10. The answer is D.

This is an example of the difficult decision nurses and other health care providers may face. Hospitals usually have policies concerning the appropriate steps a health care provider must take in a nonemergent situation. However, borderline cases occur all the time. The spiritual advisor may help clarify the patient's choice, but maybe not. The risk manager will assist the staff with following agency policy for this situation. When a patient refuses lifesaving treatment, it is important to determine the patient's competency through appropriate medical channels and to document it. It may become necessary to obtain a court order when third parties are involved. For example, the patient may be the mother of a breast-feeding infant with no other family to care for the baby or may be pregnant. There are state statutes limiting a pregnant woman's right to refuse lifesaving treatment. Health care providers must be aware of the statutes in their state. The bottom line is that each case must be evaluated individually. While laws and guidelines give health care providers rules to follow, no one case can define this area completely.

11. The answer is B.

The nurse must determine whether the pain is acute pain associated with the surgical procedure and not from a new source, such as a pulmonary embolus or deep vein thrombosis. A, C, and D are appropriate interventions, but they are secondary to B.

12. The answer is D.

According to the ANA's position, the medication should be administered for pain management even if it hastens death. It is the nurse's ethical and moral obligation. (It must be consistent with the patient's wishes.) A is wrong because the patient wishes to be pain free. B and C are appropriate but secondary to the administration of pain medication.

13. The answer is D.

The nurse needs to document the fact that the patient refuses to take part in discharge teaching. This protects the nurse and the institution if a problem arises later from this lack of follow-up by the patient. Answers A, B, and C state principles or guidelines that should be followed to ensure that the proper standard of care is met.

14. The answer is D.

Although the nurse does have the right to teach patients about alternative treatments, this needs to be done in consideration of the patient's present plan of care. Since the physician is implementing a treatment at present, the physician should be informed if the patient seeks alternative treatment. Answers A and B are incorrect because the nurse cannot just refer the patient elsewhere—this could be considered interfering with the physician-patient relationship. Answer C is incorrect because the nurse may need to make a note in the chart so that others on the health care team can consider this in their care of the patient.

15. The answer is C.

The nurse should always seek information from the most authoritative references available. Nurses are not expected to know all information about drugs and their administration but are expected to use resources. This is a reasonable action under the circumstances. Answers A and D do not reflect safe practice, because all IV medications are not given in the same way and another nurse could give incorrect information. Answer B is not the best answer because the nurse has not attempted to find out how to give the medication safely. If she did lack the skill to do so after obtaining this information, then she should refuse to give the medication.

16. The answer is B.

All answers except B reflect reasonable and expected actions to follow in this situation. Accountability requires the nurse to document the medication in the patient's medical record, take steps to monitor the patient for any untoward effects, and file an incident report according to institutional policy. These actions will ensure that the proper standard of care has been followed. This does not mean, however, that the nurse may not be liable for a malpractice claim, disciplinary action by the state nursing board, or even criminal charges if a serious error has occurred.

17. The answer is D.

Most states allow disclosure to other health care providers when the information is in the record. Disclosure should be made for the purpose of medical diagnosis and treatment, and each provider who has the information has a duty to guard it confidentially. A is incorrect because some states only permit *physicians* to tell known partners. B is incorrect because the information is confidential even to family members unless the patient has authorized otherwise. C is incorrect because nurses may disclose information in the medical record when it relates to health care.

18. The answer is B.

The purpose of the statutes is to encourage patients to seek testing and medical care for HIV infection. Providing confidentiality is a means to achieve this (answers A and C). D is true under the Americans with Disabilities Act.

19. The answer is C.

Many times patients have been abused by their adult children; however, direct confrontations (as in B and D) probably will not facilitate a solution quickly. Contacting protective services may be helpful but would not be available immediately. The social service department of many hospitals is equipped to intervene and assist with interviews and arrange appropriate referrals if necessary.

20. The answer is E.

There may be policies and protocols for the school nurse to follow in any institution when it comes to reporting suspected child abuse. However, the bottom line is that not only does the nurse have a legal responsibility to report suspected child abuse in virtually every state but also ethical codes for nurses mandate this action as well.

21. The answer is C.

Most states require notice to the family service agency when a minor under a specified age (usually 12) seeks STD treatment or birth control (check the state statute). A is incorrect because notification requirements relate to abortion services. B is incorrect because most states encourage minors to seek STD treatment by dispensing with the usual parental consent requirement (check state statute). D is incorrect because most STD confidentiality statutes require that all information go only to the minor, and this includes billing for services.

22. The answer is D.

A, B, and C are incorrect because nurses may refuse assignments for moral reasons but within the legal constraints of refusal such as assuring that proper and appropriate nursing care will be given to the patient by another nurse and that the patient will not be harmed by the nurse's refusal.

23. The answer is A.

The mother is the primary decision-maker for her child unless there is a court order declaring her incompetent or unfit or the hospital requests judicial intervention when the mother is not making reasonable medical decisions in the child's best interest. B is incorrect, although the mother will not be able to make informed and reasoned decisions unless she has the input of the physician. C is incorrect because the ethics committee is not the primary decision-maker. However, the ethics committee may be involved, especially if the mother and physician are in disagreement. Judicial intervention may also become necessary if the decision-making process breaks down.

24. The answer is B.

The court substituted the parents' preference for medical care for the infant. A is incorrect because judicial review is not a standard. C is incorrect because in a best interest analysis, it is likely the court would reason that surgery with a 90% success rate would be in the infant's best interest. D is incorrect because under the state's interest of preserving life, it is likely that the court would rule in favor of the surgery.

25. The answer is C.

Risk factors must be identified to prevent falls, and this certainly must be done before restraints are used. A, B, and D are second lines of defense.

26. The answer is B.

Restraints are only indicated for diagnostic or treatment purposes. A is incorrect because a family may not order restraint use, although their concerns should be addressed and the patient assessed for the need for restraints. C is incorrect because restraints are never used for staff convenience and their use requires more monitoring not less. D is incorrect because restraints are not used for punishment or noncompliance.

27. The answer is C.

That a patient is taking antipsychotic medications is not a factor to consider because the patient may qualify as dangerous even when taking medication. The remaining factors are necessary to consider in order to identify whether a patient is a danger to self or others.

28. The answer is D.

Civil commitment is allowed but not mandated by states. Although it recognizes that a patient is danger-ous, it does not equate to incompetency, nor does it take away the patient's right to refuse treatment. The goal of civil commitment is to afford protection while encouraging the patient to undergo treatment that will enable a safe return to the community.

29. The answer is C.

Donors who do not have donor cards can be considered. Families of potential donors may know of the patient's wishes to be an organ donor whether or not the patient has an organ donor card. Answers A, B, and C state features required in the protocols.

30. The answer is D.

Potential donors should have a card and inform family members of their wishes. These suggestions ensure that donors' rights are upheld, but donation can occur without either of them present. Families can still be asked at the time of death to donate their loved one's organs. Answer C is incorrect because one does not have to register with an agency for organ donation.

31. The answer is C.

The risks of the discharge to the mother and the fetus must be considered before a pregnant patient can be discharged AMA. It is likely that if there is a safe alternative plan (e.g., home care with IV antibiotics), and all risks and alternatives have been explained, the patient should be allowed to determine her course of treatment. Answer A is incorrect because the patient does not lose all her rights to self-determination just because she is pregnant. Answer B is incorrect because the patient does not need to be stabilized and it is not an emergency situation. Answer D is incorrect because the needs of the fetus need to be considered as well, not just the patient.

32. The answer is D.

Answers A, B, and C would constitute assault, battery, and false imprisonment. Answer D provides for respect for the patient's autonomy while offering alternatives and ongoing support, as well as explaining the risks associated with the patient's choice in an objective and nonjudgmental manner. Documentation of the above will protect the provider from future allegations of abandonment or neglect.

PART III
Documentation Issues

32 The Health Care Record

Katherine McCormack Dempski, JD, BSN, RN

A

Objective Documentation
- Give all facts necessary to communicate the patient's status.
- State facts as you witnessed them — never making assumptions.
- Give supporting facts for assessments and objective findings.
- Document patient's condition, the nursing interventions, and outcomes.
- Document that you are safety conscious.
- Document the standard of care — keep in mind complications and your steps to avoid them.
- Never add subjective comments about the patient, family members, or colleagues.

B

Make Accurate Corrections
- Draw a single line through incorrect entry; date, time, and sign the correction; never use correction fluid or scribble out incorrect entries.
- Use addendums when important data are left uncorrected; date, time, and sign the addendum; indicate date and time the addendum refers to.
- Use late entries; document date and time.
- Never rewrite a note.

Documentation in health care records serves several functions. It serves as the main source of information regarding the patient's treatment and progress. It facilitates communication to all members of the health care team, which ensures continuity of care for the patient. Additionally, various professionals of the health care agency often review records to determine if the standard of care or agency policy is followed. A complete record is the best way to protect oneself from liability.

Review of Health Care Records

Peer review committees access records to determine whether quality patient care is rendered. Infection control and utilization review committees determine if agency policy and procedures are followed. Health care records also are used by those who are not members of the health care team but may have the authority to do so, including state licensing boards, an attorney with authorization, and insurance companies.

A Complete Record

A complete record gives a detailed and accurate description of the patient's condition, nursing assessment, nursing interventions, and outcomes. The nurse should document objectively all the facts necessary to communicate the patient's status to other members of the health care team (see **Part A**). Clear and concise description of a patient's condition will assist nurses in noting subtle changes.

When documenting nursing assessments and interventions, nurses should keep the standard of care for that particular patient in mind. Nurses need to show their awareness of a patient's potential complications and show that steps are being taken to avoid them. Nurses also should document precautions being taken to safeguard the patient.

A complete record always includes the following:

1. Timeliness. Nurses' notes are best written while events are fresh in their memory. It is difficult to remember an incident years later when most liability

cases come to trial. An accurate and complete record can be used to refresh the nurse's memory. During legal proceedings, the medical record is often called the "witness that never dies." Complete and timely documentation works in the nurse's favor.

2. Date and time notes. A nurse's note is never complete without documentation of the date and time the note was written. Often the note is actually written after a nursing assessment. The correct time of the note should be written but the note can include when the assessment actually took place. Providing the chronological order of events is important to ensure the patient receives the correct progression of medical care. For example, the health care team needs to know exactly when a patient's condition began to respond well to treatment or deteriorated.

3. Name and title. A nurse's name and title in every note is part of a complete record. When a multidisciplinary team approach is being used, RNs, physicians, dietitians, physical therapists, occupational therapists, or nurse's aides are all documenting on the same progress reports. Documentation of titles explains which discipline has taken part in the medical care and who the team members are. It also shows which members of the team have performed their part in patient care. It is acceptable for the nurse to place initials on a data flow sheet, but full name and title should appear somewhere on the sheet to coincide with the initials.

4. Patient's name. The patient's name must appear on each page of the medical records. It is too easy to place a loose flow sheet from 1 patient's record or bedside into the record of another. That flow sheet will inaccurately become the permanent part of another patient's medical history. Often, specific sections of medical records are photocopied and sent to consulting health care providers. It is difficult to prove which patient these nameless records belong to. Poor record keeping could be construed as poor nursing care.

5. Neatness counts. Nurses don't have to win penmanship contests, but they do have to meet the professional standard of care in documentation. Communication between health care providers is the primary purpose of health care records. A nurse's note that is difficult to read or understand will fail to meet this standard. Sloppy records often equate with sloppy nursing care.

Objective Documentation

Nursing assessments are stated objectively and based on facts and observation. Whenever possible, the nurse should use measurable terms. For example, a wound should be described as "the size of a dime" or "2 cm wide" instead of just referred to as "small." When describing a patient's demeanor, the nurse should give an objective reason for the assessment. An example would be, "Patient's affect was flat as evidenced by his monotonous tone." The only subjective data in a nurse's note should be the patient's own statements placed in quotes. Generally, the nurse should not state conclusions without supporting facts.

When at all possible, the nurse should document facts that are personally witnessed rather than what someone else states. The exception to this would be the patient's own words in quotes or paraphrased. The nurse should be cautious about assuming anything, even what may be obvious.

Medical Abbreviations

Only agency-approved medical abbreviations should be used in medical records. Abbreviations that are not standard or agency approved through its policy and procedure manuals will only hinder communication.

Correcting Mistakes in Documentation

All mistakes made in documentation must be corrected according to the agency policy. Failure to properly correct a mistake could be construed as altering a record and is indefensible. **Part B** lists general tips on proper corrections but the nurse should always check agency policy first.

Maintain Professionalism in Documentation

A nurse's subjective comments concerning a patient or patient's family members do not belong in a medical record and will only cause legal problems for the nurse. When a patient is being uncooperative to medical care, the nurse should document the patient's behavior and subjective comments in quotes. This gives the reader notice of the uncooperative behavior in matter-of-fact terms without the nurse's subjective opinion.

Likewise, nurses and other health care providers should be careful not to express opinions concerning colleagues in a patient's medical record. Unprofessional documentation can equate unprofessional nursing judgment and care in the eyes of the patient or anyone else reviewing the medical record. Problems with coworkers should be addressed through other more appropriate channels.

Charting by Exception

Charting by exception is being practiced in some health care agencies to decrease the amount of documentation. Under a charting-by-exception policy, nurses do not document expected outcomes; they only document changes in a patient's condition outside the expected norm for that disease process and hospital course. However, nurses should document data such as daily vital signs.

Nurses need to be aware of any state or local regulation on documentation. No matter what form of documentation is used, nurses must document the standard of care for each specific patient. Hospital documentation policy must be cross-referenced with any local regulation. The department of public health and the local chapter of the ANA may be a source on state regulations.

33 Computerized Records

Diana C. Ballard, JD, MBA, RN

A   Computerized Patient Records: Key Issues for Nurses

- Authentication of entries to patient records
- Protection of confidentiality of the information
- Prevention of unauthorized access

B   Electronic Signatures Deemed Acceptable

1. Unique to person using it
2. Capable of verification
3. Under the sole control of the person using it
4. Linked to data in such a manner that if data are changed, signature is invalidated
5. Conforms to regulations adopted by the Secretary of State

C   Keys to Computer Stystem and Patient Record Security

- Password protection
- System education and training
- Control and limit user access
- Monitor access and detect breaches
- Be alert
- Overprotection is the best approach

As movement toward computerized patient records (CPR) advances, concerns grow with respect to protecting privacy and maintaining confidentiality of medical records that are stored on computers or maintained in computer databases. Advantages of such systems include the availability of patient records at the time and place they are needed, availability of large volumes of data that can assist in medical research, and streamlined billing practices due to recording of instances of treatment in a uniform manner. Risks associated with such systems include access by unauthorized users, altering of vital medical information, improper disclosure of private information, and infection by computer viruses that could impair or shut down a system entirely.

The expanding needs for medical information must be balanced against the requirement to ensure the security and personal privacy of each individual's medical record. Those responsible for management and maintenance of the system may be liable for harm caused by improper intrusions into the system.

As with traditional "paper" records, the nurse is responsible to see that CPRs remain confidential, accurate, legible, secure, and free from unauthorized access. Key issues for nurses are listed in **Part A**.

Legal Framework—Federal Protection

Privacy protects an individual's control with regard to use and disclosure of personal information. Courts are generally in agreement that patient records are protected by a privacy right grounded in the 14th Amendment of the U.S. Constitution. The Privacy Act of 1974 protects health information collected by federal agencies and includes regulations concerned with alcohol and substance abuse records. However, currently no federal law protects the confidentiality of individually identifiable health information in the private sector.

The Health Insurance and Portability Act of 1996 involves standardizing the electronic data interchange of certain administrative and financial transactions while protecting the security and privacy of the transmitted information. Other proposals continue to be under consideration at the federal level.

State Approaches

Current state laws and regulations vary from state to state and are inadequate and inconsistent. Accordingly, nurses should familiarize themselves with the laws of the state in which they practice to know what effect they might have on management of computer records and nurses' responsibility.

The National Conference of Commissioners on Uniform State Laws has developed model legislation and adopted rules regarding the disclosure of patient records. These laws can be adopted as framework for similar legislation at the state level. The vast majority of states have not yet adopted this uniform approach.

Liability for Unauthorized Disclosure of Medical Information

A common-law fiduciary duty is an obligation imposed between parties who have a relationship of special trust and confidence. Nurses occupy this trusted position with respect to their patients and with regard to maintaining the privacy of information derived out of the course of that relationship. Use or disclosure of this private information without consent or authorization may result in liability for damages.

Nurses further have a legal duty to maintain the confidentiality of a patient's medical information, a duty that arises from the obligation to perform according to the appropriate professional standard. A nurse who breaches this duty to perform according to the proper professional standard (negligence) may be liable for any resulting harm.

Authenticating Entries: Electronic Signatures

Entries made to a record, whether paper or electronic, must be signed. There are 2 categories of signatures associated with electronic transmission, electronic signatures and digital signatures, and their purpose is to guarantee a level of validity, authenticity, and security in electronic transactions that are not conducted in person. Electronic signatures are any form of electronic mark on a message or document. It is typically defined by any combination of letters, characters, or symbols entered directly into a computer or by some other electronic means. It is executed or adopted by a party to authenticate a document or entry. A digital signature is an electronic encoded message containing a unique alphanumerical notation. A "key pair," a private and a public key, is used to scramble a message and then unscramble or decrypt the information. Each digital signature is unique and can be linked back to the sender by using the appropriate public key, assuring each party that the other is who they say they are and that the message received is valid and unchanged.

Several states have imposed criteria that must be met to determine whether a particular electronic signature is legally sufficient to have the same force and effect as the use of a manual signature (see **Part B**). State and governmental agencies may be delegated the responsibility to devise rules and regulations for electronic authentication.

Maintaining Security of Information in Computer Systems

Nurses will be both key users of the CPR system and in a position to be alert to issues associated with control of access to the system (see **Part C**). Accordingly, nursing input at the outset can help design system controls that will minimize risks associated with implementation and use. Persons or entities using these technologies must adopt policies and procedures that reflect reasonable efforts to protect patient confidentiality.

The key to controlling direct access at this time is usually an individual's password. Passwords should *never* be revealed to another person and should be changed periodically. In addition, a user should not leave the computer workstation without "logging out" or "signing out" according to proper procedures.

At this time, the greatest threat to the integrity of a CPR system is inappropriate entry by someone from within the organization who has "stolen" passwords by observing users' keystroke entries or who has copied private files onto small floppy disks and carried them out of a facility or office. Maintaining alertness with regard to use of the computer itself may prevent such acts.

All staff using the system must have proper and adequate training prior to their actual use of the system.

Access to data should be permitted only according to limits based on a person's "need to know." By signing on with a unique password, users are permitted access only to the areas of the system necessary for their work.

The system must monitor and record all uses of the system to track access to the system. If a breach is detected, the "audit trail" created can provide valuable help in investigating the breach and permit corrective action and any necessary changes to the system.

Nurses must take note if they do not know who is at a terminal and intervene if they observe a person accessing a screen that he or she should not have access to or that appears improper. The alertness of nurses in the patient care workplace has prevented many problems in the past and will no doubt be critical to preventing the type of problem that can occur when there is improper access to this highly confidential information.

34 Interdependent Nursing Functions/ Implementing Orders–Part I

Katherine McCormack Dempski, JD, BSN, RN

A Verbal Order

- Clarify; repeat back the order.
- Get it in writing as soon as possible.
- Have witnesses present when possible.
- Get it directly from the physician, not from a third party.
- No proof of verbal order is practicing medicine without a license.

B DNR Orders
|
Must be written
|
Renewal per agency policy

Competent patient   Incompetent patient

Patient's written or   Family determines
verbal statement   patient's wishes

Implementing verbal, telephone, and do-not-resuscitate (DNR) orders as well as triage telenursing are interdependent nursing functions because they rely on a physician's medical assessment, diagnosis, and judgment. As such, the nurse implementing the orders must exercise independent judgment and carry his or her own legal liability.

Verbal Orders

Ideally, physicians' orders should be written to decrease the potential for errors. However, in emergency situations, verbal orders are often a necessary method of communication between physicians and nurses. Most health care agencies have policies and procedures describing situations where verbal orders must be written and signed by a physician and nurse, usually within 24 hours. Health care agencies accepting Medicare and Medicaid must follow federal regulations on the signing of verbal orders.

To minimize the potential for human error, the nurse receiving a verbal order should repeat the order back to the physician so any misunderstanding can be clarified immediately. Involving others as witnesses to the verbal orders provides proof a verbal order was given and minimizes the possibility that the physician may later change a verbal order that caused patient harm. A nurse should not take a verbal order from a physician through third parties such as the physician's office staff. This increases the potential for miscommunication, and the nurse implementing the order retains liability (see **Part A**).

Nurses should further protect themselves from liability by ensuring that the agency has policies and procedures in place for accepting and documenting verbal orders. The policy may require that a coworker witness the verbal order and cosign the written order. The policy should also determine the time frame for the physician to sign the written order. Documentation should include the time and date the verbal order was given and the time and date the order was implemented.

When the nurse believes a physician may later deny giving a verbal order, the nurse should follow agency procedure to involve the chain of command (i.e., nursing supervisor to director of medical services). The nurse should document on an appropriate agency form (documentation of a disagreement with a physician does not belong in the medical record) the circumstances surrounding the verbal order including the names of witnesses.

Questioning a Physician's Orders

The nurse's duty to the patient does not end with documentation that the nurse disagrees with the physician's orders, assessment, or diagnosis. Nurses can be held liable to a patient for injuries received from a physician's negligence when the nurse recognized (or failed to recognize) the negligence and did nothing to prevent it (failing to exercise the duty to act as the patient's advocate). The nurse should begin with discussing the situation with the physician. When a physician reacts negatively, the nurse has a duty to take the next step up the chain of command by following agency policy. The nurse should document on the appropriate agency form each level taken. While taking concerns up the chain of command, a nurse can still be liable for a patient's change in condition.

Do Not Resuscitate

The PSDA requires that health care agencies receiving federal funding ask patients whether they have advance directives (legal documents that inform health care providers of the patient's health care choice regarding receiving or refusing life-sustaining measures). The decision to receive or refuse extraordinary life-sustaining medical resuscitation belongs to the patient. The primary care physician in conjunction with other health care providers must provide the patient with the medical information necessary for the patient to make an informed decision on life-sustaining measures.

The most crucial element of the do not resuscitate (DNR) order is that the patient makes his or her specific wishes clearly known through advance directives or a written or verbal statement. In the case of a verbal statement it is prudent for the primary physician to document the circumstances surrounding the statement, including the names of any witnesses. The family of a patient who has not completed advanced directives but has suffered an incapacitation will determine the patient's wishes for extraordinary measures (see **Part B**).

The primary care physician is responsible for writing the DNR order. The order should be written according to the health care agency's policies and procedures and should clarify the specific actions to be withheld according to the patient's wishes. Agency policy may require that DNR orders be updated or reassessed periodically (usually every 72 hours). Additionally the agency bioethics committee may review the DNR process.

Nurses at the bedside bear the responsibility (and legal liability) of initiating cardiopulmonary resuscitation or making sure that unwanted attempts are not initiated. It is imperative that nurses have a clearly defined DNR order outlining the wanted versus unwanted extraordinary measures. Confusing or conflicting DNR orders and agency policies leave the nurse and the agency in an ethical and legal dilemma. To prevent the dilemma, the ANA position statement on DNR decisions recommends that nurses have a central role in the institution's DNR policy-making process. Nurses should assist in making patients and family members aware of advanced directives and the importance of having a patient's wishes identified.

Nurses must consider the possible legal liability involved when a patient does not have a DNR order but is found to have no spontaneous respirations or heart sounds. In that case the nurse may determine that resuscitation efforts would be futile. However, the nurse must be aware of the state statute on pronouncing death. Some specifically enumerate situations where a nurse may pronounce death, and others only allow physicians to do so, in which case the nurse may have to initiate resuscitation until a physician pronounces death. Depending on the language of the statute, this may be done over the phone.

Interdependent Nursing Functions/ Implementing Orders–Part II

Katherine McCormack Dempski, JD, BSN, RN

C Triage Documentation

- Caller's name
- Patient's name (if not the same)
- Telephone number (for follow-up)
- Medical history
- Allergies
- Nature of injury or illness
- Patient's age
- Whether nurse followed or deviated from protocol (document reasons)
- Discussion with physician
- Orders given
- Actions taken
- Information given to caller
- Response

D Telenursing

Nurse must know the following for each state the patients call from:

- Does telenursing fall within state NPA as a "nursing function"?
- Does state require the nurse to be licensed in that state?
- Does state require physicians to be licensed in that state before diagnosing or treating patients? (Nurse must know this before implementing physician's order.)

Telenursing

Telemedicine uses technology to communicate patient care information from one place (or institution) to another, including transmitting a patient's radiographic scan images (teleradiology) and telephone triage (telenursing).

Triage

Giving advice or triage over the telephone constitutes the practice of nursing under the NPAs of most states.

Accordingly, triage advice given by a nurse must follow applicable standards of care and should not include a medical diagnosis. Nurses performing telephone triage should follow clearly defined protocols based on medical and nursing disciplines. Scripted protocols can guide the nurse in questioning the caller for an appropriate assessment, medical history, and the nature of the injury (see **Part C**). Protocols also act as standing orders that the nurse is not making a medical diagnosis or practicing medicine. Protocols serve as

III. DOCUMENTATION ISSUES

evidence on whether the standard of care was followed should a lawsuit arise from the incident. Although the nurse is following protocols, triage nursing requires independent nursing judgment and skills. The nurse has a duty to assess when a patient's condition calls for a deviation from the protocol. In emergent situations protocol may require the nurse to stay on the phone with the caller (to ensure that the caller receives the appropriate help) and have a colleague initiate the emergency response system.

Nursing Considerations

Telenursing for regional or national HMOs or health care institutions may require nurses to speak to patients in another state. Telenursing is advancing faster than the law in this area. Because the definition of *telenursing* would be included in most NPAs, the nurse may need a license to practice nursing in the state where patients are calling from as well as the state where the nurse is. The nurse triaging across state lines should contact the state nursing boards to clarify the need for a license or check with the employer's risk management office for the protocol on multistate triaging (see **Part D**).

Although telemedicine is relatively new technology, several states have statutes regulating this practice. Some states require out-of-state physicians performing telemedicine to be licensed when making a diagnosis and ordering treatment in that state. Accordingly, nurses should be aware of this when implementing the orders of an out-of-state physician. Additionally, several states require the physician to inform the patient about the limitations of telemedicine and obtain *written* informed consent (usually informed consent can be written or oral).

36

Incident Reports

Joanne P. Sheehan, JD, RN and

Katherine McCormack Dempski, JD, BSN, RN

A Documentation in Incident Reports

- Date, time, location of incident
- Patient's name or injured person's name
- Family members notified and method of notification
- Physician, supervisor, administrator notified, time noted
- Objective and factual description
- Assessment of patient
- Treatment rendered
- Actions taken
- Information on witnesses
- Degree of injury

Defining an Incident

An *incident* is an occurrence that has the potential to put the institution at legal risk. Incidents most often involve an injury or a potential injury to a patient, patient's family member, staff member, or visitor or damage to property. Examples of incidents are burns, medication errors, abuse, equipment failure (with or without an injury), criminal activity, refusal of medica-

tion, refusal of treatment (especially when treatment is established and patient suddenly refuses), and blood exposure.

Purpose of Incident Reports

Incident reports are a risk management tool most often used for quality assurance purposes. These reports assist the facility in identifying areas of risk to patients and staff and to prevent incidents from recurring. Additionally, the reports identify system problems and act as an investigative tool for finding solutions.

Confidentiality

The incident report is intended for use within the facility itself—not for distribution to others—and therefore should remain confidential. Documenting "Confidential" on the report may prove the agency's confidential intent of the report. An incident report is not part of the patient's medical record. Nor should the nurse document in the patient's medical record "incident report completed." Doing so incorporates the incident report by reference into the medical record, and therefore could be discoverable in a legal action. The nurse should not give copies of the incident report to the patient or family members. Additionally, nurses should not keep a copy of the incident report for their personal files. This would constitute a breach of confidentiality and may be a violation of the facility's policies and procedures.

The incident report may identify an event for which the agency is liable. In most states the incident report is not discoverable to the opposing side. The agency's insurance company may require the agency to complete a report on certain incidents. The agency's policies and procedures should reflect this. If an incident report becomes part of the medical record by a breach of confidentiality, courts may allow the opposing side to obtain a copy and use it against the agency and all professionals involved.

Completing the Incident Report

All facilities have approved incident report forms to be completed when an incident occurs. Included in the incident report is an objective and factual description of the incident (without blaming anyone), an assessment of the patient, severity of the injury, treatment rendered, and any other actions taken (**Part A**). Additionally, names, addresses, and phone numbers of witnesses should be recorded. If an incident involves a staff member, the incident report should indicate the medical treatment provided for the staff member.

The most important aspect of completing an incident report is to document facts only as personally witnessed. No assumptions should be made about how an incident occurred. Preprinted agency reports may require the nurse to identify suspected causes of an event or to speculate how the incident may be avoided. If the nurse does not feel qualified to document suspicions or speculation, he or she should discuss this with the risk manager.

The incident report should be completed prior to the end of the shift during which the incident occurred. If this is not possible, it should be completed within 24 hours of the incident. The incident report should be forwarded to the appropriate supervisors and administrators pursuant to the facility's policies.

Documentation in the medical record when a patient is involved in an incident is similar but with a different focus. The focus is on the incident as it affects the patient's medical status and the medical care rendered and actions taken to ensure patient safety. For example, the nurse records many of the same facts: date and time of the incident, a concise factual description, assessment of the patient, names of family member and physician notified, and all treatment and follow-up care rendered. However, unlike the incident report, the medical record does not focus on agency policies for avoiding further incidents.

Duty to File

Because the incident report is for quality assurance purposes and internal investigations of system problems, it is the nurse's duty to file an incident report when an error is made. Witnessing a coworker's error also carries the same duty, especially if the nurse making the error does not file a report or the nurse witnessing the error has a differing factual account. To encourage the quality assurance aspect of incident reports, most states have qualified privilege immunity. Nurses completing an incident report have immunity from being sued for libel by a coworker. This privilege does not shield from liability when the nurse makes a false statement or recklessly disregards the truth when filing the report.

Falsifying a Report

A nurse who falsifies an incident report is susceptible to discipline action by the nursing board and civil penalties under state and federal regulations. Health care agencies, especially long-term care facilities, must comply with state and federal regulations. Under these regulations, civil penalties are attached to those falsifying records.

When a falsified report involves a patient incident, the nurse is susceptible to a nursing malpractice claim. A falsified report may convince the judge or the jury that the nurse tried to cover up the substandard care.

Unfortunately, supervisors or other authoritative figures may request that a nurse falsify a report. The nurse must refuse on legal and ethical grounds. The nurse who is either discharged or feels compelled to leave under these circumstances may have some legal recourse. Under wrongful discharge, the nurse must show that the discharge was against public policy for refusing to participate in illegal or unethical behavior. Under "constructive discharge," the nurse must prove that after refusing the unethical behavior, the work environment was so intolerable or hostile that the resignation was forced.

37 Forensic Issues

Regina M. DeLuca, JD, BSN and
Susan Westrick Killion, JD, MS, RN

A Documentation

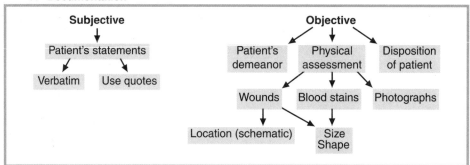

Subjective → Patient's statements → Verbatim, Use quotes

Objective → Patient's demeanor, Physical assessment, Disposition of patient

Physical assessment → Wounds, Blood stains, Photographs

Wounds → Location (schematic), Size Shape

Blood stains → Size Shape

B Evidence Collection

- Remove clothing without destroying evidence (do not cut through blood stains or entryway of penetrating object, i.e., knife, bullet).
- Document disposition of evidence.
- Label and identify specimens.

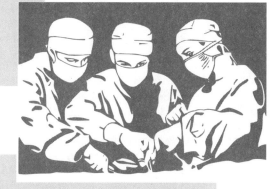

C Chain of Custody

Identify everyone handling evidence   Disposition of evidence (who receives it)

Document in medical record and appropriate agency forms

Forensic means "pertaining to the law." Forensic issues arise with victims of domestic violence or sexual assault and patients injured by trauma and accident. The victim's initial contact with the health care system is usually the nurse, and for this reason nurses share a responsibility with the legal system and must be familiar with basic forensic concepts.

Every hospital accredited by the JCAHO is required to formulate written policies and procedures related to the collection of evidence. In fact, the JCAHO has rec-

ommended that a forensic nurse be available on every shift in the emergency department. Nurses should be familiar with and adhere to an institution's guidelines on forensic evidence collection.

Documentation

Completeness and accuracy are the hallmarks of a properly documented medical record that subsequently might be used for legal proceedings (see **Part A**). The nurse's note should be factual and nonjudgmental and include the nurse's observations of the patient's appearance and demeanor. Statements of the victim should be noted in quotation marks and should be verbatim. These statements, if made for purposes of medical treatment, are usually admissible in later legal proceedings. Generally, they are obtained when taking the history from the injured patient or victim.

Documentation of the nurse's findings on the physical assessment should include a detailed description of all body wounds and marks. The use of a "body map" or a schematic of the body is a valuable tool to depict the locations of wounds and marks. The description should include the shape, size, and color of the wounds and marks. General descriptions such as "laceration" can be improved by describing wound edges as "jagged," "smooth," or "deep." Any blood stains or bloody fingerprints should be described. Physicians may report findings of a physical exam to the nurse, who should record them accurately and completely. Proper documentation also includes treatment and the patient's response to the treatment as well as the disposition of the patient.

Any photographs obtained or physical evidence collected should be carefully documented in the medical record. A photograph taken before surgery or treatment may be important in establishing facts related to the incident as based on the wound or injury.

Evidence Collection

The Emergency Nurses Association believes that nurses should have the skills needed for evidence collection and preservation since . . . "it is within the nurse's role not only to provide physical and emotional care to patients, but to help preserve the 'chain' of evidence collected in the Emergency Department." The ANA also has promulgated a statement on the scope and standards of practice in forensic nursing.

Treatment of life-threatening injuries takes precedence over evidence collection. At all times, evidence collection should not interfere with treatment. Nurses should always maintain universal precautions in collecting specimens. Each item collected should be handled and packaged separately. Most emergency departments have rape kits available for the collection of evidence in sexual assault cases. Nurses should be familiar with the proper and complete use of these kits.

Ordinarily, clothing and shoes are given to the patient's family; however, they may be evidence depending on the situation. Shoes may be very important evidence of where a victim has been and should be treated as such. When removing clothing that has blood stains or other evidence of injury, the nurse should cut away from the site of injury or cut on the seamlines, not through the site. Any foreign bodies such as bullets or knives should be handled as little as possible, being careful not to mark these items.

Any evidence collected should be labeled accurately and completely, identifying the specimen as well as who collected it (see **Part B**).

Evidence Preservation

After collection and labeling of the evidence, the chain of custody must be documented, identifying anyone who has handled the "evidence" and the responsible agency (e.g., police or medical examiner) or individual who receives the evidence (see **Part C**). This information should be contained in the medical chart for use in later legal proceedings. The number of individuals handling specimens should be kept to a minimum to ensure the integrity of the specimen.

Many emergency departments have a chain-of-custody form that is used when evidence is obtained from the patient. It documents the name of anyone who has had access to the evidence and serves as a log of where the evidence has been and who has handled it. This chain of custody becomes important as to the admissibility of the evidence at trial.

Suspected Drug Abuse or Possession

When a nurse finds drugs in a patient's possession while searching for something else (such as identification), the nurse should follow hospital policy for this situation. Often the drugs need to be confiscated, and security officers should be involved. If the nurse thinks that a patient is abusing drugs, and this is interfering with treatment, a search may be warranted. Documentation should objectively state behaviors or symptoms that lead to this suspicion. Again, the nurse should request the assistance of security officers before any search is completed, and all policies should be adhered to strictly. The physician also should be notified of the facts, as this information may affect the patient's treatment.

Accident or Trauma Incidents

Forensic nursing concepts are important in cases of accidents, trauma, or even death, not just where crimes are suspected. Thorough histories and assessments are invaluable to others trying to establish facts surrounding the incidents. Identification of bodies involves forensics, and nurses may participate in interviewing families of the deceased. Any suspicions of abuse of children or others calls for careful application of the principles of assessment, identification of any wounds, statements, and evidence collection. It may be the nurse who suspects that some aspects of either the family's or victim's statements do not "match" with other data.

Testimony

As a consequence of involvement in care and treatment of an injured victim, the nurse may testify in legal proceedings. Competency and credibility as a witness cannot be undermined if the nurse adheres to the basic principles of evidence collection and preservation as well as accurate and complete documentation in the patient's medical chart.

1. The nurse is making rounds when she notices Mr. Jones is not in his room. Mr. Jones is a 77-year-old diabetic patient who recently underwent debridement to improve healing on his left foot. He is being seen by a physical therapist to assist him with use of a walker. The therapist commented on the trouble Mr. Jones is having adjusting to the walker. As the nurse walks farther down the hall, she sees Mr. Jones lying flat on the floor with his walker on top of him. There is a small puddle on the floor next to him. Mr. Jones states, "I slipped on that wet spot and I can't seem to use this walker thing." The best way to document this incident is to write:

(A) "Mr. Jones is having a difficult time adjusting to his new walker and fell in the hallway and landed flat on his back. Vital signs are stable."

(B) "Mr. Jones was using his new walker in the hallway when he slipped on a puddle landing on his back. Vital signs are stable."

(C) "Mr. Jones was found in the hallway flat on his back with his walker on top. A puddle was beside him. Vital signs are stable."

(D) "Mr. Jones is having a difficult time adjusting to his new walker and slipped on a puddle, landing on his back."

2. At 3 PM, the nurse ends his rounds and notices he forgot to document in his 7 AM note that a patient's left ankle was swollen at 7 AM. To document, the nurse should:

(A) Put a line through the 7 AM note and rewrite the assessment to include the swollen ankle

(B) Write a 3 PM addendum to the 7 AM note

(C) Write a 3 PM late entry to the 7 AM note

(D) Any of the above

3. The nurse manager arrives on the patient unit at 6:45 AM. He notes that the computer terminal at the nurses' station is displaying a screen used to enter patient progress notes into the patient record. There is no one at the terminal. He asks all of the staff on duty if they had brought this screen up. All answer in the negative. The only other person on duty, a nurse, had left to go home at 6:30 AM. The nurse manager should:

(A) Restart the computer and clear the screen so the computer terminal will be ready for the day staff's work

(B) Isolate and freeze all activity at that terminal and call the system administrator for instructions and procedures to be followed

(C) Call the nurse who left to see whether she finished making her entries, before restarting and clearing the computer workstation

(D) Ask the unit secretary to print a copy of the work displayed on the screen and then restart the computer workstation

4. A staff nurse working on a busy acute care medical unit is approached by a professional-looking woman who requests that the nurse bring up the lab result computer screen of a particular patient so she can view and print the patient's laboratory study information. The nurse does not know the woman, and asks for identification and the purpose of her request. She said she is a consulting physician who has been asked to review the record of the patient in question. She has a driver's license but no other type of identification. What should the nurse do?

(A) The nurse should comply with the request, since the driver's license confirms her identity as she has stated

(B) The nurse should call the patient's attending physician to confirm that the woman has been requested to perform the consultation, and once verified, the nurse then complies with the request

(C) The nurse should tell the woman that since she is unable to produce anything other than a driver's license, and the nurse does not have knowledge of her authorization to view the record, the nurse cannot comply with her request without additional authorization

(D) The nurse should check the patient record to see if such a consultation is ordered, and if it is, the nurse should comply with the request

5. Do-not-resuscitate orders:

(A) Are indefinite

(B) Protect nurses and physicians from liability

(C) Must be in writing

(D) All of the above

6. A nurse believes the physician incorrectly diagnosed a patient as having a urinary tract infection. The patient is having intractable right-upper-quadrant pain not re-

lieved with narcotics. The nurse documents his assessment in the patient's medical record. His duty to the patient is:

(A) Complete upon documenting his findings in her medical record

(B) Complete when he medicates her for pain and makes her more comfortable

(C) Complete when he notifies the medical director that his assessment differs from that of the physician

(D) None of the above

7. A patient falls in the hallway and fractures his hip. The nurse records the events in the patient's medical record. The nurse completes an incident report. The patient's family requests a copy of the incident report. What should the nurse do?

(A) Give the patient's family a copy, as it is part of the patient's medical record

(B) Give the patient's family a copy and chart in the patient's medical record that a copy of the incident report was given to the patient's family

(C) Refuse to give a copy to the family but give a copy to the patient

(D) Refuse to give the family a copy and explain that the form is for the facility's use only

8. The nurse is making rounds when she hears a "thud" followed by a groan. Upon entering the next room, she notices Mrs. Smith lying on the floor next to her bed. Her feet are tangled in the sheets. Both side rails are raised. When filing the incident report, the nurse documents that:

(A) Mrs. Smith tangled her feet in the sheets and fell out of bed and onto the floor

(B) Mrs. Smith attempted to climb back into bed, tangled her feet on the sheets, and fell to the floor

(C) The nurse found Mrs. Smith on the floor beside the bed with the sheet around her feet, and both side rails were raised

(D) Mrs. Smith attempted to climb over the raised side rails, tangled her feet in the sheets, and fell to the floor

9. A nurse assessing a patient in the emergency department suspects that the patient is a victim of a crime. Which of the following is an essential nursing intervention?

(A) A thorough and descriptive assessment of all injuries including "body mapping"

(B) Telling the victim's family of the nurse's suspicions

(C) Reporting the situation to the police before verifying any more facts with the patient

(D) Notifying the risk manager since there may be litigation involved

10. A nurse suspects that a patient may have drugs in his possession. Which of the following would the nurse *not* be advised to do?

(A) Enlist the help of security officers before any other steps are taken

(B) Take control of the situation quickly and confiscate the drugs when the patient is not looking

(C) Determine whether the patient is placing either himself or others at risk

(D) Notify the physician of the outcome of the situation if drug are found

PART III: ANSWERS

1. **The answer is C.**

A, B, and D are incorrect because they make an assumption about facts that were not witnessed by the nurse documenting the incident. Even though Mr. Jones explains what happened, it is best to place the patient's own words in quotes and then describe objectively what the nurse witnessed. C is correct because it does not make any assumptions on the facts.

2. **The answer is C.**

An addendum is the best way to add to or correct a note. Late entry is used when no note was written but

one is needed. A line may be placed through an incorrect entry but this nurse's entry was not incorrect. A note should not be rewritten only corrected.

3. **The answer is B.**

The workstation is showing a confidential document that was accessed using a password with privileges assigned at least to that level of information. It appears that either the user had not logged out before leaving the computer station or someone gained access with another person's password. Thus, information of a highly confidential nature could have been accessed and even changed. The nurse manager should immediately, following the organization's procedure, notify the system administrator of the situation, take steps to safeguard the privacy of the information, and prevent any use of the station until an investigation is properly under way. The nurse manager and system administrator will need to conduct a detailed investigation that will include at least identification of the user who signed into the computer; ascertainment of exactly when that user last logged in; ascertainment of how and when the station was left in the unsecured manner; interview of all other staff as necessary to determine if any other persons had used the station; and isolation and review of all records to determine via the system's monitoring and tracking mechanism, the timing of entries during the time the station was left unsecured. In addition, the nurse manager should review procedures and training of all staff as to proper use and security procedures. Corrective procedures may also include password changes. A situation like this could be very serious indeed, since unauthorized access to the system may have occurred.

4. The answer is C.

The nurse is correct in not permitting access to the record as requested based on the information provided by the woman making the request. To make the confidential information available to the requester, the nurse must be assured that this is a proper disclosure. If the nurse fails to do this and the use and disclosure turns out to be improper, the nurse may be liable for the resulting damages. Therefore, the nurse must ask the individual to wait while the nurse takes the necessary steps to ensure the propriety of the request. The nurse should notify the superior and request guidance in managing the request. This would involve at least ensuring that this physician has been duly consulted to review this record; that the identity of the consultant is verified; that the record is not under any particular protections requiring additional consent or approval; that such consultation requests and information disclosure are proper and done according to facility guidelines; and that the necessary procedure for providing a printout is followed. This aspect is more likely to be responded to by the medical record administrator who, in most facilities, oversees any record release. Facilities should have a system in place to manage and respond to requests for information access and disclosure.

5. The answer is C.

Although verbal orders are acceptable practice, verbal DNR orders are not. The DNR order requires careful documentation of the patient's wishes, family involvement, and clearly defined orders of which, if any, medical interventions are to be implemented. A is incorrect because DNR orders are renewed every few days according to agency policy. B is incorrect because DNR orders do not necessarily protect health care providers from liability (the order may be carried out incorrectly).

6. The answer is D.

The nurse should take his concerns up the chain of command starting with the physician, who may be accessible and open to the nurse's assessment and findings. C is incorrect because the duty is not complete until after meeting a satisfactory outcome. A and B are incorrect because a nurse's duty to exercise independent judgment requires the nurse to do more than document and medicate.

7. The answer is D.

Incident reports are confidential records and A, B, and C breach that confidentiality.

8. The answer is C.

C documents the facts as the nurse witnessed them. The nurse could add Mrs. Smith's subjective statement, "I tried to get over the side rails, tangled my feet, and fell to the floor," to explain what happened but to document A, B, or D makes assumptions about facts the nurse did not see. If the nurse documents that Mrs. Smith fell out of bed because she told you, then the nurse should document, "Patient states she fell out of bed" or use the patient's own words in quotes.

9. The answer is A.

This is an essential step to confirming the nurse's suspicions and preserving evidence through documentation. The nurse will assist in gathering other information also. Answer B is incorrect because family members may be involved in the incident, and the nurse does not have enough information to inform them yet. The nurse needs to obtain information from them but not suggest causes at this point. Answer C is incorrect because the nurse does not have enough information yet to do this. The nurse needs to talk to the patient or family first, and hospital protocol may prohibit the nurse from notifying the police. Answer D is incorrect since it is premature, even though there could be litigation involved later.

10. The answer is B.

The nurse should not place himself or herself in danger and risk an unpredictable situation. Therefore, this would not be an appropriate action. Answer A is correct because security should be involved. Answer C is correct because the nurse needs to assess any danger in the situation for the patient or others and take any steps to ensure their safety without undue personal risk. Answer D is correct because the physician may need to modify the patient's plan of care based on this information.

PART IV
Employment Issues

38 Employer and Employee Rights–Part I

Doreen J. Bonadies, JD, RN

A Employee at Will
Cannot terminate for:
- Public policy violation
- Refusal to partake in unlawful/ unethical conduct
- Whistle-blowing

C OSHA Mandates for Health Care Providers
1. Develop an exposure control plan, updated annually.
2. Take precautions to protect employees from exposure to bodily fluids.
3. Provide adequate hand-washing facilities.
4. Provide protective equipment such as disposable gloves, gowns, goggles, etc.
5. Provide appropriate containers for the disposal of needles and sharp instruments.
6. Communicate presence of HIV and hepatitis hazards to employees.
7. Offer hepatitis B virus vaccinations to employees.
8. Offer postexposure evaluation if an employee has been exposed.

B Rights OSHA Grants to Employees
1. To question unsafe conditions and request an investigation.
2. To assist OSHA inspections.
3. To assist a court in determining whether certain imminent, dangerous conditions exist.
4. To bring an action to compel the Secretary of Labor to seek injunctive relief against an employer.
5. To refuse to perform hazardous job activities where there is a reasonable belief there is danger of death or serious injury and no time to seek administrative action to remedy the danger.
6. To access safety records including records disclosing the identity of toxic substances or harmful physical agents.

D Family Medical Leave Act
≥ 50 employees
12 weeks paid/unpaid leave for:

| Birth of child | Adoption or placement of foster care child | Serious medical illness | Care for family with serious illness |

Generally, nurses are employees at will of the agency they work for unless they have a contract specifically defining the terms of the employment. How an employee and employer terminate the relationship depends on the type of employment involved. Therefore, nurses need to be aware of the differences in the law governing their employment situation. Additionally, nurses should know the state and federal laws that grant employees certain rights within the work environment.

Employment At Will

Employment is considered at will when the employer or employee is free to terminate the employment relationship at any time, with or without reason, and with or without notice. Employment is considered at will unless there is a contractual agreement between the employee and employer or there is a statute dictating the terms of employment. Accordingly, an employer is under no obligation to retain an employee any more than an employee can be compelled against his or her will to work for the employer.

Exceptions to the at will doctrine are when there is (1) an express or implied contract to employ for a particular time period or (2) an express or implied contract to terminate only for certain reasons or through specific procedures. An *express contract* is typically a written agreement setting forth the terms and conditions of employment including duration of employment and cause for termination. An implied contract may be found when there are written or oral promises made to the employee to employ for a particular time or to terminate only for certain reasons or through certain procedures. Statements made in employer handbooks and policy manuals have been construed to create a binding commitment on employers to discharge only for cause (i.e., willful violation of policy, inadequate job performance, job-related misconduct, business needs) or through specific disciplinary procedures.

Another exception to the at will doctrine arises when the termination of employment violates public policy, such as when the employee refuses to do something unlawful or reports the employer for unlawful or improper conduct (see **Part A**).

Statutory Regulation

There are statutes restricting the employment at will doctrine.

1. The Occupational Safety and Health Act (OSHA) of 1970 provides that places of employment are to be free from recognized hazards that are causing or likely to cause serious physical harm or death to an employee. Employers must comply with occupational safety and health standards promulgated by the agency. Some of the rights OSHA grants to employees are listed in **Part B**. OSHA prohibits discrimination or retaliation against an employee who has filed a complaint, testified in a proceeding under the act, or exercised any of the above-mentioned rights. It is unlawful for an employer to terminate an employee who exercises his or her rights under OSHA. With respect to health care providers, see **Part C**.

2. Employers must provide their employees with employer-paid benefits for on-the-job injury, known as *workers' compensation*. Benefits include payment of a portion of wages while the worker is disabled, medical care and/or payment to health care providers, a specific payment for permanent injury, death benefits, and in many states vocational rehabilitation when the employee cannot return to his or her previous job due to permanent restrictions or disability. These remedies are available to the employee without regard to employer or employee fault. In most states, workers' compensation is the sole remedy against an employer for worker-related injuries. In other words, an employee is precluded from bringing a civil action against an employer for work-related injuries and damages. In most states it is unlawful for an employer to retaliate against an employee for filing a worker's compensation claim.

3. In 1993, Congress enacted the Family Medical Leave Act (FMLA) which mandates that employers with 50 employees grant up to 12 weeks per year of leave during a 12-month period to an employee for any of the reasons shown in **Part D**. Although leave may be unpaid, if the employer provides health benefits to the employee, the employer must continue to provide the same or similar benefits while the employee is on FMLA leave. An employer may require or an employee can elect to substitute all or any part of the statutory 12 weeks of unpaid leave with any accrued paid vacation leave or personal disability leave under the employer's personnel policies. An employee who has been denied leave or has been terminated for exercising leave under FMLA may file a complaint with the Department of Labor or file a civil action. Upon return from family medical leave, most employees must return to their original (or equivalent) position with equal pay, benefits, and other terms of employment in place prior to leave. Many states have similar statutory provisions. Some state provisions are more generous than the federal medical leave and may be applicable to employers with <50 employees.

39 Employer and Employee Rights–Part II

Doreen J. Bonadies, JD, RN

E   Federal Laws Protecting Employees from Discrimination

- Equal Pay Act of 1963 — mandates that employers pay equal wages to men and women for equal work
- Civil Rights Act of 1964 — as amended (commonly referred to as Title VII) prohibits employers from discrimination based on race, color, religion, natural origin, and/or sex including sexual harassment
- Age Discrimination in Employment Act of 1967 (ADEA) — forbids discrimination in employment of persons ≥ 40 years old
- Americans with Disabilities Act — prohibits discrimination against qualified individuals with disabilities and requires an employer to make reasonable accommodations to disabled individuals
- National Labor Relations Act — prohibits an employer from discriminating against an employee who encourages or discourages membership in a labor union
- Wage and Hour Law — bars discrimination against employees who assert rights under the Wage and Hour Law

---

Health Benefits

Health insurance is a benefit that an employer is under no obligation to provide. However, if an employer does provide health benefits, the employer must offer an employee who leaves the position or is terminated the opportunity to purchase health insurance at the employer's group rate for an 18-month period.

Protection from Discrimination

The federal laws listed in **Part E** protect employees from discrimination. Mirroring the federal laws, many states have enacted laws to address discrimination based on race, age, disability, and gender, and some states have gone further in adopting laws prohibiting discrimination because of sexual orientation, marital status, and ethnicity.

To prove discrimination, the employee generally must prove (1) that he or she is a member of the protected class; (2) that he or she is qualified for the job or promotion or other beneficial action; and (3) that the job or promotion or other benefit was instead given to a member of a different class. Members of a protected class are individuals who share the characteristics of the class of individuals the antidiscrimination statutes seek to protect. Once the employee proves the three elements referenced above, the employer has the burden of proving a legitimate and nondiscriminatory reason for either not selecting or terminating the employee. If the employer proves a legitimate, nondiscriminatory reason for termination, the employee has the burden of proving that the legitimate, nondiscriminatory reasons offered by the employer are a mere pretext for discrimination.

The general elements of a discrimination claim are slightly modified in cases brought under the Americans with Disabilities Act (ADA). Under the ADA, the employee must prove that he or she (1) is a qualified individual with a disability (i.e., has a physical or mental impairment that substantially limits 1 major activity); (2) has a record of having such a physical or mental impairment or being regarded or perceived as having an impairment; and (3) can perform the essential job duties with or without reasonable accommodation. Once an employee has shown that he or she is a qualified individual with a disability (able to do the essential functions of the job with or without reasonable accommodation), the employer is liable for an adverse employment decision (i.e., termination, refusal to hire) unless the employer can prove that the accommodation would pose an undue hardship on the employer.

Collective Rights

Under the National Labor Relations Act and Labor Management Relations Act, employees have the right to form a union (self-organize) and to engage in concerted activities without coercion, restraint, or interference from the employer. It is an unfair labor practice for employers to interfere with the right to self-organize.

40 Contracts

Susan Westrick Killion, JD, MS, RN

A Elements of a Contract

1. Offer — must be definite and certain
2. Acceptance of the offer must be clearly communicated
3. Consideration or something of value that is bargained for (quid pro quo)
4. Mutual assent or consent to the terms of the offer
5. Capacity to contract

B Defenses to Contract Enforcement

- Lack of any essential element of the contract
- Duress or undue influence of a party
- Illegal contract
- Unequal bargaining power between the parties

C Termination of the Contract

- Fulfillment of the terms and conditions
- By mutual consent of the parties
- Release of the contract obligations due to changed circumstances
- Breach of contract by 1 party not fulfilling its terms

D Remedies for Breach of Contract

- Monetary damages including compensatory and special damages
- Specific performance for contract involving unique goods, but not for personal services
- Injunction to prevent action by 1 party
- Mediation
- Arbitration

E Practice Pointers

- Do not make specific promises about outcomes of care or guarantee results from treatment.
- Be aware you may be an agent of your employer and may be contracting on his or her behalf.
- Check and follow any agency policies on contracting or witnessing contracts.
- Contract principles will be used in individual or collective bargaining for employment.

Contract law governs agreements between parties to do or refrain from doing something. A *contract* is defined as a legally binding and enforceable agreement between two or more parties. Contracts between parties are usually made and enforced as part of a business relationship. Nurses most often are involved in contracts that affect their employment. However, it is increasingly common for nurses to be involved in direct contracts with patients or others as part of an agreement to provide services. When operating a business, a nurse may be involved in contracting with others for goods or services.

Elements of a Contract

To be legally binding a contract must have certain elements (see **Part A**). In addition, there are other rules covering contract formation and enforcement such as whether modifications can be made orally and whether certain types of contracts must be in writing to be valid. State and federal statutes would need to be considered in particular situations.

Types of Contracts

Express contracts are those in which the terms and conditions have been given orally or in writing by the parties. The terms are expressed in this type of contract. Note that oral contracts are just as valid as written agreements. *Implied contracts* involve terms and conditions that were expected to be a part of an agreement by the parties. A patient going to a physician's office for services constitutes an implied contract, even though no expressed agreement takes place. It is mutually understood by the parties that this is the nature of their implied agreement. *Formal contracts* are those that the law requires to be in writing (e.g., wills, contracts that cannot be performed <1 year, and contracts for the sale of land). The idea is to prevent fraud from occurring with these types of agreements. Most other types of oral contracts are equally as binding and enforceable as written contracts but are often harder to prove. Any agreement that involves substantial consideration by the parties is recommended to be in writing.

Defenses to Contract Enforcement

Various defenses can be asserted to challenge the validity of a contract (see **Part B**). For example, one could claim that one of the essential elements was not present in the formation of the contract and that the contract should be null and void. It could be claimed that one party to the contract was under duress or some type of undue influence that should void the agreement. The contract could be illegal and thus unenforceable. In some cases the courts may not enforce an agreement if it finds there was unequal bargaining power between the parties and one party was taken advantage of.

Termination of the Contract

A contract may be terminated by various means, one of which is fulfillment of the terms and conditions of the contract (see **Part C**). Another way for the contract to terminate is for one or more of the parties to be released from the contract. A contract may be rescinded by the parties when they both agree they do not want to complete the contract. Another way that a contract can be terminated is by one party breaching the agreement. This occurs when one party fails to perform terms or conditions of the agreement. The nonbreaching party must be able to show that he or she was willing to keep performing the contract and that the breach was unilateral.

Remedies for Breach of Contract

The nonbreaching party to a contract may have certain remedies available in a claim for breach of contract against the breaching party (see **Part D**).

1. Monetary damages, the most common type of remedy, may include not only compensatory damages for the loss of the value of the contract, but also special damages such as punitive damages meant to punish a party for wrongdoing or bad faith in the agreement. The type of damages that each party is entitled to may be spelled out in the agreement and is referred to as *liquidated damages*.
2. Specific performance of the contract may be ordered by the court when no other remedy is appropriate. This may be the remedy when the contract called for a special order or unique goods. Contracts for personnel services are not usually enforceable by specific performance.
3. Injunction or an order to prevent a party from doing something might be ordered.
4. Mediation is a process that allows the parties to settle a dispute, which may be a contract, without going to court. A mediator is a neutral third party who works with the parties to reach a mutually satisfactory settlement.
5. Arbitration is another process used to avoid litigation. A neutral third party (an arbitrator) is appointed to consider both parties' interests. The arbitrator is empowered to settle the dispute in the fairest way for both parties.

Nurses and Contract Law

Nurses may be involved in negotiating a contract for employment either individually or as part of a union, which involves a collective bargaining process. During these proceedings the nurse is aided by a basic knowledge of the principles of contract law. By making the terms of the contract explicit, there will be less chance of misinterpretation in the employment situation. The rights and duties of each of the parties to the agreement will be clearer and easier to enforce.

Some types of promises that a nurse makes to a patient could be viewed by the court as creating a contract (see **Part E**). For example, a nurse should not promise any particular cure or outcome when agreeing to provide services. Nurses who contract individually with patients may be more subject to this risk than those who are employees. However, a nurse may be considered an agent of the employer and able to contract on behalf of the employer. One needs to exercise caution in entering into contracts with patients for direct services; seeking legal advice is recommended. Agency policies also may give guidelines concerning responsibilities in contracting with patients, such as in the home care situation.

41 Corporate Liability

Roberta G. Geller, JD, BS, RN

A Corporate Liability

- Safe and adequate food, equipment, supplies, and medications
- Maintain safe environment
- Adopt and follow regulations and policies
- Selection and retention of employees and privileges
- Supervision of patient care

Nurse protected from personal liability/liability imputed to corporation

Yes

When the nurse's actions are reasonable under the circumstances

No

When the nurse's actions are not reasonable under the circumstances

B Suggestions to Protect Nurses Employed by Corporate Employers

1. Be familiar with the corporate employer's rules, regulations, and policies and follow them as closely as possible.

2. Notify the corporate employer verbally and in writing of the lack of adequate and safe equipment, medications, food, and supplies.

3. Keep a lookout for an unsafe environment, taking the patient's needs into consideration. Take appropriate steps to notify the corporate employer and ensure rectification of unsafe condition.

4. Notify the corporate employer of known incompetence in accordance with policies.

Corporate liability is the corporate employer's legal accountability for matters beyond the employee's control and in certain circumstances, for wrongful conduct of the employee. Corporate liability also encompasses the concept of a collective failure of the corporate employer to adopt and implement reasonable policies. In the health care arena, corporate employers include but are not limited to hospitals, health care agencies, HMOs, and professional corporations. Five basic duties relative to the delivery of health care apply to all such corporate employers (see **Part A**). The legal standard for determining whether the corporate employer is satisfying these duties involves a reasonableness test: whether the corporate employer knew or had reason to know that a question exists.

Duty to Provide Adequate and Safe Equipment

In addition to adequate and safe equipment, the corporate employer has a duty to the patient to provide, maintain, and select adequate and safe medications, food, and supplies reasonably suited for the purpose for which they are intended. The nurse regularly deals with issues concerning equipment, medications, food, and supplies. For example, under a reasonableness test a cardiac monitor used by the nurse need not be state of the art as long as the patient's needs are met. In considering whether food is reasonably suited for its purpose, preparation of the food and suitability of the diet are paramount issues, as is whether the food is served to the patient at a proper or improper time.

If the employer does provide adequate and safe equipment and the nurse elects to utilize some other equipment or improperly uses the equipment provided, it is unlikely that liability will be attached to the corporate employer. Instead the nurse will likely be held liable for his or her own actions.

Duty to Maintain Safe Premises

The corporate employer has a duty to maintain a safe environment. The legal standard relative to maintaining a safe environment is the reasonableness test. The corporate employer must take reasonable care to maintain the premises safely. This duty incorporates a duty to protect patients, employees, and others lawfully entering the premises. It includes protection from known dangers as well as inspection of the premises for the purpose of discovering and correcting dangers. Particular emphasis must be placed on maintaining an environment appropriate for the unique infirmities of the patients (e.g., railings in hallways, wheelchair ramps). Oftentimes the employer requires that the nursing staff keep a log of defects in the patient care unit (e.g., broken side rails or wheelchairs, malfunctioning monitors or oxygen outlets) and then notify the appropriate department for rectification. If the nurse discovers an unsafe condition, steps must be taken to correct the unsafe condition and include but are not limited to such actions as removing malfunctioning equipment, blocking off spills on the floor, and notifying the supervisor or other departments.

Duty to Adopt and Follow Proper Regulations and Safety Procedures

The corporate employer has a duty to adopt and follow safety procedures that are reasonably calculated to protect patients and others, including the protocol for inspecting, discovering, and correcting dangers so as to maintain a safe environment. In addition, this pertains to the duty to reasonably anticipate safety procedures necessary to prevent attacks and injuries caused by another person, to prevent escape, and to prevent self-injury. The nurse should expect the corporate employer to have security measures in place to protect the nurse from attack in all areas on the premises, elevators, and parking areas. Furthermore, there must be protocols and policies in place for the nurse to follow when caring for a combative or self-abusive patient. Policies and procedures concerning restraints are also crucial. A claim may be brought against a corporate employer for failure to adopt and enforce proper regulations.

Duty Regarding Selection and Retention of Employees

The corporate employer must exercise due diligence in investigating the background of those working in the facility, including professional and nonprofessional staff and independent contractors (e.g., physicians, nurse practitioners, and midwives with privileges who are not employees). Investigating the background involves ordinary care in checking references, past employment history, and licensure. If such investigation reveals or even suggests a question concerning the individual's qualifications, the corporate employer has a duty to limit or deny that individual's application. Liability can also attach to nonemployees who actively participate in any such decisions. For example, a nurse serving on a review committee, board of directors, or search committee may be held personally liable for decisions made as a member of the same.

Responsibility for Supervision of Patient Care

Supervision of patient care includes the obvious professional and nonprofessional employees as well as independent contractors to whom the corporate employer has granted privileges (e.g., nurse midwives, nurse anesthetists, and nurse practitioners who are self-employed by some other professional corporation or medical/surgical group). The corporate employer has a duty to exercise reasonable care to find out if a question exists as to the competence of these individuals. The corporation may be put on notice by a particular reported event such as a nurse anesthetist being impaired. However, even if not an actual notice, the corporation has a duty to affirmatively discover any such problems. Hence, the nurse may be either required or asked to participate in quality assurance practices so that problematic trends can be detected.

Nurses' Risks and Remedies

As discussed, notwithstanding corporate liability issues, a nurse's negligent actions will prevent liability from being imputed to the corporate employer. Whether the nurse is an employee of a corporation or is granted privileges by the corporation, corporate liability will not protect the nurse from personal liability arising out of the nurse's own negligent actions. However, if liability arises out of matters beyond the nurse's control, the nurse will be protected under the corporate liability theory of law. The suggestions in **Part B** will help protect the nurse when employed by any type of corporate employer.

42 Employment Contracts and Unionization

Susan Westrick Killion, JD, MS, RN

Rights of Employees

Employee at Will

1. Employment may be terminated at will of employee or employer without cause.
2. Employee manuals usually outline rights and responsibilities.
3. There is a public policy exception to firing an employee without cause.
4. Firing related to complaints about the employer and violations of health and safety statutes may be protected by whistle-blowing statutes.

Contract, Union, or Collective Bargaining Agreement

1. Terms of agreement specify rights and responsibilities.
2. Union represents employees in contract negotiations.
3. Private sector employees are governed by NLRA and NLRB.
4. Staff nurses acting as supervisors of assistive personnel may be excluded from unions.
5. Grievances are filed when employee asserts a contract violation.
6. All steps in grievance procedure must be strictly followed.

Nurses comprise a substantial part of the employee workforce in the health care system and need to know basic rights and responsibilities related to their employment status. These are influenced by the type of employment agreement, whether there is a formal contract governing the relationship, and whether or not the nurse belongs to a union. In addition, various state and federal laws and regulations impact on particular situations.

Contractual Employee

Most nurses are employed under the terms and conditions specified by a written contract. A *contract* is a legally binding, enforceable agreement between two parties. It should specify basic features of the employment relationship such as specific duties and obligations of the employer. It should include benefits, salary, terms of employment, evaluation methods, and terms and conditions of discharge or termination. Each party must adhere to the terms of the contract. Breach of contract by one party would give rise to rights by the

other party, perhaps to terminate the agreement. For example, if an employee agrees to float to various work sites, but then refuses to do so when properly trained, a breach of contract by the employee has occurred. As long as a contract is in place, both parties are bound to its terms and conditions. If any changes in the contract are desired, they must be negotiated, agreed to, and become part of the contract.

Employment At Will Doctrine

If a nurse does not have a contract of employment, the employee at will doctrine governs (see **Table**). Under this doctrine employees are free to take a job or not, and the employer is free to terminate the employee at will. This concept gives employers freedom to hire, retain, or terminate employees with or without just cause (even if they have excellent performance evaluations). Conversely, the nurse can quit the job for any reason at any time. However, it is customary to give either party a reasonable notice to this effect, normally a period of 2 weeks.

Exceptions to the Employment At Will Doctrine

Over the years courts and laws have carved out exceptions to this doctrine that have eroded its sometimes harsh effect (see **Table**). One of the major exceptions to termination at will is the *public policy* exception. Under this exception the court has found the discharge to be wrongful if the employee was fired while promoting a desirable public policy or performing a public duty. An example is when an employee reports violation of a statute by the employer, or has been terminated for serving on a jury. Usually the court requires the public policy to be grounded firmly in constitutional or statutory rights, and some courts have cautioned against further erosion of the doctrine. Specific *whistle-blowing statutes* protect employees reporting health and safety violations of employers. Currently there is variation among states and courts as to when this exception is allowed, and decisions based on similar fact patterns have differed in various jurisdictions.

Another exception is when the employer has an *employee manual* that specifies conditions before termination. The court will require the employer to follow the manual even if it is not a formal written contract. Some courts have supported an exception based on the doctrine of "good faith and fair dealing," which protects against grossly unfair terminations.

Unions and Collective Bargaining Agreements

Recently, more nurses have become employed in organizations where employees are unionized (see **Table**). Federal or state laws govern federal government and public employees. Other employees in the private sector are governed by the National Labor Relations Act (NLRA) and the board that implements this federal legislation, the National Labor Relations Board (NLRB). Unions bargain collectively for the nurses represented by them. In most cases nurses are in their own bargaining unit, which facilitates negotiations related to their unique concerns (mandatory overtime, patient-staff ratios, salary, benefits). The collective bargaining process joins together employees and generally results in greater benefits for all than could be achieved by an individual.

As part of the collective bargaining process, both management and the union must bargain in good faith until settlement on the issues takes place. Often there is mediation or arbitration in the process by a neutral party appointed by both sides to represent them. Binding arbitration is when an arbitrator chosen by both sides makes a final decision, which is then binding on both parties. The final contract is enforceable and gives rise to significant rights by both parties to the agreement. Nurses must be familiar with the terms and conditions of any collective bargaining agreement in place where they are employed.

Representation of Nurses

Nurses may be represented by an independent union or by the state-affiliated nurses' association as the bargaining agent. The employee nurses follow rules established by the NLRB or federal or state law that governs the election process. Generally a majority of employees in an institution must support unionization and selection of the bargaining agent. Formal steps must be taken by employees to ensure compliance with the process. It is an unfair labor practice for an employer to prevent or retaliate against employees who are attempting to organize a union when this is permitted by law. However, rules and procedures need to be followed as set out by the official governmental agency, usually the NLRB.

Many nurses who favor collective bargaining prefer to be represented by the state-affiliated nurses' association because these organizations promote high-quality patient care as well as nurses' professional interests.

Staff Nurses as Supervisors

A recent concern of staff nurses involving their right to be represented by unions is the question of their supervisory status. Under the NLRA, supervisors are excluded from protection because they are considered to be management. The definition of *supervisor* under the act typically has included those who have the right to hire, fire, evaluate, assign, or direct other employees. The courts in some recent cases have supported excluding from the NLRA the LPNs working in nursing homes while supervising aides. This is of concern to nurses who also delegate and perform some of the tasks defined as *supervision*. Professional nursing organizations are currently working on clarifying this issue and are advocating to keep staff nurses under the protection of the NLRA.

Grievances

An employee who feels that the terms and conditions of employment have been violated by the employer can file a grievance. If a union is involved, the grievance is handled through union representatives. If there is no union, the employee manual should specify steps and rights in the grievance process. In all cases the employee must follow the steps carefully and adhere to all deadlines. Courts require employees to exhaust all these available internal remedies before any legal action can be taken. If there is no formal grievance procedure, nurses are advised to provide documentation in writing to their supervisor in a timely manner.

43 Employment Status Liability–Part I
Susan Westrick Killion, JD, MS, RN

A Vicarious Liability

1. Respondeat superior — employer's liability for negligent acts of employees
2. Ostensible agency — implied by the law when circumstances reasonably lead patient to conclude a non-employee is acting for the employer

B Independent Contractor

1. One who is hired for a specific purpose, usually to provide a service
2. Responsible for own liability in most cases; may share liability under some circumstances

C Employment Relationship/Setting Liability

1. **Supervisors** — liable for own decisions related to hiring and assignment of staff as well as providing supervision; not liable for acts of competent worker under supervision
2. **Student nurses** — individually liable for acts they are competent to perform; instructor or preceptor may share liability; held to standard of reasonable prudent nurse
3. **Private duty nurses** — usually independent contractors with individual liability; work as coworkers with staff nurses but does not have employment status with the institution
4. **Agency nurses** — employed by an agency that contracts with a third party for temporary employment; agency usually carries malpractice insurance; must follow NPA for state practicing in; work as coworkers with staff
5. **School nurses** — usually employed by school board but may work for a public health agency; respondeat superior typically applies with employer; employer usually carries insurance
6. **Government employed nurses** — may have special doctrines or immunities; federal employees protected by Federal Tort Claims Act, which makes the government the defendant

The employment status and practice setting of nurses impact on issues related to liability. As an employee, the nurse retains individual responsibility for actions but usually shares this liability with the employer. The patient or plaintiff is not allowed a double recovery for damages but can sue >1 person or party in alleging an injury occurred through negligence of an employee.

Vicarious Liability Theories

In addition to the principle of personal liability, there are various theories involving vicarious or substituted liability (see **Part A**). Because of a special relationship between the parties, the law makes an additional party responsible for the acts of another. The idea of vicarious liability is to allow the injured party greater access to recovery for damages, usually from the employer for the negligent acts of an employee. This extends liability to the person or agency who hired the individual who caused the harm. Doing so encourages employers to use care in hiring qualified individuals while providing adequate supervision and evaluation of their employees. Employers are usually in a better position to insure against these claims and to share the burdens and risks associated with employment. The employee is usually under the direct control and supervision of the employer, which makes the imposition of vicarious liability equitable. Thus important policies are encouraged by this practice.

The doctrine of *respondeat superior* or "let the master answer" is used when it is determined that the servant (or nurse) is under control of the master (or employer) and that the negligent act was within the scope of employment of the employee. Duties for which the nurse is employed would be included in this principle. In contrast, when a nurse acts outside the scope of employment (e.g., removing surgical stitches in an institution where only physicians are allowed to do this procedure), the principle of respondeat superior would not apply.

Another theory of vicarious liability that could be applied is *ostensible agency* (i.e., an institution can be liable for the acts of a nonemployee under certain circumstances). Ostensible agency is implied by the law when the circumstances indicate to the patient that the individual is representing the institution (e.g., student nurses or other practitioners who are nonemployees but appear to be acting as employees). The implied ostensible agency relationship would make the institution liable for the acts of the nonemployee.

Independent Contractors

There is no vicarious liability relationship with the institution when the negligent actor is an independent contractor (see **Part B**), a person who contracts with another to provide a service. A nurse hired to be a private duty nurse by the patient or the institution may be an independent contractor. The key to determining whether one is an independent contractor is whether the person is subject to the control of the other party with respect to completing the task. As nurses move into roles that are more independent and consultative, they will more often become individually liable for any negligence and be removed from shared liability with employers.

Employment Relationship/Setting Liability

The specific employment status of nurses influences their liability to patients. The setting in which nurses work also influences the situation (see **Part C**).

The nurse is often in a situation where he or she is supervising others (e.g., nurse manager or supervisor, staff nurse supervising other nurses, patient care assistants, home health aides, or student, private duty, or agency nurses). In this role the supervising nurse is independently responsible and accountable for supervisory decisions. For example, the nurse would be responsible for decisions related to assigning these individuals to patients and for providing proper guidance and supervision for them. The supervisor is not automatically responsible for any mistakes of these individuals if they become liable for negligent acts. The supervisor has the right to expect others to competently perform tasks while acting within the scope of their employment. The principle of personal liability remains in effect.

A student nurse caring for patients is also individually liable to patients for his or her actions. The student nurse is held to a standard of care that is equal to that of an RN performing the task; patients are entitled to this standard in all their care involving professional nursing interventions, regardless of whether a student provides that care. Instructors, other supervisors, or preceptors who make assignments to the student nurse based on skills and capabilities also may be held liable if they have improperly assigned or supervised the student nurse. Other entities that may be held vicariously liable include the educational institution where the student is enrolled and institutions where nurse's acts may fall under the theory of ostensible agency. Usually schools of nursing or agencies require student nurses to carry individual liability insurance for their role as a student nurse.

44 Employment Status Liability— Part II

Susan Westrick Killion, JD, MS, RN

A Vicarious Liability

1. Respondeat superior — employer's liability for negligent acts of employees
2. Ostensible agency — implied by the law when circumstances reasonably lead patient to conclude a non-employee is acting for the employer

B Independent Contractor

1. One who is hired for a specific purpose, usually to provide a service
2. Responsible for own liability in most cases; may share liability under some circumstances

C Employment Relationship/Setting Liability

1. **Supervisors** — liable for own decisions related to hiring and assignment of staff as well as providing supervision; not liable for acts of competent worker under supervision
2. **Student nurses** — individually liable for acts they are competent to perform; instructor or preceptor may share liability; held to standard of reasonable prudent nurse
3. **Private duty nurses** — usually independent contractors with individual liability; work as coworkers with staff nurses but does not have employment status with the institution
4. **Agency nurses** — employed by an agency that contracts with a third party for temporary employment; agency usually carries malpractice insurance; must follow NPA for state practicing in; work as coworkers with staff
5. **School nurses** — usually employed by school board but may work for a public health agency; respondeat superior typically applies with employer; employer usually carries insurance
6. **Government employed nurses** — may have special doctrines or immunities; federal employees protected by Federal Tort Claims Act, which makes the government the defendant

Patients may employ a private duty nurse as an independent contractor who would be solely responsible for his or her own liability. It is prudent for a private duty nurse to have a written contract with the employer. Sometimes a hospital may hire a private duty nurse for a patient, and under certain circumstances, the hospital also could be liable for the nurse's negligent acts, under the theory of ostensible agency. Staff or supervisory nurses employed by the hospital are still responsible for providing appropriate supervision for the private duty nurse and are still responsible for the patient. However, they all share responsibility for care of the patient. Private duty nurses are advised to carry their own liability insurance policy.

Nurses are increasingly employed by proprietary agencies that contract with third parties to provide temporary services. Agency nurses are employees of the agency, which typically provides liability insurance for the nurses. The agency is responsible to hire qualified and competent nurses for particular assignments. Staff and supervisory nurses in an institution remain responsible for the patients cared for by agency nurses and often share liability, even though there is no employer-employee relationship between agency nurses and the institution. Agency nurses must follow the policies and procedures of the institution. All nurses caring for patients on a particular unit need to function in a cooperative atmosphere to ensure the best care for patients. The relationship between agency and staff nurses is one of coworkers, and liability issues remain the same in most instances. Some agencies employ traveling nurses who go to other states for more extended lengths of time but are still in temporary positions. These nurses must be licensed in the state where they will be working. One must also be familiar with the specific NPA in that state and follow its rules and regulations.

The nurse who works in a school system is often employed by the school, which shares liability with the nurse. The doctrine of respondeat superior usually applies. Other school nurses are provided by public health agencies to the schools.

If a nurse is an employee of a governmental agency, special doctrines or rules may apply. Some governmental agencies have immunity from liability for their employees. Federal government employees have the protection of the Federal Tort Claims Act, which substitutes the federal government as the defendant in most cases.

In all situations the principle of individual accountability is still present. While liability may typically shift to employers or others, the judgment against a nurse can remain as an individual responsibility. This underscores the need for nurses to be protected adequately with individual or employer liability insurance, or both.

45 Staffing Issues and Floating

Roberta G. Geller, JD, BS, RN

How to Float Safely — Essential Steps

1. Find out as much as possible about the assignment.
2. Assess skill, experience, and training.
3. Utilize all resources.
4. Refuse assignment if unqualified and seek alternative sources of care.
5. Express specific concerns to supervisor.
6. Follow up in writing as soon as possible if assignment is refused.
7. Consider whether refusing the assignment leaves the patient without any nurse.
8. Never "walk off" the job.
9. Familiarize yourself with your employer's policies and regulations.
10. Request inservices/training for new information and refreshing skills.

Always put patient safety first!

Employer's Right to Assign Nurses According to Staffing Needs

With few exceptions (see last section in this chapter) employers have the right to designate the nursing unit to which a nurse is assigned in accordance with the needs of the patient population. The employer has a legal duty to provide professional nursing staff in sufficient numbers to meet the needs of the patients. Any unit that does not meet this standard is considered understaffed. Therefore, the employer has an affirma-

tive obligation to "float" nurses to units that are otherwise understaffed.

The Nurse Should Be Qualified for the Assignment

Because the employer must provide nursing staff to meet the needs of patients, the nurse must be qualified to meet those needs. First and foremost, the nurse is personally liable for his or her own conduct. If the nurse knowingly undertakes actions for which the nurse is

112

not qualified, the care provided is likely to deviate from the standard of care. In such an event the nurse is at risk for a nursing malpractice claim. The fact that the employer assigned the nurse to the nursing unit is not a defense. Therefore, the nurse must first ascertain the unit to which she is being "floated" and the nature of the responsibilities on that unit. It's imperative that the nurse ask the supervisor as much as possible about the type of unit, diagnoses/needs of the patients, and whether the assignment entails "charge" responsibilities.

If the nurse is told to provide care for which he or she is unqualified, it's very important for the nurse to ask whether an experienced staff member or inservice instructor is available to instruct or supervise. If so, then the nurse is competent to provide the specialized care under the instruction and supervision of the experienced staff member unless it is established that certification in a procedure or classroom/inservice instruction is mandatory. If an experienced staff member or inservice instructor is available to teach the procedure and answer questions during the nurse's shift, the nurse should consider these factors.

Once such information is obtained, the nurse should then assess his or her own skills and experience to determine whether he or she is qualified. If the answer is yes, the nurse must do so. If the answer is no, the nurse must put the employer on notice.

The Employer Must Be Put on Notice if the Nurse Is Not Qualified

Once the nurse has determined that his or her level of skill and experience is unsuitable for the assignment, the nurse must advise the person making the assignment. This applies regardless of whether the person making the assignment is the charge nurse, nurse manager, or supervisor, etc. The nurse should be as specific as possible about the reasons for refusing the assignment rather than simply refusing to take care of the patient. If the person making the assignment will not or cannot change it and appropriate supervision is not available to the nurse, the nurse should voice the specific concerns to that person's supervisor. Soon after the nurse should document this verbal exchange in the nurse's notes. Doing this most often shifts the burden of liability to the employer who has the control over staff assignments. It's also a good idea for the nurse to keep a personal, written account of the events for the nurse's own records.

From a practical standpoint, the nurse has only two choices, either the assignment can be accepted or refused. If the nurse accepts the assignment, all efforts should be undertaken to prepare as much as possible. The nurse should utilize all resources available; consult with coworkers, review equipment manuals, review hospital policy and procedure manuals.

If the nurse elects to refuse the assignment, it's imperative to keep in mind that doing so may subject the nurse to disciplinary action or even termination. In most instances, the nurse is an "at will" employee of the employer. This means that the employee can self-termi-nate at any time for any reason and the employer can terminate at any time for any reason. However, if the employer has terminated the nurse for refusing an assignment that would place patients at risk, the nurse may have recourse against the employer for wrongful discharge. A wrongful discharge claim will be successful if the employee can prove an improper reason for the dismissal. An "improper reason" in this context is generally defined as a violation of public policy. In one case, a nurse anesthetist claimed that she was constructively discharged (compelled to resign due to intolerable conditions) from the employer hospital for refusing to work with an impaired anesthesiologist. The nurse asserted that the alleged constructive discharge was in violation of public policy or, in other words, injurious to the public. The court held that there was no violation of public policy because the nurse did not prove the physician was impaired. Hence the wrongful discharge claim did not prevail because the nurse could not prove the public was at risk because of an impaired anesthesiologist.

Patient Safety Comes First

The paramount priority for both the nurse and the employer is the safety of the patient. The hospital/employer had a duty to provide *adequate* staff. The nurse has a duty to exercise a *reasonable* degree of care and skill. Less than optimal staffing requires a balancing of safety issues. Remember the standard for care is not perfection but rather is a standard requiring reasonable care. If no other option for the patient exists, the nurse should accept the assignment and proceed in a manner as safe as possible.

Exceptions to the Employer's Right to Float Nurses

There are limited exceptions to the employer's right to "float" nurses. If the nurse is a member of a collective bargaining unit (union), the collective bargaining unit's contract with the employer may specify if and when a nurse may be "floated." The nurse should be familiar with the terms of the contract. In the event that an employer attempts to float a nurse in contravention of the terms of any such contract, the nurse should still express concerns to the person making the assignment as described above. In addition, the collective bargaining unit will very likely have an established procedure for the nurse to follow under these circumstances.

The other exception is if the nurse has an employment contract directly with the employer. If so, the terms of the contract control. If the contract is silent relative to the "floating" issue, the best course of conduct is for the nurse to proceed in the manner described above.

It's important to be aware that an employee handbook can be the basis for an implied contract between the employee and the employer, especially if the employee relies on the information and policies therein. Therefore, it's always prudent to refer to the handbook and, if not already available, this document should be requested.

46 Americans with Disabilities Act

Katherine McCormack Dempski, JD, BSN, RN

A Americans with Disabilities Act

- Title I prohibits employers from discrimination against disabled but otherwise qualified job applicants. All aspects of employment are covered including the application process, hiring, training, promotion, compensation, and any other terms, conditions, or privileges of employment. It applies to private employers with ≥15 employees, state and local governments, and labor unions.
- Title II prohibits state and local government programs and activities from discrimination against disabled individuals including structural accessibility requirements.
- Title III prohibits private entities that provide public accommodations and services (such as health care institutions and physician's offices) from denying their goods and services to disabled individuals based on the disability. Structures must be accessible.
- Title IV requires that telecommunication devices and services such as interpreters be available for the hearing and speech impaired.
- Title V includes the miscellaneous provisions necessary for the construction and application of the act.

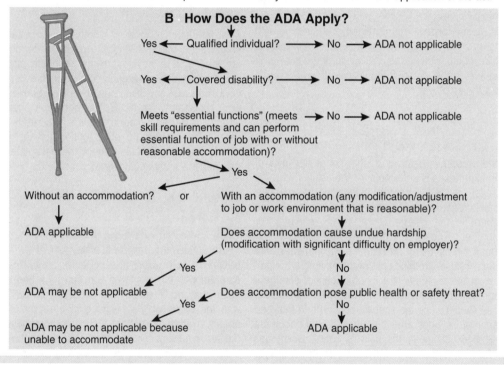

B How Does the ADA Apply?

Qualified individual? → Yes / No → ADA not applicable

Covered disability? → Yes / No → ADA not applicable

Meets "essential functions" (meets skill requirements and can perform essential function of job with or without reasonable accommodation)? → No → ADA not applicable / Yes

Without an accommodation? → ADA applicable

or

With an accommodation (any modification/adjustment to job or work environment that is reasonable)?

Does accommodation cause undue hardship (modification with significant difficulty on employer)?

Yes → ADA may be not applicable

No → Does accommodation pose public health or safety threat?

Yes → ADA may be not applicable because unable to accommodate

No → ADA applicable

Congress passed the ADA in 1990 with the goal of encouraging disabled individuals to participate in work and social environments by discouraging discrimination. The law is intended to balance the needs of disabled citizens with the ability of public and certain private entities to reasonably accommodate those needs without causing an undue hardship. The act does not give an individual any unfair advantage. It seeks to end discrimination of qualified disabled individuals by removing barriers that would prevent them from the same opportunities as others. The ADA has 5 titles (see **Part A**).

Who Is Covered?

The ADA applies to those with an impairment that substantially limits major life functions such as seeing, hearing, speaking, walking, breathing, performing manual tasks, learning, caring for oneself, and working. The act is more clear on what it does not cover such as nonchronic illnesses and impairment from current illegal drug use. Covered impairments are constantly evolving, but generally the act applies to alcoholism, epilepsy, paralysis, HIV infection, AIDS, mental retardation, and specific learning disabilities.

A qualified individual with a disability is one who meets the skill, experience, education, or other requirements of employment and can perform the "essential functions" of the position with or without a "reasonable accommodation." The term *essential functions* refers to the ability to perform the job requirements with the exception of marginal or incidental job functions. *Reasonable accommodation* is any modification or adjustment to the job or work environment that will assist the qualified individual to perform essential job functions. This includes adjustments that give the qualified individual the same rights and privileges enjoyed by the employees. When a qualified individual can perform essential job functions except for marginal functions, the employer must consider whether the individual could perform those functions with a reasonable accommodation. The employer is only required to accommodate a known disability. Employers are not required to lower the quality of standards and are not obligated to create a position that does not exist. *Undue hardship* is an "action requiring significant difficulty or expense." An accommodation for the qualified individual must not pose an undue hardship on the employer. Undue hardship is not the only limitation on an employer's requirement to reasonably accommodate a qualified individual. Public safety and health must always be considered (see **Part B**).

Public Accommodations in the Health Care Setting

Physicians' offices, pharmacies, inpatient and outpatient health care institutions, and long-term care facilities fit into the act's definition of *public accommodations*. The act also considers establishments providing a "significant" amount of social services to be places of public accommodations. Therefore, certain group homes, independent living centers, and retirement communities will come under the act if they provide enough social services.

How the ADA Affects Nurses as Employees

The employer may not ask an applicant to take a medical examination before a job offer is made. Employers may not make a preemployment inquiry into a disability but may ask about a disability as it applies to the performance of specific job functions. Employers may condition job offers on a post–job offer physical examination that is required of all employees at the same level. The reason for not hiring an applicant after a post-offer physical examination must be related to business necessity. Testing for illegal drug use is not considered a medical examination; therefore, an employer may test and make employment decisions based on the results. However, this information must be treated the same as a confidential medical record.

Uniformly applied leave policies do not violate the ADA when there is no apparent discrimination to the disabled worker. However, the employer may be required to modify a leave policy upon a qualified individual's request unless it would cause an undue hardship.

The ADA differs from workers' compensation programs in that workers' compensation applies when an employee is injured on the job. A work injury would have to fit into the act's criteria for "qualified disabled individual" to fall under the protection of the ADA.

How the Act Affects Nurses as Health Care Providers

Health care institutions and physicians' offices must provide auxiliary aides and services. Individuals with hearing impairments should be provided with qualified interpreters, assistive listening devices, note takers, or written material. Vision-impaired persons must be provided with qualified readers, taped texts, or large print or Braille materials.

There are limits to the length a public accommodation must go to reasonably accommodate disabled individuals. Maintaining public health and safety is always a primary consideration. For example, if an auxiliary aide animal at the hospital bedside presents a threat to public health and safety, the physician will need to document the reasons for the health threat. Nurses should document the auxiliary aides and the support given to replace the auxiliary aide animal.

As patients' advocates, nurses must always be aware of their institution's policy on providing auxiliary aides to a disabled patient or the patient's disabled family member. Having such a policy in place did not shield a California hospital from liability when the nurses did not know how to implement the policy.

Remedies for Noncompliance

The ADA provides plaintiffs in private causes of action with an injunction against the defendant. Upon finding a violation of the act, the court may order an injunction, which prohibits the defendant from continuing the unlawful behavior or commands the defendant to correct any wrong done to the plaintiff. Monetary remedies are not generally available under the act except in specific circumstances. The attorney general must be involved in the case and make a request of the court for the plaintiff to be awarded monetary damages. The attorney general will only make the request in cases where the defendant has established a pattern of discriminatory behavior or exhibits discriminatory conduct that rises to the level of public concern. In those cases the court may grant an injunction, award monetary damages to the aggrieved party, and assess a civil penalty. The court will take into consideration any good faith effort by the defendant to comply with the act.

47 Employees with AIDS/HIV Infection and Needle Sticks

Katherine McCormack Dempski, JD, BSN, RN

A Responsibility of the Nurse after a Needle Stick Injury

- File an incident report within statutory deadline.
- Inform the patient's primary physician who will seek consent from the patient.
- Submit to baseline HIV test.

B Rights of HIV-infected Nurses

- Right to confidentiality as an employee and a patient
- Right to maintain employment status while competently performing professional duties (HIV is protected disability under the ADA)
- Right to anonymity following an exposure to a patient
- Right to be free from mandatory HIV testing

C Duty of HIV-infected Nurses

- Health and safety of patients is primary duty.
- Safeguard patients and the public from spread of HIV.
- Use universal precautions and follow agency policy on proper disposal of infectious waste.
- Avoid high-risk areas of practice for blood exposure and invasive procedures.

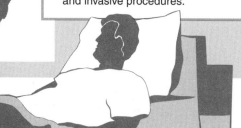

Nurses have a duty to not negligently expose patients to infectious diseases, including diseases from other patients as well as from the nurses themselves. Although there are state and federal statutes that protect the confidentiality of HIV-positive employees; HIV-positive nurses must find the balance between maintaining their own confidentiality and not exposing others to the infectious disease while performing professional duties. Likewise, health care agencies have a duty to not negligently expose its employees in performance of their duties and must have in place policies and procedures to protect staff from needle stick injuries.

Work-Related Exposure

Health care facilities may be liable to health care providers and others within the facility when exposure to HIV occurs due to negligence. The viability of the case depends on the individual facts, the legal theory the case is brought under, and the state's laws. A plaintiff will have to prove either that actual exposure (such as a needle stick with HIV positive blood) to the infectious disease occurred or that the fear of becoming HIV positive due to the exposure is "reasonable." Usually under tort law a plaintiff cannot sue for mental anguish unless it is associated with a physical injury but some courts have ruled the reasonable fear of being HIV positive is a compensable injury.

Under individual state workers' compensation statutes, an employee's disease or injury must be work related. The status of HIV infection as a recognized occupational risk is evolving. Most states do not recognize it as such although some disability insurance companies are beginning to compensate health care workers who contract HIV in the work setting.

Needle Stick Injuries: Nurse Rights When a Patient Refuses an HIV Test

Health care providers must follow strict statutory guidelines when obtaining a patient's informed consent for HIV testing. Even nurses who are exposed to a patient's blood products must receive the patient's informed consent before testing the patient. When the patient refuses to have an HIV test, the exposed health care provider must consult the state HIV informed consent/confidentiality statute and strictly adhere to it.

The statutes vary in each state but the following is a general example of the process (see **Part A**). The health care worker must have a "significant exposure" during his or her occupational duty. A *significant exposure* is generally defined as a parenteral exposure (such as a needle stick or cut) or mucous membrane exposure (splash to the eye) or prolonged exposure to skin (which may be capped, cut, or abraded). An incident report describing the incident and identifying witnesses must be completed. A physician must seek to obtain the patient's voluntary consent. Upon the patient's refusal, the exposed health care provider will need to submit to a baseline HIV test. An evaluation committee made up of impartial health care providers will review the incident. This group determines whether the statute's criteria have been met. The health care provider may need to seek a court order. The employer of the exposed nurse bears the cost of this process. Once the test is done, the confidentiality statute must be followed. The test results may not go in the patient's health care record unless the results related directly to the current medical care. If the patient wishes to receive the test results, then HIV counseling must be offered.

Nurses' Rights as Employees to Confidentiality

The HIV confidentiality statutes that protect patients give health care providers the same rights (see **Part B**). A hospital has a duty to keep the results confidential under the HIV confidentiality statutes. The ANA supports confidentiality regarding the HIV-positive nurse.

Americans with Disabilities Act

HIV-seropositive employees are protected from job discrimination under the ADA (see **Part B**). An employer may not fire an employee solely because he or she is HIV seropositive. An employee may be excluded from his or her job position if the infection becomes so disabling as to prevent the employee from competently performing the job functions.

The HIV-Infected Nurse

Health care providers are not required by law to reveal personal information on their health status, including their HIV status. In the absence of a legal duty, however, professional organizations such as ANA and the American Dental Association have issued position statements on the ethical obligation of disclosure. The ANA believes that HIV-positive nurses may deliver safe and effective care without compromising the patient and should not be removed from patient care based on HIV status alone.

All nurses have a duty to protect their patients from harm. Therefore, the HIV-infected nurse should avoid exposure-prone invasive procedures. If an exposure to a patient does occur, the HIV-infected nurse has a duty to inform the patient of the exposure and potential risk for HIV infection. This can be done while protecting the anonymity of the nurse. The HIV-infected nurse must understand the duty to not compromise patient care by remaining in a high-risk area of practice for blood exposure. (see **Part C**). Universal precautions as recommended by the CDC must always be followed, to minimize risk. Nurses with personal risk factors for HIV have an ethical obligation to know their own HIV status so steps can be taken to minimize risk to their patients.

Agency HIV Policies

The primary goal of HIV policies is to ensure the health and safety of all employees, patients, and visitors. Policies should reflect the most up-to-date medical and scientific information on the prevention of HIV transmission, postexposure management, and the implementation of infection control. Staff education and training should focus on infection control and the HIV-positive individual's right to privacy, whether as a patient or employee. Staff must have useful guidelines on postexposure protocol such as HIV testing for those involved and hazardous waste cleanup. Agency policy must be written to comply with the federal laws involving HIV such as the ADA and the Rehabilitation Act as well as state laws on workers' compensation and HIV informed consent/confidentiality.

48 Impaired Nurses

Melinda S. Monson, JD, MSN, RN

A Indications of an Impaired Nurse

1. Physical and mental
   - Slurred speech
   - Unsteady gait
   - Flushed face
   - Reddened eyes
   - Rapid mood swings
   - Poor personal hygiene

2. Work performance
   - Difficulty concentrating or remembering
   - Tardiness or frequent absences
   - Inability to complete work in a timely fashion
   - Prolonged use of private areas and bathrooms
   - Illegible documentation
   - Failure to follow through on tasks and assignments

3. Evidence of diversion
   - Patients complaining of ineffective pain relief
   - Frequent trips to the medication room or cart
   - Discrepancies in narcotic count
   - Reports of excessive waste, breakage, use of prn medications, and illegible or altered medical records

---

B

Do's	Don'ts
• Carefully consider/monitor and document suspicions by way of *factual*, nonjudgmental information (i.e., discrepancies), patient complaints, and observations and then report information to nursing management for further review and follow-up. • Participate in education and peer assistance programs to increase personal awareness and to assist in the impaired nurse's reentry into the workplace. • Strive to prevent legal implications involving yourself and your employer by responding to the impaired nurse in a timely and professional manner.	• Enable by excusing, ignoring, defending, or justifying. • Confront nurse on your own. • Allow personal beliefs, judgments, or feelings of betrayal interfere with your professional responsibility to assist the impaired nurse. • Look the other way and fail to address the issue of an impaired colleague in the hope you can avoid professional or legal involvement.

One indirect but not insignificant issue that must be considered in patient care is the impaired nurse. As a pattern of impairment unfolds and evolves, the impaired nurse becomes increasingly unable to function cognitively, physically, and emotionally, resulting in unsafe practice.

Definition of Impairment

The definition of *impairment* typically includes a dependency on alcohol, drugs, or both. Impairment also has been associated with psychiatric illness and psycho-logical conditions. *Dependency* is defined as a state of psychological or physical addiction to a chemical substance. Impairment results from the use of these mood-altering substances and leads to an inability to perform professional duties in a reasonably acceptable manner.

Incidence and Etiology

In 1987, the ANA estimated that approximately 6%–8% (130,000–170,000) of the practicing RN population was addicted to drugs or alcohol. In 1995, an average

65% of the nursing disciplinary hearings conducted in the United States involved allegations of substance abuse. The most commonly abused drug is meperidine hydrochloride (Demerol), with workplace theft noted as the most frequent means of obtaining drugs.

Although no definitive conclusion has been reached as to why nurses become impaired, the frequently cited reasons include chronic pain, depression, job stress (especially related to critical care nurses), sense of powerlessness, increased workload, extended shifts, and loneliness. Likewise, researchers have struggled to find an explanation as to the process by which impairment occurs. While some believe that chemical dependency is a disease process grounded in physiological and psychological factors, others believe that social factors (e.g., peer influence, exposure to high-risk behavior, ready access to chemical substances, awareness that drugs are effective in solving patient problems such as pain and anxiety, shift in work setting to less supervised areas such as outpatient and community health) also play a role.

Current Attitudes

In 1984, the ANA took steps to publicly recognize substance abuse as a problem among nurses. Since then, the goal has been to treat and rehabilitate the impaired nurse and to allow the individual to safely return to practice. This goal has found support in a variety of other professional models including state NPAs and the NCSBN. Both the ANA and the NCSBN have established formal resolutions seeking the implementation of assistance programs, as well as an increase in education and research. Additionally, many hospitals have enacted policies and procedures governing and addressing issues related to the impaired nurse.

Identification of an Impaired Nurse

Part A lists signs indicating impairment.

Ethical and Legal Obligations

Coworkers of an impaired nurse often struggle with the ethical issue of whether or not to report their suspicions. Reasons cited for not reporting include loyalty, uncertainty, fear of jeopardizing another's job, fear of being labeled a "whistle-blower," and feelings of inadequacy regarding what to do and say. By failing to report, nurses engage in enabling behavior (e.g., ignoring or excusing the activity, taking blame for the situation, defending or justifying the impaired nurse's actions), which serves as an inadequate and improper response.

The ethical dilemma has been resolved, however, by the legal obligation to report, as mandated by many state reporting laws. Such laws generally require that drug and alcohol abuse be reported to the state licensing board. Likewise, the ANA *Code for Nurses* mandates intervention when patient safety is at issue. It provides that "[t]he nurse acts to safeguard the client and the public when health care and safety are affected by the incompetent, unethical or illegal practice of any person."

The guidelines for handling the situation and for reporting are presented in **Part B**.

Effective Programs

The key to helping an impaired nurse succeed in recovery and return to practice is an effective diversion program. More than 25 states have implemented such programs, which have been defined by the NCSBN as voluntary, confidential alternatives to licensure disciplinary action. The goal is to enable the nurse to regain productivity, health, and self esteem.

Additionally, many facilities offer employee assistance programs, which generally provide the employees and family members with access to free, confidential counseling, evaluation, and referral. Sometimes the state board of nursing implements similar programs. The programs usually consist of networks of supervisors who refer the nurse for rehabilitation and document the course of treatment and compliance. In addition, they provide the employer with assurance that the employee is receiving effective treatment and will be able to return to the clinical setting as a solo practitioner.

In addition to a monitored employee assistance program, other tools have been effective in aiding the recovery of an impaired nurse: (1) random urine testing for drugs and alcohol; (2) mandatory attendance to Alcoholics Anonymous/Narcotics Anonymous meetings; (3) back-to-work agreements outlining conditions of continued employment; and (4) restricted practice areas to preclude high stress, high medication usage, and unsupervised shifts and settings. Failure to participate in these programs may prompt the employer to report the RN to the state board of nursing for possible disciplinary action.

Costs

A coworker and the health care facility may invite litigation if they fail to reasonably recognize an impaired nurse and follow through in an appropriate manner. The implementation of organizational policies and procedures, as well as the promotion of staff education, will aid in effective rehabilitation of the impaired nurse and the avoidance of liability.

Given that impaired nurses commonly divert medication from the workplace as a means of supporting their habit, health care facilities should use this cost as a further incentive to timely identify and treat these individuals. Likewise, the financial losses associated with the amount of management time devoted to the issue, as well as the rate of employee turnover or retention, should hasten the decision to implement an effective assistance program.

Certain intangible costs associated with impaired nurses such as staff morale, quality of care, and erosion of public confidence are crucial and must be prevented.

49 Sexual Harassment in the Workplace–Part I

Susan Westrick Killion, JD, MS, RN

A Rights and Responsibilities of Employees and Employers

Employee

- Right to a workplace free of sexual harassment including a nonhostile environment
- Right to have a clearly defined policy by management against sexual harassment in the workplace
- Responsibility to confront harasser, document incident, and report to supervisor
- Right to confidential and timely investigation of a claim by employer
- Right to potential remedies under the law including damages, injunctive relief, and disciplinary action against the harassing employee

Employer

- Responsibility to communicate a clearly defined policy against sexual harassment to employees
- Responsibility to consistently enforce the policy
- Responsibility to conduct fair, confidential, and timely investigation of complaints
- Right to expect employees to report incidents of sexual harassment and to cooperate fully with all investigations
- Responsibility to take steps to prevent incidents of sexual harassment in the workplace

B Steps to Take When Sexual Harassment Occurs

1. Confront the harasser and make it clear that the specific behavior is unwelcome and is interfering with your work performance. Do not send out ambiguous messages through your behavior that could be misinterpreted. Some authorities recommend that you send a return-receipt letter to the harasser so that there is no question that the person has received a clear message.

2. Document the incident in your own notes so that you have a record of the incident or incidents. Record any witnesses to the circumstances and include who you notified of the incident. If the harasser is a patient, you should document the facts objectively in the patient's record and the outcome. In any event, you should keep your own notes of the incident. Employers may have other policies that you need to follow in these situations.

3. Report the incident to your supervisor, who will then be on notice of the situation. If you have a union contract, you may need to report the incident to a union representative who will help you resolve the issue, perhaps through a grievance process.

4. Keep other evaluations of your job performance to show that you have evidence of performing well on the job, if a claim is made by the harasser about your poor job performance in retaliation for your claim of sexual harassment.

Sexual harassment in the workplace has become a growing concern for employees and employers in health care settings. Both the intimate nature of contact with patients and a work environment in which there is often power disparity among workers contribute to this problem. Almost all claims of sexual harassment involve complaints by females against male harassers, but females also may be the subject of a complaint. Same-sex harassment can occur and may be the basis of a valid claim. Sex role stereotypes, socialization of males and females, and traditional power disparities between men and women have contributed to making sexual harassment a sometimes pervasive and underreported situation.

Sources of Protection

The primary source of protection against sexual harassment in the workplace is Title VII of the Federal Civil Rights Act of 1964, which bans job discrimination on the basis of sex. Prior to 1980, Title VII did not clearly include sexual harassment as a form of sexual discrimination. Throughout the years courts have extended protection under this law so that various forms of sexual harassment are included. The Civil Rights Act of 1991 contains definitions of sexual harassment that are operative at this time. The Equal Employment Opportunity Commission (EEOC), a federal agency that enforces Title VII and is where a complaint would be filed, has further clarified definitions of conduct and circumstances that constitute sexual harassment. These definitions have been upheld in the federal courts.

Many states have laws that provide an additional source of protection for workers. Union contracts for employees may explicitly deal with this issue, and most employers provide employment manuals with policies on sexual harassment.

Definitions and Types

Sexual harassment is defined as unwelcome sexual advances or requests for sexual favors, or other verbal or physical conduct that unreasonably interferes with job performance.

There are 2 major categories of sexual harassment as defined by the Civil Rights Act of 1991:

1. *Quid quo pro* sexual harassment involves conditioning job privileges or advancement on granting of sexual favors by the other party. It occurs most often when there is a supervisor relationship with the victim of harassment, and the supervisor has control over the victim. The alleged harassment must have resulted in a loss of job benefits or in a detriment to one's job. Employers have been held strictly liable for the acts of their supervisors in such circumstances. The EEOC has included in its guidelines that the unwelcome sexual advances may have been made explicitly or implicitly a condition of the job.

2. Sexual harassment in a *hostile work environment* involves sexual conduct such as dirty jokes or lewd remarks, sexual remarks or gestures, pinup calendars or posters, or even sexually suggestive looks or job assignments. The EEOC has included conduct that has the purpose or effect of unreasonably interfering with an individual's work performance or creating an intimidating, hostile, or offensive work environment. Victims of this type of harassment do not need to prove that they suffered an economic loss. It is enough to show that the conduct affected the psychological well-being of the victim. The conduct or behavior complained of is viewed from the perspective of the victim, and courts have used the "reasonable woman standard" if the victim is a female. Although there is no universal standard to determine what specific conduct or behavior falls within these definitions, the courts have interpreted the language broadly.

50 Sexual Harassment in the Workplace-Part II

Susan Westrick Killion, JD, MS, RN

A   Rights and Responsibilities of Employees and Employers

Employee

- Right to a workplace free of sexual harassment including a nonhostile environment
- Right to have a clearly defined policy by management against sexual harassment in the workplace
- Responsibility to confront harasser, document incident, and report to supervisor
- Right to confidential and timely investigation of a claim by employer
- Right to potential remedies under the law including damages, injunctive relief, and disciplinary action against the harassing employee

Employer

- Responsibility to communicate a clearly defined policy against sexual harassment to employees
- Responsibility to consistently enforce the policy
- Responsibility to conduct fair, confidential, and timely investigation of complaints
- Right to expect employees to report incidents of sexual harassment and to cooperate fully with all investigations
- Responsibility to take steps to prevent incidents of sexual harassment in the workplace

B   Steps to Take When Sexual Harassment Occurs

1. Confront the harasser and make it clear that the specific behavior is unwelcome and is interfering with your work performance. Do not send out ambiguous messages through your behavior that could be misinterpreted. Some authorities recommend that you send a return-receipt letter to the harasser so that there is no question that the person has received a clear message.

2. Document the incident in your own notes so that you have a record of the incident or incidents. Record any witnesses to the circumstances and include who you notified of the incident. If the harasser is a patient, you should document the facts objectively in the patient's record and the outcome. In any event, you should keep your own notes of the incident. Employers may have other policies that you need to follow in these situations.

3. Report the incident to your supervisor, who will then be on notice of the situation. If you have a union contract, you may need to report the incident to a union representative who will help you resolve the issue, perhaps through a grievance process.

4. Keep other evaluations of your job performance to show that you have evidence of performing well on the job, if a claim is made by the harasser about your poor job performance in retaliation for your claim of sexual harassment.

Employer's Liability

Sexual harassment can occur from supervisors, fellow employees, or patients. Employers have a duty to investigate complaints by employees, maintain confidentiality of complaints, and document claims and their outcomes (see **Part A**). Along with strict liability for supervisors, employers have been found liable for acts of their employees if they knew about the conduct or behavior but did not respond appropriately. Successful claims can result in large legal expenses for employers and have been cited as a cause of impaired productivity, emotional distress, absenteeism, and high turnover of employees.

Employers have a legal and ethical duty to provide employees with a safe work environment, which includes an environment free of sexual harassment. In addition, clear policies against this conduct should be communicated to employees and followed by employers.

Steps to Take When Sexual Harassment Occurs

A series of actions should be taken when a harassment situation occurs (see **Part B**). In all instances the nurse should follow policies set out by the employer for such situations and follow procedures for internal solutions to the problem. If the nurse is not satisfied with this process, he or she can file a complaint with the EEOC and the state human rights commission or retain an attorney to pursue the claim.

Remedies for Successful Claims

Injunctive relief in the form of a court order that would require the employer to discontinue the activity or to take steps to prevent the harassment may be available to an employee. If an employee is terminated due to harassment, the court can order reinstatement along with an award of back wages. Courts may grant punitive damages to the employee if the claim involves an especially egregious case against an employer.

Termination of employment of the harasser or transfer to another job is another possible remedy. Disciplinary action of some type is expected against employees who are guilty of sexually harassing other employees. Other types of relief may be granted through state statutes or union contracts.

Prevention

Both employees and employers can take steps in the workplace to help prevent sexual harassment. One way is for both groups to recognize the seriousness of this issue and its detrimental effects on the work environment. All employees need to know that they have a right to work in an environment free of these concerns (see **Part A**). Employers need to identify high-risk areas for sexual harassment and implement preventative strategies.

There must be top-level commitment to issuing clear and strong policies against tolerating any form of sexual harassment. Employers must strictly enforce these policies and give careful attention and response to alleged claims of sexual harassment. It is unwise to endorse in any way a culture or work environment that condones this type of harassment.

As a victim of sexual harassment, an employee needs to deal with the issue. Not doing so jeopardizes not only the victim's work environment, but also that of others. By dealing with the situation, the victim may find that others have been victimized, which makes it easier to establish a pattern of unacceptable behavior or conduct. This prevents the harasser from controlling the situation and will help prevent the physical and emotional cost to the victim and other potential victims.

Staff education regarding specific aspects of the law as well as prevention strategies can be an effective way to decrease exposure of employees to situations involving sexual harassment.

51 Violence in the Workplace-Part I

Susan Westrick Killion, JD, MS, RN

A Suspected Violence against a Patient

- Must protect the patient.
- Legal duty is often based on statutes (e.g., child abuse laws requiring mandatory reporting)
- Ethical duty is based on ANA *Code for Nurses*.
- Maintain confidentiality of patient and integrity of evidence.

B Violence by Health Care Workers

- Includes verbal, physical, or sexual abuse.
- Includes claims for forcing medications, food, or misuse of restraints or medication for control.
- Must be reported to nurse manager or administration.

C Violence against Health Care Workers

- Exposed to verbal and physical abuse or injury by patients or families in high-risk settings or by colleagues.
- Can recover workers' compensation claim for injury.

D Documentation and Reporting

- Maintain objective record of all events.
- File any required incident, police, or other reports.

E Prevention and Strategies to Minimize Violence

- Detect early and intervene.
- Teach strategies to deal with stress.
- Make referrals to social or mental health agencies.
- Implement emergency protocols such as for restraints.
- Institute workplace safety programs and security devices.

Health care agencies and other parts of the community in which nurses work have been increasingly exposed to the effects of violence. Nurses are especially vulnerable to violence in high-risk areas of practice such as the emergency department and psychiatric settings. Patients also may be exposed to violence by health care workers. It is imperative that nurses be able to safely intervene with effective strategies that must incorporate an awareness of legal rights and responsibilities for all involved.

Suspected Violence Against a Patient

A nurse who suspects that violence or abuse has occurred against a patient must document the findings, gather more information from the victim or others, and protect the patient (see **Part A**). In many instances (e.g., child abuse) the nurse has a legal duty to report the abuse, based on mandatory reporting statutes. However, in the case of domestic abuse, states vary as to whether reporting can be done by health care workers. Some states require permission of the victim before police or state agencies are notified.

Whether reporting is mandatory or not, the nurse has an ethical duty to protect the patient, as clearly articulated in the ANA *Code for Nurses* (1985). In addition, a charge of malpractice or other claim could be successful against a nurse for not reporting a suspected incident. This can happen if it can be proved that harm came to the victim because of the failure to report.

In all cases, confidentiality regarding the situation and the victim must be maintained. Permission must be obtained if photographs are to be taken of evidence. Any evidence must be accurately marked, labeled, and stored in containers that will preserve it and not disturb the "chain of custody." The storage of evidence and the names of who has had access to it are extremely relevant to whether it can be used in any subsequent legal proceeding.

Violence by Health Care Practitioners Against a Patient

Violence by health care workers against a patient can take many forms: physical abuse, verbal abuse, rough handling, and sexual abuse (see **Part B**). Nurses have been charged with calling patients names, using medications or restraints inappropriately to control patients and forcing patients to take medicines. If a nurse has knowledge of this behavior against patients it is suggested that the nurse confront the other health care worker about the behavior and report it to the nurse manager or appropriate administrator. Each agency should have a protocol as to how to deal with such situations that must be followed.

Violence Against Health Care Workers

Staff may be vulnerable to violent situations because of their practice settings (e.g., community health center in high-crime area, emergency department, psychiatric setting). Nurses can be exposed to physical violence as well as verbal abuse and harassment by patients and their families (see **Part C**). Although nurses should be eligible for workers' compensation from physical injuries incurred as a part of their job, the effects of these injuries can be far-reaching (e.g., change of jobs or practice settings, permanent disability, HIV-positive status).

Another type of abuse that nurses can be exposed to is physical or verbal abuse by colleagues. The nurse-physician interaction is an all too frequent source of interpersonal conflict that occasionally results in violence or abuse.

Violence in the Community

When traveling to agencies or patients' homes in high-crime areas, nurses must be especially vigilant of personal safety. If a nurse is uncomfortable visiting a patient alone, the nurse's employer should request a security escort. The employer has a legal duty to provide reasonable measures to ensure the safety of employees. Some agencies will not permit home visits in especially high-crime areas because of these concerns. The nurse must be aware of and follow all agency policies regarding employee safety.

52 Violence in the Workplace—Part II

Susan Westrick Killion, JD, MS, RN

A Suspected Violence against a Patient

- Must protect the patient.
- Legal duty is often based on statutes (e.g., child abuse laws requiring mandatory reporting)
- Ethical duty is based on ANA *Code for Nurses*.
- Maintain confidentiality of patient and integrity of evidence.

B Violence by Health Care Workers

- Includes verbal, physical, or sexual abuse.
- Includes claims for forcing medications, food, or misuse of restraints or medication for control.
- Must be reported to nurse manager or administration.

C Violence against Health Care Workers

- Exposed to verbal and physical abuse or injury by patients or families in high-risk settings or by colleagues.
- Can recover workers' compensation claim for injury.

D Documentation and Reporting

- Maintain objective record of all events.
- File any required incident, police, or other reports.

E Prevention and Strategies to Minimize Violence

- Detect early and intervene.
- Teach strategies to deal with stress.
- Make referrals to social or mental health agencies.
- Implement emergency protocols such as for restraints.
- Institute workplace safety programs and security devices.

Suspected Drug Possession

If a nurse has suspicions of drug possession or weapons, the nurse should call security and notify the nurse manager. A nurse should not conduct a search of a patient's or visitor's belongings because doing so would violate the person's right of privacy. However, a nurse may act on knowledge of what is in "plain view" since this does not require a search. The nurse should note in the chart if the patient has symptoms or behaviors that could indicate use of drugs (other than those prescribed) but should not draw a conclusion about the source. As in all documentation, statements must be objective.

If the nurse suspects a coworker possesses or uses drugs, the nurse should follow the same procedure and notify the nurse manager. The nurse should document the situation in personal notes or wherever required to do so by agency policies. If the situation involves personal risk to the nurse, the nurse should notify security. In no case can the situation be ignored.

Documentation and Reporting

A thorough and objective record of events or evidence involving violent situations needs to be compiled (see **Part D**). Notes should be made in patient records, and incident reports or police reports may need to be completed. In all cases agency or institution policies must be followed. These notes may be used as evidence in subsequent legal proceedings and may be invaluable to successful claims. Reports may need to be filed with state agencies. Employees need to follow through with necessary documentation of work-related injury for workers' compensation claims.

Prevention of or Strategies to Minimize Violence

The best way to deal with violence is to prevent it by early detection and intervention (see **Part E**). Nurses should be aware of situations that could become violent and actively work to deter this from happening. Teaching strategies such as how to effectively handle stress can help to prevent child or domestic violence. Appropriate referrals to social service or mental health agencies can be made as an early intervention strategy. A nurse suspecting that an employee is abusing patients must deal with the situation promptly.

If a patient or coworker becomes violent, the nurse needs to assertively state that the behavior should stop. Nurse managers and security may need to be called if the individual is not calmed. In all cases, personal safety and the safety of others (including the perpetrator) must be considered. If a patient leaves the facility while threatening harm to someone, the police may need to be notified. In some extreme cases, health care workers may have a legal duty to warn identifiable third persons.

Workplace safety can be enhanced by programs that teach employees principles of personal safety and by the presence of physical barriers and security devices designed to prevent unauthorized access to high-risk areas. Protocols and procedures that deal with these situations proactively can minimize problems when they occur.

53 Intentional Torts–Part I

Susan Westrick Killion, JD, MS, RN

A Elements of Intentional Torts

Battery
- Unconsented touching
- Contact with person or objects on or close to them
- May result from lack of permission for a procedure (no informed consent)

Assault
- Fear or apprehension of a battery
- Present, not future harm intended
- Must be a reasonable fear of harm
- Mere words are not enough, need to include an overt act

False imprisonment
- Physical restraint or intimidating words
- Victim aware of restriction of movement
- May include withholding means to leave (car keys, wheelchair)

Intentional infliction of emotional distress
- Conduct that is outrageously distressing
- Victim experiences severe emotional distress

Defenses
- Consent (could be implied)
- Necessity
- Justification
- Self-defense

B Elements of Quasi-intentional Torts

Defamation
- False statements that injure one's reputation
- Libel — by the written word (includes charting)
- Slander — by the spoken word
- Publication to a third party or parties
- May need to show economic harm or business interference
- Claim not usually valid if made in a business relationship to supervisors or others up the chain of command who need to know the information
- Claim not usually valid if statement made by a former employer for a reference — "qualified privilege"

Invasion of privacy
- Interference with right to be left alone
- Revealing private facts publicly
- Using likeness or photos without permission
- Less rights for public figures, based on newsworthiness of private facts

Defenses
- Truth as an absolute defense to libel or slander
- Privilege or qualified privilege in a business relationship
- Public figure or newsworthiness exception

The law of torts protects individuals against private wrongs by another person. A *tort* is defined as a legal or civil wrong committed by one person against the person or property of another, independent of a contract. A tort involves some type of intentional conduct on the part of the actor (who could be a nurse) that invades the interest of another. In situations where the intent is less clear, the tort is termed a *quasi-inten-tional tort*. The type of intent that is required to prove an intentional tort is that of intent for purposeful conduct on the part of the actor. What is necessary is that the actor intended the act. The actor is then responsible for all the natural consequences that follow from that act, even if the specific harm that resulted was not intended. Intentional and quasi-intentional torts are contrasted with *negligent torts* in which there is no

128

intent on the part of the actor, but rather a failure to uphold a standard or duty that was owed to the injured party. No expert witness would be needed in proving intentional tort cases since there is no requirement of a standard to be proved in the situation. Sometimes a particular act (such as a battery) could have criminal as well as civil consequences, although this is not the usual case in health care situations.

Intentional Torts

Part A reviews the elements of intentional torts. In health care situations, *battery* (unconsented touching) can apply when a patient has not consented to a procedure. This would also then become a claim for lack of informed consent. The unconsented touching does not always have to be direct touching for a claim to prevail. It may include instances of touching the patient's clothing or purse or other objects that are in the person's hands. Nurses are cautioned to ask for the patient's permission in any doubtful situation.

Assault is defined as threat to do harm or the immediate fear of a battery. Usually assault and battery are claimed together even though they involve 2 separate torts. Mere words are not enough to prove assault. Together with an overt act of threatening, the 2 factors may be enough. The threat must create a reasonable apprehension, it must be immediate (not in the future), and the victim must be aware of the threat. The actual touching, or battery, does not have to occur for a claim of assault to be successful.

False imprisonment is defined as the act of preventing the free movement of a person or detaining a person without legal cause. The patient needs to prove that he or she was restrained physically or by intimidation. Thus, the person must be aware of the actor's

intent to restrain movement. It is sufficient to show that there was essential restraint, such as removing the person's outdoor clothing from the room or car keys to prevent him from leaving. Misuse of chemical or physical restraints can result in successful claims of false imprisonment if all other elements are present. However, there are some justifications for physically restraining patients, including preventing harm to themselves or others.

Intentional infliction of emotional distress involves outrageous conduct that inflicts severe emotional disturbance on the victim. This situation is rare in the health care setting but could occur if a patient was intentionally told some false and extremely upsetting news such as that he or she had a fatal illness. What is more common is when there is negligent (but unintentional) infliction of emotional distress. Persons with successful claims need to show that some damage has occurred, such as inability to work or health problems that resulted from the incident.

Defenses

One valid defense is that the patient consented. A patient may claim that an assault and battery took place when he or she did not give verbal consent to an injection. However, a valid defense could be that the patient turned over and got in position for the injection, thus inferring consent. Another defense could be necessity or justification, when it may have been necessary to touch a patient to prevent the patient from a fall or harm. Self-defense is another defense. Even a claim of intentional infliction of emotional distress could be justified under some circumstances, if there was an emergency or disaster that warranted the nurse's action.

54 Intentional Torts—Part II

Susan Westrick Killion, JD, MS, RN

A   Elements of Intentional Torts

Battery
- Unconsented touching
- Contact with person or objects on or close to them
- May result from lack of permission for a procedure (no informed consent)

Assault
- Fear or apprehension of a battery
- Present, not future harm intended
- Must be a reasonable fear of harm
- Mere words are not enough, need to include an overt act

False imprisonment
- Physical restraint or intimidating words
- Victim aware of restriction of movement
- May include withholding means to leave (car keys, wheelchair)

Intentional infliction of emotional distress
- Conduct that is outrageously distressing
- Victim experiences severe emotional distress

Defenses
- Consent (could be implied)
- Necessity
- Justification
- Self-defense

B   Elements of Quasi-intentional Torts

Defamation
- False statements that injure one's reputation
- Libel — by the written word (includes charting)
- Slander — by the spoken word
- Publication to a third party or parties
- May need to show economic harm or business interference
- Claim not usually valid if made in a business relationship to supervisors or others up the chain of command who need to know the information
- Claim not usually valid if statement made by a former employer for a reference — "qualified privilege"

Invasion of privacy
- Interference with right to be left alone
- Revealing private facts publicly
- Using likeness or photos without permission
- Less rights, for public figures, based on newsworthiness of private facts

Defenses
- Truth as an absolute defense to libel or slander
- Privilege or qualified privilege in a business relationship
- Public figure or newsworthiness exception

Quasi-Intentional Torts

Part B reviews the elements of quasi-intentional torts. *Defamation,* an invasion of the right to one's good name or character, involves the two torts of *libel* (written communication) and *slander* (oral communication). Defamation consists of publication of a false statement to a third party or parties that injures the person's reputation. The defamatory statements must be made as a statement of fact and be of the type that would be seen as derogatory, adverse, or harmful to a person's reputation. The tort is a personal one and only living persons can be defamed. Statements made about a group are not defamatory.

Claims for defamation may arise when false or derogatory statements are made about patients in a public place or written in a chart. Nurses are reminded to chart objectively and to not state opinions that may be considered defamatory.

A claim of defamation also may arise when an employer writes or gives an oral negative reference about a former employee (who may be a nurse). The nurse may claim that a job was not obtained because of this. However, this circumstance involves a qualified privilege by the employer; because of the work situation, the employer is privileged to disclose negative information about former employees and in some instances has a duty to do so. In fact, courts have recognized a qualified privilege for statements made up the chain of command when they are made in good faith. The discussion must be held with supervisors or others who have a legitimate need to know and not just with coworkers or others. One needs to be cautious in making statements about colleagues, physicians, or other workers that could be considered defamatory.

Invasion of privacy protects the person's interest in being left alone, free from unwarranted intrusions into one's privacy. Claims by patients may include public release of private facts or appropriations of one's likeness without permission. Courts have allowed such claims when pictures of patients have been published in medical texts without their permission. All agencies should have policies for obtaining written permission from patients for photographs, even for publicity purposes.

Defenses

Truth is an absolute defense to a claim of defamation. Another defense could be privilege or qualified privilege. A defendant may also claim that false statements made about another were intended as a joke and that no harm was caused. Sometimes the defense of fair comment in the public interest may overcome a claim of defamation. Consent may be a defense to invasion of privacy. The defendant may also claim that the victim is a "public figure" so that there may be less protection against invasion of privacy. Most courts do embrace this concept since public figures may fall into an exception for "news worthiness" of facts that would otherwise be considered private. Under limited circumstances the public may have a right to know certain information.

Damages and Liability

Damage awards from successful claims of intentional and quasi-intentional torts can be substantial. Some torts require actual damage to be proved, but others do not. In addition to compensatory damages, the court may award punitive damages against an individual for a particularly harmful or malicious act. These intentional acts usually are not covered by malpractice insurance policies, and the nurse would be individually liable if found guilty. In some cases the employer also may be held liable for the intentional conduct of the employee.

1. An employee at will reports to a state agency that his employer is violating health and safety codes, and the employer is fined. The employee is subsequently terminated and brings a lawsuit against the employer for wrongful discharge. The likely outcome of the case will be:

(A) The employer will win since an employee at will can be terminated at any time

~ (B) The employee will win because of the public policy exception

(C) The court will need to look at the employee handbook before any decision could be made

(D) Since there is not a contract for the employment situation, the NLRB will handle the employee's claim

2. A nursing supervisor who is 62 years old believes she was terminated because of her age. She brings a lawsuit under the Age Discrimination in Employment Act (ADEA). Which of the following is *not* an essential component of the claim?

(A) She must show she is a member of the protected class

(B) She must prove she is qualified for her position

(C) She must show that the position was given to someone else who is not a member of the class that the ADEA seeks to protect

~ (D) She must show specific intent on the part of the employer to discriminate

3. The nurse employed by a home care agency is working with a patient in his home. The nurse makes the statement, "I know that if you do these exercises each day your hand will regain all of its former function." This statement could cause a problem for the nurse or the employer because:

(A) The nurse has created an implied contract for the employer

~ (B) The statements of the nurse could be interpreted by the patient as a promise to guarantee results and could create a contract

(C) There is unequal bargaining power between the parties so a contract has not been created

(D) Statements such as this can be misinterpreted by the patient and are therefore unethical

4. A patient requests that the nurse take care of him when he leaves the hospital and specifies an hourly rate and other conditions. Which of the elements of creating a contract are *missing* from this scenario?

(A) There is no offer or acceptance

(B) There is no consideration that would be exchanged by the parties

~ (C) There is an offer but no acceptance or mutual assent ·

(D) There is no capacity to enter into the contract

5. A nurse speaks out in the local newspaper about the short staffing at her hospital. She claims that there are violations of state-mandated nurse-patient ratios on a regular basis by her employer. The nurse does not have an employment contract and is an employee at will. If she is fired because of this:

(A) She will have no recourse against the employer because she is an employee at will

~ (B) There may be recourse against her employer's action if it is found that she was promoting an important public policy while making these statements

(C) The employer will have to reinstate the employee unless he can show cause as to why the employee was fired

(D) She can win a claim that her employment is secured because she can make any statement she wants as protected speech under the First Amendment

6. Staff nurses who assign other nurses to patients or who evaluate them may be excluded from the protection of unions. This means that:

~ (A) Some charge nurses could be considered "supervisors"

(B) Nurses should refuse to undertake these duties in the workplace

(C) The employer can keep nurses from joining unions if they perform these tasks

(D) The NLRB cannot rule on a claim that the nurse's rights have been violated if the union refuses to allow nurses to join

7. A nurse is assigned to a patient diagnosed with Alzheimer's disease and requires assistance with all activities of daily living, including eating. The patient is

on a "soft" diet and his dinner tray, which is prepared by the hospital, contains tea, pureed vegetables, pureed chicken, and chocolate pudding. The pureed chicken appears somewhat "lumpy" but no more so than usual. The nurse spoon-feeds the patient, who thereafter appears quite comfortable. Two hours later the patient begins vomiting bright red blood. Radiographs reveal the presence of a very small metal object, probably from the pureed chicken, in the patient's stomach. A claim is brought against the nurse and the hospital and the likely outcome is:

(A) Both the nurse and the hospital are liable

(B) Only the nurse is liable

(C) Only the hospital is liable

(D) No party is found liable

8. The operating room calls for a patient after a 6-hour delay. The nurse helps the patient move onto a stretcher, which doesn't have an IV pole attached to it. The nurse locates one that is too slender to fit into the "pole hole" in the stretcher. Instead of taking the time to locate the nursing unit's IV pole on wheels, the nurse wraps tape around the base of the slender IV pole until it is thick enough to fit into the hole on the stretcher. During transport to the operating room, the IV pole topples over, lacerating the patient's forehead. A claim is brought against the hospital and the nurse. The likely outcome is:

(A) The nurse is not liable because this is accepted practice on the nursing unit

(B) The hospital is not liable because the stretcher did not have an IV pole

(C) The nurse is liable

(D) Both parties are liable

(E) The hospital is solely liable

9. A nurse midwife is employed by Obstetrics, Inc., a corporation formed by a group of obstetricians. The nurse midwife and all physicians in Obstetrics, Inc. have admitting privileges at Best Hospital. While the nurse midwife is attending to a laboring mother, she notes that the baby's heart rate has dropped significantly and is concerned that the amniotic fluid will contain meconium. The written policy of Obstetrics, Inc. is that under these circumstances the nurse midwife must call the on-call obstetrician in the group and notify him or her of the situation. Rather than doing so, the nurse midwife follows her typical pattern (as demonstrated at this hospital before) and elects to wait and see what happens. The baby has cerebral palsy. A claim is brought against Obstetrics, Inc. and Best Hospital. Liability is imputed to:

(A) Obstetrics, Inc.

(B) Best Hospital

(C) Both Obstetrics, Inc. and Best Hospital

(D) Neither

10. A student nurse is working at a hospital as a paid nursing assistant. During this time the student performs a negligent act for which liability is found. The student also has clinical experiences at this hospital and sometimes cares for the same patients as a student nurse and as a paid assistant. Which of the following would be true?

(A) The student is personally liable

(B) The hospital would be vicariously liable under a theory of respondeat superior

(C) The hospital is liable under a theory of ostensible agency

(D) The educational institution is liable since it placed the student in this assignment

(E) Both A and B

11. An agency nurse travels across state lines to work. Which of the following factors determines liability for the nurse's actions if negligence is found?

(A) Which agency or individual carries malpractice insurance for the nurse

(B) Whether or not the nurse is licensed by the state where the negligence occurred

(C) Who employs the nurse as well as who controls her practice in this patient situation

(D) Whether or not the nurse has personal assets to satisfy any judgment that the patient may be entitled to

12. A nurse with 10 years of medical nursing experience in the neurology intensive care unit (NICU) arrives at work one night and learns he is being "floated" to the cardiothoracic intensive care unit (CTICU) for the shift because that unit is short one nurse. When the nurse tells the supervisor that he has never taken care of a CT patient the supervisor says "You're an intensive care nurse, you can do it. Besides the whole hospital is understaffed tonight." On arrival in the CTICU, the nurse is assigned to a patient who is due to be admitted directly from the operating room after undergoing a quadruple coronary artery bypass. The nurse's best course of action is:

(A) Explain to the CTICU charge nurse that he or she has never taken care of a CT patient before

(B) Ask if there is a stable patient already in the unit that can be assigned instead

(C) Ask if one of the regular CTICU nurses can be available to assist

(D) Ascertain the procedure for taking care of a fresh, postoperative patient in that unit

(E) All of the above

13. A nurse has an employment contract with the employer hospital. The contract explicitly states that the employer will not require the nurse to "float." One day the supervisor approaches the nurse and asks if she will "float" to another unit that is particularly understaffed. Considering the contract the nurse:

(A) Must refuse to "float"

(B) May walk out

(C) May agree to "float"

(D) Must take legal action against the employer

(E) All of the above

14. An employer may be required to perform all of the following as a reasonable accommodation for a qualified disabled nurse except:

(A) Reassign the nurse to another job position

(B) Create a job position that fits the nurse's skills

(C) Allow an auxiliary aide animal into the workplace

(D) Assign someone else the nonessential job functions

15. Which of the following action by an employer is considered unlawful under the Americans with Disabilities Act?

(A) Pre-employment inquiry into a disability

(B) Job offer conditioned on an examination

(C) Drug testing of applicants

(D) Uniformly applied leave policy that causes hardship on a disabled employee

16. After being exposed to a patient's blood products, a nurse may do all of the following except:

(A) Review the chart for the patient's HIV status

(B) Draw blood on the patient and send it for HIV testing

(C) Have a physician request the patient's consent to be tested

(D) Fill out an incident report and submit it to the evaluation group

17. Nurses have a legal duty to:

(A) Know their own HIV status if they have risk factors

(B) Transfer to a specialty area without invasive procedures if they are HIV positive

(C) Identify safety risks to a patient and take steps to prevent harm

(D) Inform their own partners if they are HIV positive

18. An effective diversion program includes:

(A) Automatic termination

(B) Mandatory treatment including Alcoholics Anonymous/Narcotics Anonymous attendance

(C) Revocation of license

(D) Encouragement to seek employment elsewhere

19. In the process of reporting suspicions that a coworker is impaired, the nurse should do everything except:

(A) Document the factual basis for the suspicions

(B) Confront the nurse with the findings

(C) Notify the nurse manager

(D) Participate in education programs

20. For a claim of sexual harassment to prevail when a complaint is filed with the EEOC, a victim must:

(A) Prove there was physical contact between the harasser and oneself

(B) Have taken steps outlined in any employment policies, unless there are compelling reasons not to do so

(C) Prove that the alleged conduct resulted in an adverse job-related decision

(D) Be a federal employee since the EEOC enforces a federal law

21. An acceptable action to take if one is being sexually harassed in the workplace is to:

(A) Ignore the behavior if the harasser is a patient

(B) Calmly state to the harasser that you do not approve of what he or she is doing

(C) Document the incident the next time it happens

(D) Confront the harasser and make it clear that the specific conduct is unwelcome and unacceptable

22. A nurse is assigned to a patient admitted for drug withdrawal on the evening shift. As the nurse enters his room, he quickly shoves his hand under his pillow as if to conceal something. Nursing interventions should include which of the following?

(A) Conduct a search of his room

(B) Tell him he must show what he is hiding

(C) Document the incident and any behavior changes he may have

(D) Notify the supervisor and possibly security if the nurse strongly suspects he is hiding illegal drugs

(E) Both C and D

23. Which of the following is *not* an appropriate action to take if a community health care nurse suspects that a patient is being abused by a nursing assistant from her agency?

(A) Document the incidents that led to this conclusion in personal notes

(B) Follow up with any procedures required by the employer

(C) Confront the nursing assistant if it can be done safely

(D) Detain the employee until security or the police can be called

24. The nurse is talking to a coworker in the cafeteria about a physician. The nurse makes statements about the fact that the physician does not know what he is doing and often makes mistakes when treating patients. A visitor in the cafeteria later reveals to the physician that she overheard these statements, and she identifies the nurse who made the statements. Could the physician sustain a successful claim of slander against the nurse?

(A) No, since the statement was made in the work environment

(B) No, since the statement was just overheard by the visitor and was not published by the nurse

(C) Yes, since the statements injured the work reputation of the physician and were spoken so a third party could hear them

(D) Yes, because the statements were intended to cause harm to the physician and were only partially true

25. A patient claims that a nurse struck his arm intentionally when she was helping him get back in bed and used threatening language that there was more to come. What claims can be substantiated as based on these facts?

(A) Assault, since the nurse made unconsented contact with the patient

(B) Battery, since there was threatening language and fear of another harmful touching

(C) Both assault and battery, for reasons included in A and B

(D) No claims, since the nurse was only doing what was necessary

PART IV: ANSWERS

1. **The answer is B.**

Reporting bona fide claims to a state agency will most likely meet the standard of the public policy exception to firing at will employees for any reason. An important public policy is served by encouraging these violations to be reported. Answer A is incorrect because of the public policy exception. Answer C is incorrect because the employee manual is irrelevant to the facts given, although some courts may look to it for other exceptions to the employee at will doctrine. Answer D is incorrect because the NLRB only handles claims when there is a collective bargaining agreement governing the employment situation.

2. **The answer is D.**

It is not necessary to prove a specific intent on the part of the employer to discriminate against the employee. This intent often can be inferred on the basis of proving the other essential elements. Specific intent would place too high a burden of proof on the employee. However, after all the other components of the claim are shown, the employer can present a nondiscriminatory reason for the termination which the court may accept. Answers A, B, and C contain components that must be shown in order to shift the burden of proof to the employer to present a nondiscriminatory reason for the termination.

3. **The answer is B.**

The statement could be construed by the patient as creating a promise or a guarantee by the nurse as to specific results if the patient follows the directions. The nurse is also considered an agent of the employer and could bind the agency to the agreement if a contract was found by the court. Answer A is incorrect because this would be an express contract since specific statements were made. Answer C is incorrect because there is no indication of a situation of unequal bargaining power by either party. Answer D is not correct because misinterpretation by a patient is not automatically unethical.

4. The answer is C.

Although there is an offer, it has not been accepted and there is no mutual assent. Answer B is incorrect because there is consideration that would be exchanged—services for money. Answer D is not correct because there is no information in the question to indicate a lack of capacity to contract on the part of either party.

5. The answer is B.

This is the public policy exception to the usual case that the employee at will can be fired for any reason (even for no cause). If these allegations are proved true, the employee has a valid claim against the employer for reinstatement. Answer A is incorrect for the same reason. Answer C is incorrect because cause does not have to be shown to fire an at will employee. Answer D is incorrect because even though this speech may be found to be protected, it is too broad to state that anything said will be protected.

6. The answer is A.

A nurse who is in charge generally performs the tasks described in the question and could be considered a "supervisor" by the courts. Supervisors are considered management and would be excluded from participation in a union. Answer B is incorrect because the employer has a legitimate right to expect an employee who is qualified to perform this task, even if union protection may not necessarily be available to the employee. Answer C is not correct, since all the circumstances would be looked at, not just these particular tasks. Answer D is incorrect because the NLRB can still rule on the claim even if the nurse eventually would be excluded from participation in the union.

7. The answer is C.

The hospital is liable for negligently prepared food since the pureed chicken was not adequate and safe, as it was not reasonably suited for the purpose intended. B is incorrect since there is no indication that the nurse knew or should have known there was a metal object in the pureed chicken. A and D are incorrect for the same reasons.

8. The answer is C.

The nurse selected the equipment to be used and did so notwithstanding the fact that an adequate and safe IV pole on wheels was made available for use by the hospital. The nurse knew or should have known that such an injury to the patient would occur. Therefore, it is not likely that liability will be imputed to the hospital. E is incorrect for the same reasons. B and D are not the best answers because although it could be argued that the hospital failed to provide a stretcher reasonably suited for the purpose intended, a reasonable alternative was provided to the nurse who elected to forego using it. That it was common practice on the nursing unit to tape the IV pole is not sufficient to protect the nurse from liability absent a written hospital policy to do so.

9. The answer is C.

Although the nurse midwife has ignored Obstetrics, Inc.'s written policy and Obstetrics, Inc. argues that for that reason it is not liable, the nurse midwife has done this before. Therefore, there is a pattern of conduct on the part of the nurse midwife, and both Obstetrics, Inc. and Best Hospital knew or should have known that there is a question concerning the nurse midwife. A, B, and D are incorrect under the same reasoning.

10. The answer is E.

Both A and B are correct statements. A is correct because the principle of personal liability always remains. B is correct because when the negligent act occurred, the student had an employee-employer relationship with the hospital. C is incorrect because the theory of ostensible agency is not applied in the employee-employer relationship. D is incorrect because the student was not participating in clinical experiences when the negligent act occurred, and no one from the school was supervising the student.

11. The answer is C.

In addition to his or her personal liability, the employer would be liable under respondeat superior. The institution where the nurse is working could also be liable if it exerts so much control over the nurse's practice that he or she is considered an agent. Also the patient may view the agency nurse as an agent of the institution so that ostensible agency may be implied. A is not relevant to whether liability is found or as to who is liable. The fact of whether one is protected by insurance is not considered in determining liability. B is not correct because liability could still be found even if the nurse was not licensed by the state. D is not a factor to determine liability since the judgment could be satisfied from future wages. The fact that there are no assets or future assets does not determine liability.

12. The answer is E.

The actions described in A–D all serve to protect the nurse and protect the patient. As in A, by telling the charge nurse in the CTICU that the nurse doesn't have experience in CTICU nursing, the nurse is giving further notice to the employer that he or she may be unqualified for the assignment. By asking for a more stable patient as in B, the nurse is seeking to take care of a patient for which the nurse is more qualified. In C and D, the nurse is taking efforts to be as prepared as possible so as to provide adequate, safe nursing care.

13. **The answer is C.**

If the nurse is willing to "float" and, after obtaining as much information as possible about the assignment believes he or she is qualified, the nurse may "float." Absent contractual language to the contrary, that the hospital agreed not to "float" the nurse does not preclude the request that the nurse do so. If the nurse accepts the assignment, the contract will not protect the nurse from personal liability. All steps must still be taken to provide safe, reasonably proficient nursing care. The nurse is not obligated to refuse to "float" as in A. The agreement not to require the nurse to float does not allow the nurse to walk out simply because the employer asks as in B nor does it mandate taking legal action as in D.

14. **The answer is B.**

The employer is not required to create a job, under reasonable accommodation. An employer is required to reassign a qualified individual (A) or reassign nonessential job functions (D). The employer must accommodate an auxiliary aide animal (C) unless there is documentation that it poses a health or safety risk.

15. **The answer is A.**

A is unlawful because employees may not make pre-employment inquiries into disability but may inquire about ability to perform specific job functions. B is lawful, while an employer may not require an applicant to take a medical exam prior to a job offer, the job may be conditional on a post offer examination. C is lawful because employers may base job offers on results of drug testing and D is legal under the act as long as the leave policy is uniformly applied to all employees and does not specifically target disabled employees. If the employee asks for a modification, the employer may accommodate.

16. **The answer is B.**

A nurse may not draw blood for an HIV test without verifying that a physician has properly documented informed consent in the medical record.

17. **The answer is C.**

C is the only *legal* duty (this is the standard of care in nursing). All the other answers are *ethical* duties that should be performed within the bounds of ethics. Ethical duties are often guidelines for nurses to follow and occasionally become the standard of care in certain circumstances. Therefore under some circumstances A, B, and D could turn from an ethical duty to a legal duty.

18. **The answer is B.**

A, C, and D represent past remedies. Currently, the goal is to encourage recovery through formal rehabilitation including inpatient and outpatient programs (B), random drug testing, education, and back-to-work agreements that define the terms of continued employment.

19. **The answer is B.**

The nurse should not confront the impaired nurse. It is important to make certain that the suspicions are reviewed and confirmed by the nurse manager and that when confronted, a plan is outlined and treatment resources are immediately available.

20. **The answer is B.**

Courts and agencies that deal with claims generally require that an employee exhaust all internal remedies before a claim will be processed. An exception to this would be if an employee could not follow the policy because the immediate supervisor was the harasser. This would constitute a compelling reason for not following the policy. A victim does not have to prove that actual physical contact occurred with the harasser (A) or that there was a negative effect on one's job (C), especially in cases involving a hostile work environment. These elements may be a part of the victim's case, especially in quid quo pro harassment. Title VII of the Civil Rights Act applies equally to private and public employees and employers (D).

21. **The answer is D.**

One needs to be firm and clear about what conduct is unacceptable, and the first step in doing this is to confront the harasser. A is incorrect because sexual harassment by patients needs to be dealt with in a constructive way. B is incorrect because the message to the harasser is somewhat ambiguous. C is incorrect because each incident of harassment should be documented.

22. **The answer is E.**

The nurse should provide objective documentation of the incident and any assessment of the patient in the patient's record. It is also appropriate to tell him that for his medical care to be effective, the health care team needs to know about anything he is taking that is not a part of his care plan. The supervisor should be notified, and if the nurse thinks there is an issue of safety, security should be notified. Answer A is incorrect because a nurse cannot conduct a search without the patient's permission. Answer B is incorrect because a nurse cannot demand that a patient do this, since it is the patient's decision. The nurse can ask to see what is under the pillow in a nonthreatening manner.

23. **The answer is D.**

The nurse should not attempt to detain anyone suspected of abuse, since doing so could jeopardize personal safety. However, the supervisor or security needs to be notified. Answers A and B state correct actions to be taken to document the incident and follow agency protocols. Answer C is a correct action if it can be done safely. The nurse is putting the employee on notice of the incident and making it clear that the behavior is not acceptable.

24. **The answer is C.**

The statements were made as facts not just opinion and were of the type that would harm the business relationships of the physician (although economic harm may need to be shown). Publication has occurred even if the nurse did not intend this, since he or she is responsible for the natural consequences that flow from acts. Answer A is incorrect; just because a statement is made in a work environment would not exempt it. Answer B is not correct because publication has taken place. Answer D is incorrect because it does not matter what the specific intent was, and being partially true means that some of the statements were false and thus were actionable.

25. **The answer is C.**

The facts indicate that the elements for both claims of assault and battery are present. There are no facts to support that the actions constituted a necessity or were justified by the nurse, so answer D is incorrect. Answer A or B alone would be incorrect because each only contains one part of the claims that could be sustained.

PART V
Ethics

55 Ethical Decision-Making

Cynthia Keenan, JD, BA, RN

Moral Principles of Ethical Decision-Making

Autonomy — the ability to allow the patient to independently make decisions regarding care and treatment, based on information provided so that the patient can effectively reason in his or her own way.

Freedom — the patient's ability to freely determine what method of treatment is most consistent with protecting his or her autonomy and independence. The nurse has an obligation to ensure that the patient receives the relevant information needed to make these decisions.

Beneficence — the expectation of the patient that the nurse will *do good* and prevent harm to the patient. The patient has a right to expect beneficence.

Nonmalfeasance — to protect the patient from harmful circumstances or decisions and to promote, not ignore, treatments that will not harm and forbid those that will cause harm.

Veracity — information given to the patient must be truthful so that informed decisions can be made by the patient. This protects the patient's autonomy.

Confidentiality/privacy — endorses the theory of self-ownership, the right to privacy and freedom from harm due to a breach of that privacy. The patient expects that this right will not be violated by the nurse.

Fidelity — the patient has the expectation and right to expect that the nurse will remain faithful and trustworthy to each understanding and agreement.

Justice — the nurse's moral obligation to treat all people fairly, without prejudice or regard for their socioeconomic status, personal characteristics, or disease process.

Nurse's Role

According to the ANA's *Code for Nurses with Interpretative Statements,* the nurse is committed to respect the dignity of each patient and to foster each patient's freedom to make choices to receive that to which he or she is entitled. *Respect for the patient* is the basis for this commitment. As such, the nurse has a duty to respect the patient regardless of socioeconomic status, personal character, or nature of the illness. Every patient should be treated with dignity and worth, taking into account the differences and special needs of each patient.

To further ensure this respect, the nurse must make decisions through a reasoning process that incorporates professional judgments, clinical observations, and the practical matters of technical feasibility. This process is a vital component of nursing. In doing so, the nurse needs to be certain that any approach that is taken does not violate the moral principles that need to be considered when assessing an ethical dilemma.

As part of the process, the nurse needs to consider the consequences of the actions taken and to determine in what manner any objections to the decisions that have been made will be handled. This justifies the decision from a moral standpoint while satisfying all of the principles of decision making.

Principles

- *Autonomy.* The nurse allows a patient to maintain character, values, and uniqueness, regardless of the nurse's own values. The nurse helps the patient to understand the nature, extent, and possible outcome of treatment so the patient can make health care decisions based on information provided in an easily understood manner. The nurse has the responsibility to continue to provide information to the patient and to evaluate the patient's understanding of that information in order to satisfy the moral obligation of maintaining the patient's autonomy.
- *Freedom.* This enables the patient to function independently and be allowed to freely make informed decisions in an autonomous manner. The nurse cannot interfere with the patient's desires or actions.
- *Beneficence.* The nurse has a moral obligation to do good, and the patient has a right to expect that he or she will derive some benefit from that good. This obligation also includes preventing harm and reducing the risk of harm. This is not done merely by instructing the patient as to what is good or not good for him or her, but rather providing the information that will enable the patient to reduce the risk of harm or prevent harm from occurring by making informed choices about the best approach, i.e., the one that will "do good."
- *Nonmalfeasance.* The nurse has a moral obligation to avoid harm to the patient. The nurse's primary obligation is to the patient, always. Ignoring the treatment and efforts required to protect the patient's well-being or allowing actions that will cause harm to the patient is unacceptable.
- *Veracity.* In order to function in an autonomous manner and make health care decisions, the patient expects the nurse to provide truthful information. Without the truth, the patient cannot make informed decisions based on reason, and his or her rights to do so have been violated.
- *Confidentiality/privacy.* This moral obligation endorses the theory of self-ownership and privacy; i.e., the patient has the right to expect that the nurse will guard against the unwarranted or unethical release of information about the patient. This principle protects the patient from harm that may be caused by breach of confidentiality or privacy.
- *Fidelity.* The nurse is obliged to stay faithful to the agreement or the understanding reached with the patient regarding the care to be given. This allows the patient to be able to predict his or her environment, based on the expectations of the established trustworthy relationship.
- *Justice.* The nurse is required to treat all people fairly without regard to socioeconomic status, personal attributes, or nature of the patient's health problems.

Influences

The Patient's Rights

Over the years, several medical and hospital organizations have set forth agendas that enumerate the rights of patients who are under their care. Many of these patient's rights have mirrored the principles involved in ethical decision making: the rights to confidentiality, to truthful information, and to be treated equally regardless of personal circumstances. Although each bill of rights is worded differently, the message is the same: the patient has the right to be treated with respect and dignity and to determine what is to be done with his or her body.

As with most ethical decisions, however, these rights can conflict with the nurse's responsibility to the patient and present a difficult challenge for the nurse. For example, a patient receives truthful information about an anticipated procedure during the informed consent process, but the patient refuses the procedure. Certainly, the nurse's ethical obligation to "do good and avoid harm" would be defeated if the patient does not undergo the procedure. On the other hand, the patient's right to refuse the surgery would be violated if the refusal were ignored. This sort of dilemma requires a reasoning process based on the nurse's observations and clinical judgments. In doing so, the nurse must find a balance between any preconceived notions and acting blindly, without regard for the individual characteristics and needs of each patient, with the solitary goal of influencing the patient. The goal is to reach a decision based on a mindfulness of the patient's rights and freedoms while adhering to the principles of decision making, with a full understanding of the consequences of that decision.

The ANA Code of Ethics

The *ANA Code of Ethics* requires that nurses justify their ethical decisions and the consequences of those decisions on universal moral principles, the most basic of which is respect for all humans. This requires a promotion of patient autonomy.

Inherent in the duty to enhance the patient's responsibility to maintain an autonomous existence is the duty to assess and evaluate, in an ongoing manner, the nurse's clinical competence, decision-making capabilities, and clinical judgments.

56 Reporting Illegal, Unethical, or Unsafe Conduct
Susan Westrick Killion, JD, MS, RN

Legal and Ethical Framework
- Professional codes
- Standards of care
- Statutes (e.g., child abuse)

↓

Consequences of not reporting
- Malpractice or other legal action
- State board of nursing action

Steps to ensure proper reporting
- Document facts objectively
- Confront person or notify authorities
- Notify supervisor and follow internal chain of command
- Report to outside agencies if no response

Risks of reporting illegal or unethical conduct
- Unpredictable situation; use caution
- May be threatened with lawsuit for libel or slander
- May experience animosity of coworkers

The nurse is often in a position to recognize conduct of others that is potentially detrimental to the welfare of patients. In such situations, the nurse must seek a satisfactory solution for all parties involved but that ultimately protects the patient's health and safety. In seeking this solution the nurse must weigh the risks and benefits of any action to be taken, as well as the consequences of not taking any action. As in all situations, the nurse is responsible and accountable for such action or inaction (see **Figure**).

Legal and Ethical Framework for Duty to Report

1. **Professional codes.** These provide guidance in many situations that confront the nurse involving the practice of other health professionals. For example, the ANA *Code for Nurses* (1985) and the *International Code for Nurses* (1973) mandate that the nurse take appropriate action to safeguard the individual when care is endangered by a coworker or any other person. While these codes identify ethical and not legal duties, they do form standards of care for professional practice that are often used in legal proceedings. It is certainly a part of prudent practice to follow all professional codes for conduct.

2. **Standards of care.** The profession has determined that certain standards of care are required for particular situations. Thus, when a nurse is aware that a standard is not being adhered to by either a person or an agency, an ethical and sometimes a legal duty arises to take corrective action. An example would be if a nurse is aware that OSHA standards are being violated. This becomes a duty to report the situation to the appropriate authorities, and in some cases the nurse might face serious consequences for not reporting violations.

3. **Statutes.** Most states have mandatory statutes requiring health care workers to report child or elder abuse and other kinds of information such as gunshot or homicide incidents. There are usually fines or other types of sanctions for not reporting.

   Other statutes that impact on reporting situations involving health and safety are whistle-blowing statutes. These federal or state statutes are designed to protect persons who "blow the whistle" on employers or others who can retaliate for such action. For example, an employee may be fired for reporting unsafe conditions or inaction of supervisors related to patient safety concerns. In some cases, a whistle-blowing statute could provide protection for the worker in seeking reinstatement or it may prevent the worker from being fired. Some state nurses' associations are actively working to improve whistle-blowing protection for nurses who have been fired for complaining about shortages of staff and other concerns related to patient safety.

A federal statute known as the False Claims Act (FCA) encourages uncovering fraud against the federal government and can be used in medical and agency billing fraud. A civil suit known as *qui tam* lawsuit can be filed to recover lost money in the government's name. This statute provides whistle-blower protection to the one who makes the claim, and the person is entitled to a portion of the recovery by the government. While it is sometimes difficult to obtain evidence in these cases, nurses have reported fraud under this statute.

Consequences of Not Reporting

1. Malpractice suit or other legal action can be taken against a nurse for not reporting illegal or unsafe practice by another that results in harm to the patient. In some cases it is the patient who becomes the plaintiff and alleges that the harm could have been prevented by others who did not report it to proper authorities. The ANA *Code for Nurses* can be used as evidence in malpractice cases to determine the standard of care for nurses' conduct.

   Some states have mandatory reporting statutes for health care professionals suspected of drug abuse or diversion of drugs. Nurses who do not report these violations risk penalties for nonreporting and could be the subject of actions against them.

2. State board of nursing action imposes penalties for unprofessional conduct by nurses. Unprofessional conduct could include not reporting persons who were harming patients or who were creating issues of health and safety.

Steps to Ensure Proper Reporting

1. Document the facts. The nurse should first document the incident or incidents in a thorough and nonjudgmental manner. The chart should not be used for such comments, but an incident report may be used in some circumstances. The nurse needs to keep thorough personal notes with specific dates, information, witnesses, and any action taken. This invaluable reference is necessary to validate the person's conduct or the circumstances of concern.

2. Confront the person or notify the proper authorities. It is recommended that the nurse confront the person whose conduct is in question to clarify the situation and inform the individual of the specific concern

for the health or safety of others. Having another person present is recommended since the individual may become defensive or may later misrepresent the information to others. This is especially so if the nurse is confronting a colleague or a physician who may be in a position of power or authority.

3. Notify a supervisor and follow the internal chain of command and channels. A supervisor should always be notified of the situation and the nurse should be careful to respect the chain of command. If there is an internal mechanism for reporting such incidents, such as to a committee or union, this should be followed. Many nurses are mistaken in the belief that once they report the situation to supervisors, their responsibility ends. However, it has been confirmed by the courts that the duty does not end there. If there is no response to satisfy the situation and the patient is harmed, the nurse can be responsible for not taking further action. For example, if a physician is still causing harm to a patient and it has been reported to the supervisor with no outcome, the nurse needs to go to a higher authority such as the medical director.

4. Report to outside agencies or practice boards. An outside agency may need to be contacted as the next step in seeking a resolution to the problem. The state medical or nursing board should be notified if it involves harmful practice by a health professional. A regulatory agency such as OSHA may need to be notified if it is within its area of control.

Risks of Reporting Illegal or Unethical Conduct

While the benefits and obligations to reporting questionable conduct that is a threat to health and safety of others outweigh the consequences of not doing so, there are often detrimental effects from reporting. One needs to proceed with care and caution since the risks can be very serious. The accused individual may threaten libel or slander claims against a nurse for reporting his or her conduct. However, the reporting nurse is assured that the truth is an absolute defense to claims that are made in good faith. One may face the animosity of coworkers who consider the reporting nurse to be a traitor or worse. Other forms of retaliation that can occur include job reassignment, demotion, or job loss.

Fulfilling Professional Responsibility

In reporting the illegal, unethical, or unsafe practice of others, the nurse is preserving a sense of moral integrity for the profession. The public has a right to expect protection against such harmful conduct by others and to rely on professional nurses to participate fully in its elimination.

57 Maternal versus Fetal Rights– Part I

Cynthia Keenan, JD, BA, RN

A Mother's Rights

- Right to maintain autonomy, bodily integrity, due process, and privacy
- Moral right to determine what will be done with her own person
- Right to be given accurate information, and information necessary to make informed judgments
- Right to be assisted with weighing the benefits and burdens of options in their treatment
- Right to accept, refuse, or terminate treatment without coercion
- Right to be assured that the release of all medical information be prudently restricted

B Situations Where Mother's Rights May Be Diminished

- Requests do-not-resuscitate order
- May not be able to refuse a blood transfusion in some situations (to save the life of the fetus or where she has other children who depend on her)
- Emergency admission during labor or acute illness where mother refuses treatment; questionable whether mother has the capacity to give consent or refuse treatment
- Where the 4 stringent conditions required prior to court intervention have been met

With the development of patient's rights, a pregnant woman presenting in her final trimester creates an inherent conflict to the medical provider. To whom do physicians or nurses owe their first duty—the pregnant woman or the unborn child? Are the rights of the mother subordinated to those of the unborn child? The nurse's role in these situations is a cautious one, but the moral and professional obligation inherent in that role is to treat, regardless of the magnitude of the emotional and moral issues involved. The nurse needs to ensure that the patient's rights as set forth in the *Code of Ethics for Nurses with Interpretative Statements* are adhered to in the treatment and care plan of each patient.

Rights of the Unborn Child and the Mother

The unborn child has a right to be born healthy. *Roe v Wade* delineated the rights of the fetus and mother based on the degree of viability. The more viable the fetus, the greater degree of rights. When abortion is deemed necessary to save her life, however, the mother's life and health take precedence regardless of the consequence to the fetus.

The rights of the mother are similar to those of any other patient: the right to maintain autonomy and integrity of her body, access to due process, and the right to privacy. The mother's rights according to the *Code of Ethics for Nurses with Interpretative Statements* are listed in **Part A**.

The pregnant woman being asked to undergo an extremely invasive procedure to save the baby's life has the right to refuse the treatment and to be free of coercion, even if the fetus is viable. Generally, the more invasive the procedure, the greater degree of maternal rights. In its position statement *Patient Choice and the Maternal-Fetal Conflict,* the American College of Obstetricians and Gynecologists suggest three approaches to dealing with the competent pregnant woman who refuses treatment: (1) to abide by the patient's decision, allowing her to autonomously determine the course of action, regardless of the consequences; (2) to offer that the woman be cared for by a different provider if the original physician refuses to abide by her request, to give the mother a better chance to be supported; and (3) to petition the court for authorization to proceed against the mother's wishes (the less frequently exercised option).

Courts have been involved in determining the rights of pregnant women in instances of forced monitoring, forced cesarean section, compulsory amniocentesis, and drug testing. Before the decision is made to involve the judicial system, however, the facts of the case must be scrutinized to ascertain the presence of 4 conditions: (1) a high probability that the fetus will suffer serious harm if the patient's refusal is honored; (2) a high probability that the treatment will prevent or substantially reduce harm to the fetus; (3) no comparable treatment options available; and (4) a high probability that the treatment will also benefit the mother, or that the risks to her are minimal. Unless these four conditions are met, the woman's right to autonomy risks being violated with the use of judicial authority.

In these cases, providers need to be cognizant of the fallible nature of testing and the possibility that an ordinarily low-risk procedure such as cesarean section could result in serious maternal complications. These unpredictable realities need to be considered when attempting to persuade a pregnant woman to undergo a procedure she has refused.

Diminished Maternal Rights

The pregnant woman's right to autonomy is not always absolute (**Part B**). When the four conditions for judicial review are met, the court will often balance this right with the fetus's chances of survival, the risks of the procedure, and other factors specific to that case. Under this balancing test, some pregnant women have not been required to undergo a medically intricate cesarean while others have been under court order to receive a life-saving blood transfusion. Besides judicial intervention, some states have diminished maternal autonomy by passing advance directive statutes that remove the DNR option as a health care choice for the duration of the pregnancy.

Drug Abuse

The prevalence of drug abuse has risen among pregnant women. For the most part, the long-term effects of illegal drug use on the fetus are negative. In some states, drug-addicted women are prosecuted for using drugs while pregnant. If arrested and prosecuted prior to the period of viability of the fetus, the mother can be charged with possession, while after viability she is charged with "distribution to a minor." Other states have laws that act to curtail parental rights. Few give pregnant drug users the option of priority access to treatment facilities.

The nurse in this situation is an information provider, discussing options about and assistance with seeking admission into a treatment center. If the mother chooses not to seek treatment and continues to use illegal drugs, she runs the risk of losing her parental rights, and the newborn child may be placed in protective custody. This can cause a "backlash": if the mother knows she risks arrest or that her newborn child may be taken from her, she is less likely to seek the treatment required.

Although in many instances drug screening may seem warranted, it is not done routinely. Many institutions believe that if a mother refuses to be tested, the quality of her care will be compromised. As one cannot be forced to undergo testing, the risk of doing so without consent jeopardizes the patient's right to privacy. Although testing may be done with the best interests of the child in mind, the possible ramification of a positive finding, that of losing her rights as a parent, would be the direct result of the illegally obtained blood sample.

58 Maternal versus Fetal Rights– Part II

Cynthia Keenan, JD, BA, RN

A Mother's Rights

- Right to maintain autonomy, bodily integrity, due process, and privacy
- Moral right to determine what will be done with her own person
- Right to be given accurate information, and information necessary to make informed judgments
- Right to be assisted with weighing the benefits and burdens of options in their treatment
- Right to accept, refuse, or terminate treatment without coercion
- Right to be assured that the release of all medical information be prudently restricted

B Situations Where Mother's Rights May Be Diminished

- Requests do-not-resuscitate order
- May not be able to refuse a blood transfusion in some situations (to save the life of the fetus or where she has other children who depend on her)
- Emergency admission during labor or acute illness where mother refuses treatment; questionable whether mother has the capacity to give consent or refuse treatment
- Where the 4 stringent conditions required prior to court intervention have been met

AIDS

AIDS is one of the most serious sexually transmitted diseases, as it can be life-threatening to the newborn. Many states require that medical personnel report all incidences of AIDS to their local health department. The CDC has set forth guidelines both to preserve the patient's privacy and to promote public health through disclosure of the HIV infection. In cases where the reporting of AIDS cases is mandatory, the nurse can breach a patient's confidentiality; the required documentation overrides the patient's privacy.

Mandatory HIV testing has acted to subordinate the usual requirement of obtaining informed consent from the mother, for the sake of the fetus. Those who support mandatory HIV testing do so on the grounds that this will enable them to provide the optimum level of care to the newborn. At the same time, mandatory testing acts to violate the mother's right to individual liberty and privacy. To ascertain whether mandatory HIV testing of the newborn takes precedent over the rights of the mother, an analysis of the test or procedure is required. If the test or procedure is found to be effective, accurate, and proportionately beneficial to serve its purpose—to protect the health, safety, and welfare of the public—interfering with one's right to privacy and individual liberty will be considered constitutional. With the development of medications that reduce perinatal transmission of HIV and prophylactic regimens that prevent potentially fatal complications, the necessity of mandatory testing is less clear.

American Medical Association Position Statement

Overall, the American Medical Association advocates that the rights of the mother should prevail, except in unusual circumstances. It also adheres to the belief that a decision-making process be in effect to resolve these conflicts. Areas to explore and consider as part of that process include the patient's physical state, the disease process, treatment options, religious beliefs, cultural values, family dynamics, and the legal and financial aspects of the case. In terms of treatment options, technological advances now allow for genetic testing, perinatal diagnosing, fetal surgery, and extensive fetal intensive care facilities. This fact, coupled with the providers' desire and ethical responsibility to do good, further complicate the issue of whose rights prevail.

59 Futile Care

Katherine McCormack Dempski, JD, BSN, RN

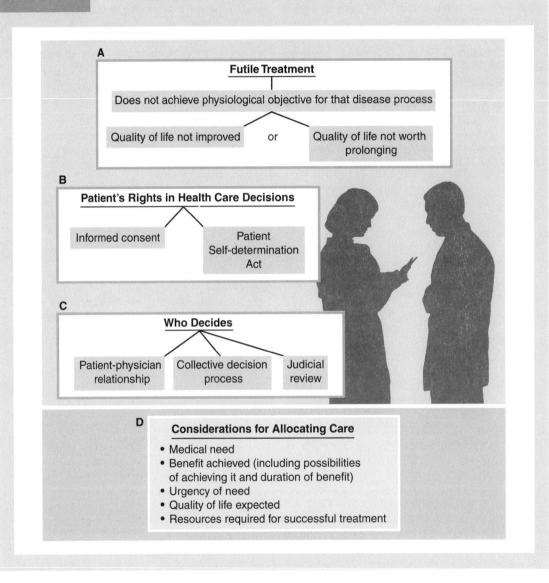

A

Futile Treatment

Does not achieve physiological objective for that disease process

Quality of life not improved   or   Quality of life not worth prolonging

B

Patient's Rights in Health Care Decisions

Informed consent   Patient Self-determination Act

C

Who Decides

Patient-physician relationship   Collective decision process   Judicial review

D

Considerations for Allocating Care

- Medical need
- Benefit achieved (including possibilities of achieving it and duration of benefit)
- Urgency of need
- Quality of life expected
- Resources required for successful treatment

The American Medical Association's code of medical ethics states that physicians are not obligated to deliver medical care that in their best judgment will not have a reasonable chance of benefiting the patient. Denial of medical treatment must be based on acceptable standards of care and openly stated ethical principles. Health care providers must be aware of the federal statutes and case law that have further compli-cated the issue of futile care. Although treatment may not be medically indicated, recent court decisions may make it legally necessary.

Defining Futile Treatment

Futile treatment is not easy to define (see **Part A**). The Hastings Center defines *futility* as care that will not achieve its physiological objective and so offers no physiological benefit to the patient. The term *futility* almost always is used when some treatment is available and may possibly work but the patient's quality of life is either not worth prolonging or treatment will not improve it. Although futile treatment is often considered "medically unnecessary," that definition alone would encompass such procedures as cosmetic surgery, circumcision, sterilization, in vitro fertilization, etc. Futile care usually is characterized as treatment that does not return the patient to full function or meaningful "quality of life," or life as the patient knew prior to the injury or disease. *Futile* also is used to describe medical treatment that is effective but the patient's quality of life is not perceived as worth prolonging. For example, for an anencephalic infant in acute respiratory distress, intubation is an effective treatment to solve the acute respiratory distress but it will not cure the anencephaly. In this respect, futile care should not be confused with ineffective treatment. Ineffective treatment does not achieve the desired result.

Self-Determination Vs Futility

The doctrine of informed consent ensures that a patient's decision to consent to or refuse medical treatment is an educated one (**Part B**). The PSDA outlines a patient's right to predetermine his or her own life-and-death decisions regarding medical care. Through advanced directives a patient informs the health care provider of his or her decision regarding resuscitation, nutrition, hydration, and pain relief when the patient becomes permanently unconscious or terminal (as defined in each state's advanced directive statute).

Informed consent and the PSDA preserve the patient's right to refuse medically indicated treatment, but a patient's right to demand medically futile treatment remains uncertain. The President's Commission for the Study of Ethical Problems in Medical and Biomedical Research found that medical professionals are not obligated to "accede to" the patient's demands when it violates acceptable medical practice. The commission defined informed consent as a "choice among medically acceptable and available options." Informed consent does not translate into a self-determined right to demand what is medically futile. The Hastings Center *Guidelines,* in accord with the American Medical Association, view physicians as having no ethical obligation to provide futile care.

Who Decides

Medical-legal scholars suggest one of three approaches to the issue of medical futility (see **Part C**). The first avenue is to give deference to the physician-patient relationship. Weight is given to the physician's professional judgment, with the patient's informed consent used as the boundary.

This approach allows the physician and patient the freedom to choose whether the relationship is right for them. The patient has an option to continue care when the physician believes treatment is medically futile. With the physician's help, the patient may transfer to another physician who shares the patient's belief in continuing care. In this approach, the patient's own financial resources or medical insurance may be the limiting factor on receiving care.

The second process involves the collective decisions of the physician, the patient, the family members, the agency, and the judges. An agency's ethics committee is another type of collective decision process. Ethics committees are made up of physicians, nurses, hospital administrators, attorneys, and community members.

When the issue of futile care comes before the courts, it is often because family members wish to continue medical care the hospitals and physicians determined is futile. In the majority of cases, courts hold that medical care should be continued. Several courts have used federal statutes to determine the issue of medical futility. Congress passed the EMTLA to prevent physicians and hospitals from transferring unstable emergency and in-house patients to another facility for insurance purposes. Several courts stated that the EMTLA requires hospitals and physicians to medically treat and stabilize all patients who present to the hospital with a medical condition even when the treatment may be futile. For example, an anencephalic infant continuously presented to the emergency department in acute respiratory distress, and the court held that the physicians must mechanically ventilate the infant even though the physicians believed it was ultimately futile.

Using Ethics to Allocate Medical Care

To safeguard a patient's interest, only medical need may be considered when the allocation of limited medical resources is necessary. Other criteria that are appropriate to consider are listed in **Part D**.

According to the American Medical Association's ethics committee's statements on allocation of medical care, when medical resources are limited, it may be necessary to prioritize patients so death or poor quality of care is avoided. Nonmedical criteria such as social standing, financial ability to pay for treatment, patient age, or patient contribution to illness (drug use, smoking, etc.) should not be considered. When there is little difference among the patients with a medical need and the potential for successful outcome, then equal opportunity criteria such as first come–first served is appropriate. The American Medical Association also recommends that allocation procedures be disclosed to the public and be subjected to the peer review process.

60 Advance Directives

Cynthia Keenan, JD, BA, RN

A Durable Power of Attorney for Health Care

- Surrogate is chosen by the patient, most often a family member or close friend.
- Surrogate has the authority to make decisions regarding health care and treatments as well as end-of-life decisions.
- Power is in effect only upon incapacity or at the time when the patient lacks decision-making capacity.
- Surrogate's intent is to protect the patient's wishes or promote the best interests of the patient.
- This directive has broad application.
- Patient's preferences always take precedence, unless to do so would cause more harm than good.

B Living Will

- Living will allows the patient to choose what life-support measures should be provided or withheld when the patient is determined to be terminally ill or permanently unconscious.
- *Terminally ill* means an incurable or irreversible medical condition that without the administration of life-support systems will result in death within a relatively short period of time.
- *Permanently unconscious* means a permanent coma or persistent vegetative state that is an irreversible condition; patient is at no time aware of himself or herself or the environment and shows no behavioral response to the environment.

C Advanced Care Medical Directive

- Specific instructions by patient as to type of care consented to and type of care refused.
- Surrogate may be appointed to assist in interpretation of the instructions.

As required by the PSDA, all patients must be advised of their right to make decisions about their health care, including the right to establish written advance directives. Under the umbrella term *advance directives,* a durable power of attorney for health care and a living will and advance care medical directive are the means by which the patient's autonomy can be protected in the medical environment.

Durable Power of Attorney for Health Care

The person who is named in the durable power of attorney for health care document is called a *surrogate* (see **Part A**) or *proxy.* The surrogate, chosen by the patient, has the authority to make decisions about the patient's care and treatment in the event the patient becomes incapable of making such decisions (i.e., the reasoning required to make informed decisions is lacking). Ideally, the patient chooses a surrogate with whom a trusted relationship has been established, often a family member or close friend who knows the patient well enough to have had discussions pertaining to end-of-life decisions and treatment choices.

The surrogate's intent should be to protect the patient's wishes or to act in a manner that fosters the best interests of the patient if the patient's wishes are not known. If the surrogate is not acting in a manner consistent with this or is making what appear to be inappropriate decisions, the nurse needs to protect the patient from the harm that could incur from these acts. These incidents should be reported to the patient's physician, the nursing supervisor, and the ethics committee.

The application of the durable power of attorney for health care is broad and can range from temporal requests such as obtaining information about past medical conditions, to those relative to discontinuing life-support systems. In all cases of decision-making, if the patient's preference is known, it should take precedence. The surrogate also should have broad authority to interpret vague statements relative to health care choices made by the patient prior to incapacity. If the surrogate is unaware of such statements, whatever action that advances the best interests of the patient should follow.

Living Will

Under a written living will, if the patient's condition is deemed "terminal" or if the patient is determined to be "permanently unconscious," life-support systems including artificial respiration, cardiopulmonary resuscitation, and artificial means of nutrition and hydration may be provided, withheld, or removed (see **Part B**). Often a statement from one or two physicians indicating that the patient's condition is not expected to improve is required prior to any action. The patient needs to be aware that foregoing life-support measures does not mean that the patient will not be provided measures of pain control or comfort.

Some states recognize an oral living will as valid. Any statements made by the patient relative to withdrawing or withholding life support should be documented in the chart and made known to the primary physician. These statements become part of the patient's medical record and provide the primary means of communication regarding end-of-life decisions. Not communicating the fact that a written living will exists or that the patient made statements regarding end-of-life decisions acts to deny the patient's rights of autonomy and self-determination. Advance care medical directive is a combination of the living will and the health care proxy but with specific instructions on the type of care desired or not (**Part C**).

Nurse's Role

The nurse has a duty to ensure that the patient is a full participant in the choice to initiate advance directives.

In its position statement *Nursing and the Patient Self-determination Act,* the ANA suggests that nurses question patients upon admission as to the existence of any advance directives. If none are in place, they should ask if the patient desires to create such a directive. If so, the nurse has the responsibility to see that the patient has the information needed to make an informed decision about treatment and options. The nurse should encourage the patient to ask questions about medical issues as well as the mechanics of advance directives. The nurse also should encourage the patient to be as clear as possible about the choices. If the statements by the patient are of a general nature, such as "no machines to keep me alive," it is the nurse's responsibility to educate the patient. Going through each life-support system and its respective functions educates the patient in a manner that provides for a more sound and effective directive. This will have the effect of making adherence to the directive unequivocal.

When the provisions of a living will contradict either the desires of the family or the physician's orders, the nurse who recognizes this needs to advise all those involved in the patient's care of the contradictory requests. One cannot follow through on one directive when others are inconsistent. Consulting with those involved in the patient's care as a means of determining what actions are in the best interests of the patient is the appropriate and professional practice under these circumstances.

Liability

If medical providers do not follow the instructions of an advance directive, they subject themselves to the same scrutiny and consequences that would occur if they disregarded a refusal to treatment. Some statutes state that health care providers must comply with the instructions in a living will. However, in some cases a physician who cannot do so for reasons of conscience can opt to not follow through with the directive. The patient and the patient's family need to be advised of this policy at the time of admission to the facility, so that they may be given the option of transferring the patient to a provider who will.

Finally, nurses or other medical personnel should not sign as witnesses for any advance directive. The nurse works too closely with the patient, and in certain circumstances, the allegations of undue influence could surface. In most states, the law prevents nurses or other health care providers from acting as surrogates for health care for patients. In most states, the advance directive statutes prevents nurses or other health care providers from being named as their patients' health care agent.

61 Life-Ending Decisions/ Terminating Life Support

Maureen Townsend, JD, RN

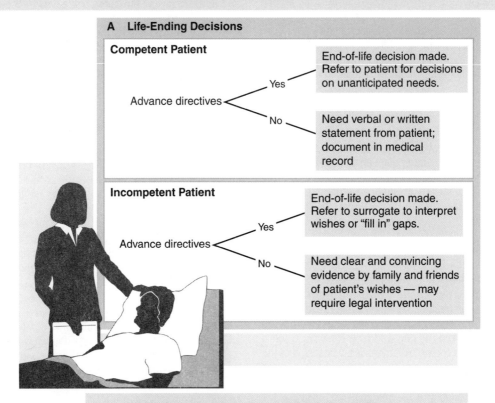

A   Life-Ending Decisions

Competent Patient

Advance directives
- Yes → End-of-life decision made. Refer to patient for decisions on unanticipated needs.
- No → Need verbal or written statement from patient; document in medical record

Incompetent Patient

Advance directives
- Yes → End-of-life decision made. Refer to surrogate to interpret wishes or "fill in" gaps.
- No → Need clear and convincing evidence by family and friends of patient's wishes — may require legal intervention

B   Health Care Provider's Responsibilities to Patients

- Educate patients to make decisions before incapacitation.
- Communicate with patient regarding end-of-life decisions.
- Provide patient a copy of institution's policy on end-of-life decisions.
- Document in the medical record that advance directive is complete and that copy is in medical record.

The Patient Self-Determination Act

Critical health-related decisions should be made before a person or the family is faced with a stressful, traumatic situation, before the person is in a life-ending situation. To encourage meaningful discussions regarding life-sustaining as well as life-ending concerns, the PSDA was created (Omnibus Budget Reconciliation Act of 1990) with the intent "to ensure that a patient's right to self-determination in health care decisions be communicated and protected."

Competent versus Incompetent Patient's Rights

A notable case that has thrust the issue of termination of life support as well as communicating your wishes regarding life-sustaining measures to the forefront is *Cruzan v Director, Missouri Department of Health*. Nancy Beth Cruzan, a 25-year-old woman, lost control of her car in Jaspur County, Missouri. When the paramedics found her, she had no detectable breathing or heart beat, and the paramedics proceeded to resuscitate her. Cruzan lay in a persistent vegetative state—a condition in which a patient exhibits motor reflexes but no significant cognitive function. The family, realizing that there was no chance of Cruzan regaining any of her mental faculties, asked hospital employees to terminate artificial nutrition and hydration procedures. Because that act would cause her death, hospital employees refused to honor the request without court approval. The lower court granted the family's request, finding that Cruzan's informed conversation with a friend indicated that she would not wish to continue living in her current condition. The Missouri Supreme Court reversed that decision. The higher court recognized a common law doctrine of informed consent but not a broader constitutional right of privacy to refuse medical treatment. The Missouri Supreme Court concluded that the Missouri living will statute embodied a state policy favoring the preservation of life except where the wish to die was established by "clear and convincing evidence." The Missouri Supreme Court also rejected the argument that Cruzan's parents were entitled to order termination of treatment on behalf of their daughter.

Seven years later, the U.S. Supreme Court considered whether life support could be withdrawn from Cruzan's body. The question before the U.S. Supreme Court was whether Cruzan had a right under the U.S. Constitution that would require the hospital to withdraw life-sustaining treatment. The Supreme Court noted that the U.S. Constitution grants a *competent* person the constitutionally protected right to refuse lifesaving hydration and nutrition. Because an *incompetent* patient's rights were in question, the court looked to (and recognized) the Missouri requirement that evidence of the incompetent patient's wishes as to the withdrawal of treatment must be proved by "clear and convincing evidence" (see **Part A**). As such, the U.S. Supreme Court ruled in June 1990, in a 5-4 decision, that Cruzan's family had not provided clear and convincing evidence to the Missouri court that Cruzan would refuse the life support if she was competent.

After the Supreme Court's decision, a Missouri probate judge ruled that Cruzan's parents had amassed "clear and convincing evidence" that she would not want to persist in her present state of "life." Artificial maintenance procedures were terminated and Cruzan died 12 days later.

Advance Directives

Competent individuals can make their wishes known via an advance directive, defined by the PSDA as a written instruction, such as a living will or durable power of attorney for health care recognized under state law when the individual is incapacitated. Three legal instruments currently meet the act's definition of advance directive (the nurse should refer to each state-specific legislation to ensure the validity of each):

1. Living will. Many states have enacted a living will statute under which a competent adult may prepare a document providing direction as to his or her medical care in the event this individual may become incapacitated or otherwise unable to make decisions personally.
2. Durable power of attorney/health care proxy. A durable power of attorney/health care proxy enables a competent individual to name someone (usually a spouse, parent, adult child, or other adult) to exercise decision-making authority, under specific circumstances, on the individual's behalf.
3. Advance care medical directive. An advance care medical directive can be considered a hybrid of the living will and the durable power of attorney/health care proxy. Via this tool, an individual will provide precise instructions for the type of care he or she does or does not desire in a number of scenarios. The individual may also appoint a proxy decision maker to help interpret the application of the specific instructions or fill in unanticipated gaps.

Even though the PSDA has provided an avenue for the health care user to make his or her wishes known, many issues regarding end-of-life decisions remain open: (1) Many patients historically have demonstrated a reluctance to actually complete a living will. (2) What is the effectiveness or reliability of the actual advance directive (will the health care institution or provider act on the document or instructions)? (3) Will the act create another piece of worthless paper that will be added to the ever-amounting mass of paperwork? (4) When is the best time to initiate discussions? (5) Will the skyrocketing costs of medical care influence those put in a position to make a life-ending decision to make the wrong decision?

Health Care Providers' Responsibilities

In the aftermath of the Cruzan case, every person in the United States should have the opportunity to make provisions for decision making about his or her health care. As such, the PSDA focuses on education and communication, not the creation or modification of substantive legal rights. Each state must provide information to an individual about its laws that govern these advance directives. Health care providers' responsibilities to each patient are listed in **Part B**. Health care providers receiving Medicare or Medicaid funds must ensure that such information is distributed on a timely basis, along with information on the institution's own policies regarding implementation of these advance directives.

62 Assisted Suicide

Maureen Townsend, JD, RN and
Katherine McCormack Dempski, JD, BSN, RN

A Assisted Suicide

- Deliberate act with intent to aid in ending another's life

- Providing means (lethal dose) to end another's life

 With knowledge of patient's intent to end life

Example: administering pain medication with intent to end patient's life even when motivated by mercy, compassion, and quality-of-life considerations

B Permissive End-of-Life Nursing Care

- Alleviation of pain (even if hastening death)

- Withholding life support

- Termination of life support

 With competent patient's exercised right to refuse medical treatment

Example: administering pain medication with intent to alleviate pain even if hastening death

The terms *assisted suicide* and *euthanasia* generally mean aiding or assisting another person to kill himself or herself, or killing another person at his or her request, often called "active voluntary euthanasia." The U.S. Supreme Court upheld two state statutes that prohibited assisted suicide in all instances, including patients with a terminal illness. Providing palliative treatment for those in intractable pain and near death or terminating life support per the patient's wishes are generally not considered assisted suicide. Nurses should be aware of these differences.

State Interest in Preserving Life

Assisted suicide involves a decision concerning one's own body; as such it falls within the realm of personal liberty that government may not enter. However, the state has an obligation to protect life simply because of its existence. This conflict between personal autonomy (which includes the right to refuse medical treatment) and the state's interest in preserving life leaves the nurse in the middle of a legal and ethical entanglement.

Distinguishing Assisted Suicide from Personal Autonomy

Nurses providing patient care are concerned with defining assisted suicide versus honoring the patient's wishes regarding palliative care and termination of life support. Two notable cases involving terminating life support provide some guidelines. The first began with Karen Quinlan, a young adult hospital patient who had been in a coma for approximately 1 year and was being kept alive by a respirator. The New Jersey Supreme Court, in a unanimous decision based on the patient's right to privacy, permitted the father to seek physicians and hospital officials who would agree to remove the respirator. The court said that if the responsible attending physician concluded that there was no reasonable possibility of Karen Quinlan's return to cognitive and sapient life and that the life-support apparatus be discontinued, they should consult the hospital ethics committee, or similar group at the institution where she was hospitalized. If the ethics committee agrees, the life-support system may be withdrawn and the action will be without any civil or criminal liability on the part of any participant, whether guardian, hospital, physician, or others.

In its ruling, the New Jersey Supreme Court laid down a procedure insulating the physician from liability. Ethics committees were formed to free health care providers from using their own self-interest and fear of legal ramifications to make decisions on the well-being of their dying patients.

In the second case, *Cruzan v Director, Missouri Department of Health,* a 25-year-old woman sustained life-disabling injuries after a car accident. The family asked to have any and all life-sustaining measures removed. Both the hospital and the courts of Missouri denied this family request. The U.S. Supreme Court upheld the state court decision, citing the state's right to legislate the type of evidence it will accept to prove an incompetent person's desires for life-support termination. The court emphasized that preservation of life was paramount unless there was clear and convincing evidence that the patient wished otherwise under those circumstances (such as a persistent vegetative state).

The difference between assisted suicide and permissive termination of life support is the question of intent. For the latter, a patient's *informed* refusal of treatment is recognized as legal and even a constitutionally mandated right, the patient's right to personal autonomy. Assisted suicide, even in the face of intractable pain or terminal illness, is not legal because the *intent* is to kill and usually involves the deliberate act of providing a means to cause death (see **Part A**).

Nurse's Role

The ANA position statement on assisted suicide concludes that nurse participation in assisted suicide violates the *Code for Nurses.* The role of the nurse in end-of-life decisions includes promoting comfort, pain relief, and permissive withdrawal or withholding of life support (see **Part B**). The ANA acknowledges that administering pain medication with the intent of alleviating pain may risk hastening death but that this does not constitute assisted suicide. The underlying cause of death is the natural disease process. A nurse may not deliberately aid in the termination of another's life.

Conflicting Professional Views

It has been long cultivated for health care professionals to respect the patient's wishes to refuse or to discontinue life-prolonging treatment. Physicians and nurses may hold some views that make it difficult to act in ways that would be consistent with their own express support for patient autonomy. Most clinicians are uncertain about what the laws, ethics, and the respected professional standards state. In addition to this uncertainty, clinicians are less likely to withdraw treatments than to withhold them for a variety of other reasons, including psychological discomfort with actively stopping a life-sustaining intervention; discomfort with the public nature of the act, which might occasion a lawsuit from disapproving witnesses even if the decision were legally correct; and fear of sanction by peer review boards.

Arguments against Assisted Suicide

Legalization of physician-assisted suicide creates fear of abuses resulting from undue influence and coercion, financial incentives, inadequate determinations of mental competence, mistaken diagnosis of illness as terminal, inadequate diagnosis of depression, inadequate treatment for pain, ineffective communication, and impatience of medical personnel. However, not recognizing and setting forth some sort of framework in which to operate in the realm of assisted suicide may exacerbate the risk of abuse of decision-making power.

Protection against Claims

In 1974 and 1980 the American Medical Association proposed that decisions not to resuscitate be formally entered in the patient's progress notes and communicated to all staff. When applied and followed correctly, it provides evidence that the health care providers followed the patient's wish (and right) to refuse unwanted medical treatment. Many hospitals have published policies about withdrawal or nonapplication of life-prolonging measures. It is paramount that health care providers be very aware of these standards, protocols, and procedures.

1. A 44-year-old obese woman is admitted to the hospital for an evaluation of numerous vague complaints. She has seen several physicians and undergone several tests over the years, but her symptoms have not been diagnosed. She has been taking narcotics for her pain, as prescribed by her private physician. When the nurse is in her presence, she moves in a painful manner, making frequent references to her discomfort and inability "to do anything." However, when the nurse is observing her without her knowledge, she has no difficulty moving and does not reveal any signs of pain on movement. The admitting physician writes an order for the narcotics as requested by the patient. What should the nurse do?

(A) Pick up the order and give her a dose upon her first request

(B) Talk to the physician about the observation

(C) Refuse to give her the medication when she requests it, and telling her why

(D) Spend some time talking with the patient before she requests a pill in order to try to get an understanding of her needs, both physical and emotional

2. The nurse is treating two patients with the same condition. The nurse believes that all patients should be fully informed as to their conditions and prognoses. One of these patients is very interested in learning more about the condition, while the other could care less. In fact, he stated, "I don't want to know. This whole thing scares me to death. I just want to get it over with and get out of here." The nurse should:

(A) Walk away in frustration, complaining to colleagues about the incident

(B) Talk to the physician about the patient's denial, suggesting a psychiatric evaluation is in order

(C) Tell the patient that the nurse understands and start talking about the condition

(D) Speak to the patient privately about his concerns, to ascertain what in fact he does know about the condition and prognosis

3. Which of the following steps should the nurse take *first* in fulfilling a professional duty to report a colleague who is not completing nursing tasks in a safe manner for patients?

(A) Report the conduct to the nurse's supervisor

(B) File a complaint with the state board of nursing

(C) Check to see if others have noticed this by seeking validation from other coworkers

(D) Confront the individual and state specific concerns

4. A nurse has witnessed a physician diverting drugs for his own use and signing them as given to patients. The physician told the nurse to "keep quiet" about it. If the nurse does not report this potentially harmful conduct for patients, the nurse:

(A) Should be safe from consequences since the physician has the authority to prescribe drugs

(B) May be subject to disciplinary action by the state board of nursing

(C) Will only be at risk if actual harm does come to a patient because of this

(D) Will fulfill professional responsibility if the nurse confronts the physician and documents in personal notes what was seen

5. A pregnant woman comes into the emergency room. She is talking incoherently and acting paranoid. Her labor is processing rapidly, and the nurse has difficulty hearing a fetal heart tone. The physician examines her and makes the decision to perform a cesarean section. When the patient hears this, she reacts violently, shouting that she "will not be cut!" What should the nurse do first?

(A) Get an immediate order for diazepam

(B) Tell the physician that in spite of the patient's drugged state, she has refused to undergo a cesarean section

(C) Question the patient about her fears, if able to, and try to determine if it is feasible to educate her as to the risks and benefits of cesarean section

(D) Leave her to attend to other patients who are more cooperative and less combative

6. A woman comes into the emergency department and is 8 months pregnant. She is experiencing contractions. She tells the nurse she has had no prenatal care. She also tells the nurse she has had multiple sexual partners and in fact does not know which one is the father of her unborn baby. The nurse should:

(A) Listen, take the patient's vital signs, and make a note of it in the chart

(B) Tell the patient that she will need to undergo AIDS testing and remind the physician to order it as part of regular blood work

(C) Advise the patient that she should have an AIDS test and that if the result is positive, this finding will have to be reported to the local health agency

(D) Do nothing

7. When allocating medical care in an equality situation, it is necessary that:

(A) The patient's physician assist in the decision

(B) The patient's age and quality of life be considered

(C) The allocation be based on first come–first served basis

(D) The patient's contribution to the illness be considered because a smoker who refuses to quit smoking should not be given a lung transplant prior to someone who never smoked

8. In a community hospital emergency department, an 80-year-old man presents with chronic obstructive pulmonary disease complicated by a 65-year history of smoking two packs of cigarettes per day. He arrives in the department with his family at least once a month in acute respiratory distress requiring intubation and respiratory support. After a few days in the intensive care unit, he is discharged back to a hospice program. There is no indication that he is incompetent, but his condition is terminal. The medical and nursing staff agree that he is wasting hospital resources since there is no cure and he continues to smoke even as he is hooked up to his oxygen tank. The appropriate action to take the next time he comes to the emergency department is to:

(A) Refuse to intubate him and get a court order to declare him incompetent (no one who continues to smoke while on oxygen is competent)

(B) Continue to intubate him as needed for the acute respiratory arrest

(C) Refuse to intubate and get a physician to order DNR

(D) Do none of the above

9. A 24-year-old victim of a serious motor vehicle accident told the nurse that he does not want heroic measures to save his life. The nurse first should:

(A) Ignore the statement and attend to other patients

(B) Tell him he is not thinking clearly and walk away

(C) Ask him to be more specific and report the results of this conversation to the charge nurse and attending physician

(D) Talk to family members about how they feel about his decision

10. An 84-year-old mother of 6 has been hospitalized after fracturing her hip. The incident caused a major setback in her independence, and she will no longer be able to manage her affairs. One of her sons has approached her about signing a durable power of attorney for health care, which would name him as having that authority. The nurse notices that he speaks to her rudely and in a manner that is a little threatening. The nurse first should:

(A) Encourage the mother to sign the document, assuring her everything will work out

(B) Speak to the mother privately about her concerns, if any, and preferences, and report your findings to the charge nurse and social worker in charge of her case

(C) Speak to the family members about the options available and leave it to them to decide

(D) Report the observations about the son to the charge nurse only

11. The Patient Self-determination Act (PSDA) requires that:

(A) Patients make living wills when admitted to hospitals

(B) Health care providers receiving Medicare or Medicaid funds apprise patients of their right to make advanced directives

(C) All inpatient facilities must provide special counselors to help patients fill out advance directives

(D) Nurses discuss living wills or health care proxies with any patient who is terminal

12. A landmark case in the area of life-ending treatment is the Cruzan case. This case involved the family's desire to end life-sustaining treatment for Nancy Cruzan, who was in a persistent vegetative state. The outcome of this U.S. Supreme Court case was that the Court:

(A) Would not allow the termination of life support because the patient was not competent and could not express her wishes

(B) Required that states have statutes in place before decisions like this could be made

(C) Stated that the U.S. Constitution would grant a competent person a constitutionally protected right to terminate life-sustaining treatment, and extended this to incompetent patients when consistent with state statute's requirements

(D) Struck down the provision of the state statute that required "clear and convincing" evidence of the incompetent patient's wishes in such situations

13. Arguments that have been advanced against legalizing assisted suicide include all *except:*

(A) Patients may be influenced by financial concerns to select this option

(B) Medical personnel may make a mistaken diagnosis of a terminal condition

(C) Disabled persons may be urged to die as a form of conserving resources

(D) There has been no Supreme Court decision about the issues surrounding assisted suicide

14. A nurse is administering large doses of morphine to a terminally ill patient. The nurse is concerned that these actions may be considered assisted suicide. The law permits this intervention if:

(A) The nurse has a physician's order that allows the nurse to set the patient's dosage of the morphine without any dosage parameters

(B) The patient's family has requested this action

(C) The nurse is implementing pain relief as a therapeutic intervention with no intent to harm the patient or cause his death

(D) There is a statute permitting assisted suicide by physicians in the state

PART V: ANSWERS

1. **The answer is D.**

Although talking to the physician may be in order, to give the patient the respect she deserves, a conversation with her is the first action. This recognizes the patient's autonomy and gives the nurse a chance to obtain information about the patient. Ultimately, the nurse will be able to draw upon that information when making ethical decisions. Giving her the medication in spite of the nurse's beliefs would be contrary to beneficence. Refusing to give the medication denies the patient's rights to autonomy and acts to create an adversarial, authoritarian relationship.

2. **The answer is D.**

The nurse needs to comprehend this patient's level of understanding and can only do that by speaking with him. He may have unfounded fears about his health and prognosis that the nurse could help to correct and alleviate. Although the nurse's duty is to provide truthful information to all patients, to do so in this case could cause harm and therefore violate the principle of nonmalfeasance. A specialized approach to each patient is necessary to give patients the respect they deserve.

3. **The answer is D.**

The person whose conduct is questioned should be confronted before other actions are taken. Specific facts and circumstances should be addressed, and the nurse should document these facts in personal notes. Answer C is a step that can be taken but with caution—the nurse does not want to appear to be influencing the opinion of others, and it is safest to confront the person first. Answer A would occur after the person is on notice but could occur shortly after this. Answer B may be necessary in some instances but would not be the first step.

4. **The answer is B.**

The nurse risks disciplinary action by not reporting, based on the idea that the nurse is not protecting patients from potential harm. This is a serious unethical and illegal act that needs to follow all the steps for proper reporting of such incidents. Answer A is incorrect because these acts are not permitted even with prescriptive authority. Answer C is incorrect because actual harm does not have to be shown; placing patients at risk is enough. Answer D does not go far enough in taking definitive action to prevent harm.

5. **The answer is B.**

This is the first response in this situation. One should also consider C, however. In spite of her drugged state, the patient has a right to be informed and educated about what is at stake. By ascertaining the comprehensive ability of the patient and relaying the risks and benefits to both herself and her baby, the nurse may provide her with enough information to at least make an informed refusal. Assuaging her fears regarding the surgery should be part of the information process as well. This should all be done in a noncoercive manner.

6. **The answer is C.**

The nurse needs to advise the patient, without emotion or coercion, of the effect of HIV on her unborn baby, with the hope that the information will encourage the mother to undergo the test for the sake of her child's health. The nurse should also inform the patient that most states mandate the reporting of positive AIDS test results. A and D fall below the standard of care and B is incorrect because HIV testing of pregnant women is voluntary in an overwhelming majority of states. Currently only one state has mandatory HIV testing of pregnant women.

7. The answer is C.

A is incorrect because usually the ethics committees make the allocation determinations. Although it may be necessary for the treating physician to add medical input and answer quality-of-life questions, ethicists advise that the treating physician not be in the forefront of the decision because it may damage the physician-patient relationship, which is based on trust. B is incorrect because ethicists advise that patient's age not be considered. D is incorrect because ethically the patient's contribution to the disease should not be considered.

8. The answer is B.

Unless there is a court order to the contrary, the staff must continue to intubate the patient. The nurse could request a team meeting with the patient and family and an ethics committee review. A is incorrect because there is no indication (even smoking) to declare incompetence, and even if he was incompetent, his guardian could seek medical care on his behalf, so the issue of futile care is not solved solely by this action. C is incorrect because the sequence is wrong (DNR status must be determined first). Furthermore, physicians must have a competent patient's agreement for DNR status (DNR status is a collaborative decision and not unilaterally done by a physician).

9. The answer is C.

If a patient makes a clear statement about an end-of-life decision, it needs to be taken seriously. Reporting his statement to the charge nurse and attending physician is required. Document the statement in the chart. Unless the patient has a history of suicidal tendencies or his prognosis is not deemed to be poor, discussion with the family is not the first action to take. He needs to be educated as to the mechanics of life-support systems and needs to be made aware of his options to withhold or discontinue one or all systems.

10. The answer is B.

The nurse's first obligation is to the patient. Assuming the patient is capable, the nurse must inform the patient of the options available (durable power of attorney for health care and living wills) and what signing these documents means to her care and ability to make decisions. The nurse needs to encourage the patient to be honest about her concerns, with assurances that anything said will be held in confidence from those whose interests may be affected. Reporting the incident to the charge nurse is necessary, but the nurse's responsibility does not stop there. An assessment of the patient's capacity is also necessary. This should be pointed out to the physician as well.

11. The answer is B.

Any health care provider who receives these federal funds must provide information to individuals about the laws that govern advance directives (living wills or health care proxies or agents) in their state. The PSDA does not create these rights but refers to patients and others being informed of the rights under these state statutes. Answer A is incorrect because there is no requirement that a patient complete an advance directive. Answer C is incorrect because it is often health care personnel (nurses, social workers, etc.) who implement the PSDA. Answer D is incorrect because there is no requirement that nurses do this, although often it is the nurse who provides this information. Also it applies to all patients, not just those who are terminally ill.

12. The answer is C.

The court upheld the state statute that required "clear and convincing" evidence of the incompetent's wishes while finding a constitutional right to terminate life-sustaining nutrition and hydration. Answer A is incorrect because the right was extended to incompetent patients while upholding states' rights to implement standards for determining the incompetent's wishes. Answer B is incorrect because statutes are not required by states. Answer D is incorrect because the "clear and convincing" standard required by the state statute was upheld by the Court.

13. The answer is D.

This is not one of the arguments against assisted suicide because the Supreme Court has decided that there is no constitutional right to assisted suicide. However, the door was left open to let states deal with the issue with the possibility that a statute could be upheld in the future. Answers A, B, and C contain reasons that have been advanced for possible abuse of any legalized assisted suicide law.

14. The answer is C.

The nurse is clearly within legal and ethical boundaries if there is no intent to cause the patient's death and the medication is being administered to provide for pain relief. Answer A is incorrect because the order would not be valid if it permitted the nurse to adjust the dosage without dosage parameters. Answer D is incorrect because even if there is a statute, the nurse would not be allowed to implement this since the statement says this is permitted for physicians. B is incorrect because this must be done with a physician order to relieve pain not hasten death. Dosage should be set at the minimum to relieve pain.

References

Chapter 3

Helmlinger, C., and Milholland, K. (1997). Telehealth discussions focus on licensure. *American Journal of Nursing* 97:61.

Trossman, S. (1998). ANA voices concern over multistate licensure plan. *The American Nurse* 30 (2): 7.

Chapter 8

American Nurses Association (1992). *Position statement: registered nurse utilization of unlicensed personnel.* Washington, DC: American Nurses Publishing.

Chapter 9

Geller, R. (1998). The nurse's role as a witness. *The Nursing Spectrum, New England Edition* 2 (17):6.

Chapter 10

Forward, D. (1998). Managing malpractice insurance. *American Journal of Nursing* 98:16BB–16II.

Lippman, H. (1993). Malpractice protection—how much is enough? *RN* 56(5):61–67.

Rhodes, A. (1994). Personal liability insurance. *MCN American Journal of Maternal Child Nursing* 19:309.

Chapter 11

American Nurses Association (1985). *Code for Nurses: With Interpretive Statements.* Kansas City, MO: American Nurses Association.

Powers, J. (1993). Accepting and refusing assignments. *Nursing Management* 24:64–68.

Sullivan, G. (1995). When assignments don't match skills. *RN* 57–60.

Chapter 13

American Hospital Association (1972). *A Patient's Bill of Rights.* Chicago, IL: American Hospital Association.

American Medical Association (1998–1999). *Code of Medical Ethics.* American Medical Association.

American Nurses Association (1976). *Code for Nurses.* Washington, D.C.: American Nurses Association.

American Nurses Association (1976, 1985). *Code for Nurses with Interpretative Statements.* Washington, D.C.: American Nurses Association.

American Nurses Association (1991). *Position Statement—Nursing and the Patient Self-determination Act.* Washington, D.C.: American Nurses Association.

Annas, G.J. (1998). A national bill of patient's rights. *New England Journal of Medicine* 338:695–699.

Chapter 15

Sullivan, G. (1997). Protecting patient's privacy. *RN* 60(6): 55–56.

Chapter 18

Sullivan, G. (1998). Getting informed consent. *RN* 61(4): 59–62.

Chapter 19

Appelbaum, P.S., Lidz, C.W., and Meisel, A. (1987). *Informed Consent: Legal Theory and Clinical Practice.* New York: Oxford University Press.

Cruzan v Director, Missouri Department of Health, 497 U.S. 261 (1990).

Hackathorn v Lester Cox Memorial Center, 824 S.W.2d 472, (Mo. 1992).

Veatch, R. (1989). *Death, Dying and the Biological Revolution.* New Haven, CT: Yale University Press.

Chapter 20

Agency for Health Care Policy and Research (1992). *Acute Pain Management: Operative or Medical Procedures and Trauma (Clinical Practice Guidelines).* Rockville, MD: U.S. Department of Health and Human Services.

Agency for Health Care Policy and Research (1994). *Management of Cancer Pain (Clinical Practice Guidelines).* Rockville, MD: U.S. Department of Health and Human Services.

American Nurses Association (1992). *Compendium of Position Statements on the Nurse's Role in End-of-Life Decisions* (M-30). Washington, DC: American Nurses Association.

American Pain Society. Glenview, IL. 60025 www.ampainsoc.org.

Cushing, M. (1992). Pain management on trial. *American Journal of Nursing* 92(2):21–22.

Chapter 21

Chamberlain v Deaconess Hospital, Inc. 324 N.W.2d 172 (Ind. Ct. App. 1975).

Crawford v Earl Long Memorial Hospital, et al. 431 S. 2d 40 (LA 1983).

Tuma v Board of Nursing, 100 Idaho 74, 593 P.2d 711 (1979).

Chapter 23

Fiesta, J. (1997). Legal update—1996—part 2. *Nursing Management* (6):16–17, 19.

Fiesta, J. (1998). Legal aspects of medication administration. *Nursing Management* 29(1):22–23.

Plum, S. (1997). Nurses indicted. *Nursing 97*. 27(7), 34–35.

Smetzer, J. (1998). Lessons from Colorado—beyond blaming individuals. *Nursing Management* 29(6):49–51.

Smetzer, J. (1998). Voices from Colorado. *Nursing Management* 29(6):52–53.

Chapter 24

American Nurses Association (1991). *Position Statement: Guidelines for Disclosure to Known Third Parties about Possible HIV Infection*. Washington, DC: American Nurses Association.

American Nurses Association (1994). *Position Statement: Risk versus Responsibility in Providing Nursing Care*. Washington, DC: American Nurses Association.

Chapter 25

All, A.C. (1994). A literature review: Assessment and intervention in elder abuse. *J. Gerontol. Nurs.* 20(7):25–32.

American Medical Association (1992). *Diagnostic and Treatment Guidelines (Child Physical Abuse and Neglect, Child Sexual Abuse, Domestic Violence, Elder Abuse and Neglect)*. Chicago: American Medical Association.

Anetzberger, G.J., et al. (1993). Elder mistreatment: A call for help. *Patient Care* 27(11):93–130.

Capezuti, E., et al. (1995). Meeting the challenge of elder abuse. *Nursing Dynamics* 4(1):5–9.

Chez, N. (1994). Helping the victim of domestic violence. *American Journal of Nursing* 94(7):32–37.

Janez, M. (1990). Clues to elder abuse. *Geriatric Nursing* 11:220–222.

Lachs, M.S., and Fulmer, T. (1993). Recognizing elder abuse and neglect. *Clinics in Geriatric Medicine* 9:665–681.

Lachs, M.S., and Pillemer, K. (1995). Abuse and neglect of elderly persons. *New England Journal of Medicine* 332:437–443.

National Clearinghouse on Child Abuse and Neglect Information. 330 C Street, SW, Washington, D.C. 20447. (800) FYI-3366 or (703) 385-7565. E-mail: nccanch@calib.com

Paris, B.E., et al. (1995). Elder abuse and neglect: How to recognize warning signs and intervene. *Geriatrics* 50(4): 7–53.

Wolf, R.S. (1998). Elder abuse: Ten years later. *Journal of the American Geriatrics Society* 36:758–762.

Chapter 26

American Nurses Association (1989). *Position Statement: Reproductive Health*.

Bellotti v Baird, 443 U.S. 622 (1979).

Planned Parenthood v Danforth, 428 U.S. 52 (1976).

Roe v Wade, 410 U.S. 113 (1973).

Chapter 27

American Academy of Pediatrics (1996). Policy statement—ethics and cure of critically ill infants and children. 98:149–152.

Stokley, J. (1994). Withdrawing or withholding medical care from premature infants: Who should decide, and how? *North Dakota Law Review* 70:129–157.

Chapter 28

Braun, J. (1998). Legal aspects of physical restraint use in nursing homes. *Health Lawyer* 10(3):10–16.

Richman, D. (1998). To restrain or not to restrain. *RN* 61: 55–60.

Chapter 29

Appelbaum, P. (1995). Civil commitment and liability for violating patients' rights. *Psychiatric Services* 46:17–18.

Engleman, N., et al. (1998). Clinician's decision making about involuntary commitment. *Psychiatric Services* 49:941–945.

Fiesta, J. (1998). Psychiatric liability: Part 2. *Nursing Management* 29(8):18–19.

Hughes, D. (1996). Implications of recent court rulings for crisis and psychiatric emergency services. *Psychiatric Services* 47:1332–1333.

Mindvich, D., and Hart, B. (1995). Linking hospital and community. *Journal of Psychosocial Nursing* 33:25–28.

O'Connor v Donaldson, 442 U.S. 563, 95 S. Ct. 2486, 45 L. Ed. 2d 396 (1975).

Ries, R. (1997). Advantages of separating the triage function from the psychiatric emergency service. *Psychiatric Services* 48:755–756.

Tarasoff v Regents, 17 Cal. 3d 425, 551P2d 334 (1976).

Chapter 31

George, J.E. (1985). Potential liability for the patient signing out against medical advice, law and the ED nurse. *Journal of Emergency Nursing* 11(2):110.

Jeremiah, J., O'Sullivan, P., and Stein, M. (1995). Who leaves against medical advice? *Journal of General Internal Medicine* 10(7):403–405.

Chapter 33

Ballard, D., and Cohen, J.W. (1994). Confidentiality of patient records in the computer age. *Journal of Nursing Law* 2(4):49–61.

Maddox, P.J. (1998). Update on patient privacy legislation. *Nursing Economics* 16:212–214.

Chapter 35

American Nurses Association (1992). *Position Statement: Nursing Care and Do Not Resuscitate Decisions*. Washington, DC: American Nurses Association.

Gobis, L. (1997). Reducing risks of phone triage. *RN* 60(4): 61–63.

Grande, P. (1997). Brave new world of telemedicine. *RN* 60(7): 59–62.

Horsley, J. (1997). When you go toe to toe over doctor's orders. *RN* 60(11): 54–61.

Sloan, A. (1996). Don't resuscitate, lose your job? *RN* 59(8): 51–54.

Chapter 37

American Nurses Association (1997). *Scope and Standards of Forensic Nursing Practice.* Washington, DC: American Nurses Association.

Easter, C.R. (1995). An ED forensic kit. *Journal of Emergency Nursing* 21:440–444.

Emergency Nurses Association (July 1998). *Emergency Nurses Association Position Statement: Forensic Evidence Collection.* Des Plains, IL: Emergency Nurses Association.

Hoyt, C., and Spanlger, K.A. (1996). Forensic nursing implications and the forensic autopsy. *Journal of Psychosocial Nursing* 34(10):24–31.

Lynch, V.A. (1991). Forensic nursing in the emergency department: A new role for the 1990s. *Critical Care Nursing Quarterly* 14(3):69–86.

Lynch, V.A. (1995). Clinical forensic nursing: A new perspective in the management of crime victims from trauma to trial. *Critical Care Nursing Clinics of North America* 7:489–507.

Pasqualone, G. (1996). Forensic RNs as photographers, documentation in the ED. *Journal of Psychosocial and Mental Health Nursing* 34(10):47–51.

Chapter 45

Fiesta, J. (1994). Staffing implications: A legal update. *Nursing Management,* 25(6): 34–35.

Chapter 46

Aikens v St. Helena Hospital, 843 F. Supp. 1329 (N.D. Cal. 1994).

Mahoney, R., and Gibofsky, A. (1992). The Americans with Disabilities Act of 1990. *Journal of Legal Medicine* 13(1):51–75.

Schmidt v Methodist Hospital, 5 AD Cases 1340 (7th Cir. 1996).

Chapter 47

American Nurses Association (1992). *Position Statement: HIV Infected Nurse, Ethical Obligations and Disclosures.* Washington, DC: American Nurses Publishing.

Cushing, M. (1992). The courts confront occupational HIV. *American Journal of Nursing* 92(10):26–27.

Chapter 48

American Nurses Association (1985). *Code for Nurses: With Interpretive Statements.* Kansas City, MO: American Nurses Association.

Bugle, L. (1996). A study of drug and alcohol use among Missouri RNs. *Journal of Psychosocial Nursing* 34(7):41–45.

Ellis, P. (1995). Addressing chemical dependency. *Nursing Management* 26(8):56–58.

Lowell, J., and Massey, K. (1997). Sounds of silence. *Nursing Management* 28(5):40H–40L.

Perry, B., and Rimler, G. (1995). Chemical dependency among nurses. *Nursing Management* 26(5):52–56.

Pullen, L., and Green, L. (1997). Identification, intervention and education: Essential curriculum components for chemical dependency in nurses. *Journal of Continuing Education in Nursing* 28:211–216.

Smith, L., Taylor, B., and Hughes, T. (1998). Effective peer responses to impaired nursing practice. *Nursing Clinics of North America* 33(1):105–118.

Thompson, N., Handley, S., and Uhing-Nguyen, S. (1997). Substance abuse in nursing. *Nursing Management* 28(2):38, 40, 42–43.

Torkelson, D., Anderson, R., and McDaniel, R. (1996). Interventions in response to chemically dependent nurses: Effect of context and interpretation. *Research in Nursing and Health* 19:153–162.

Chapter 50

American Nurses Association (1993). *Sexual Harrassment: It's against the Law.* Washington, DC: American Nurses Association.

Davidhizer, R., Erdel, S., and Dowd, S. (1998). Sexual harassment: Where to draw the line. *Nursing Management* 29(2):40–44.

Editors (1994). Confronting sexual harassment. *Nursing94* 24(10):48–50.

Fiesta, J. (1999). When sexual harassment hits home. *Nursing Management* 30(5):16–18.

Chapter 51

American Nurses Association (1985). *Code for Nurses: With Interpretive Statements.* Kansas City, MO: American Nurses Association.

Chapter 55

American Hospital Association (1972). *A Patient's Bill of Rights.* Chicago, IL: American Hospital Association.

American Nurses Association (1976). *American Nurses Association Code for Nurses.* Washington, DC: American Nurses Association.

American Nurses Association (1976, 1985). *American Nurses Association Code for Nurses with Interpretative Statements.* Washington, D.C.: American Nurses Association.

American Nurses Association Task Force on End of Life Decisions (1991). *Position Statement—Nursing and the Patient Self-determination Act.* Washington, DC: American Nurses Association.

Chapter 56

American Nurses Association (1985). *Code for Nurses with Interpretive Statements.* Kansas City, MO: American Nurses Association.

International Council of Nurses (1973). *International Code for Nurses.* Geneva, Switzerland: International Council of Nurses.

Chapter 58

American College of Obstetricians and Gynecologists Committee on Ethics (1999). *Patient Choice and the*

Maternal-Fetal Relationship. Washington, DC.: American College of Obstetricians and Gynecologists.

American Nurses Association (1976). *American Nurses Association Code for Nurses.* Washington, DC: American Nurses Association.

American Nurses Association (1986). *Code of Ethics for Nurses with Interpretative Statements:* Washington DC: American Nurses Association.

Honig, J., and Jurgrau, A. (1999). Mandatory newborn HIV testing. *Journal of Nursing Law* (6):33–37.

Mohaupt, S.M., and Sharma, K.K. (1998). Forensic implications and medical-legal dilemmas of maternal versus fetal rights. *Journal of Forensic Science* 43:985–992.

Pinkerton, J.V., and Finnerty, J.J. (1996). Resolving the clinical and ethical dilemma involved in fetal-maternal conflicts. *American Journal of Obstetrics and Gynecology* 175:289–295.

Roe v Wade, 410 U.S. 113 (1973). In re Angelu C., 573 A.2d 1235 (1990).

Chapter 59

American Medical Association Code of Medical Ethics. (1997). *Futile Care.* Chicago, IL.

American Medical Association Code of Medical Ethics (1997). *Allocation of Medical Care.* Chicago, IL.

Cultice, P.N. (1994). Medical futility: When is enough, enough? *Journal of Health and Hospital Law.* 27:225–232.

Grant, E.R. (1992). Medical futility: Legal and ethical aspects. *Law, Medicine and Health Care* (92):330–335.

Hastings Center (1987). *Guidelines on the Termination of Life-Sustaining Treatment and the Care of the Dying.*

In re Baby K, 16 F.3d 590 (4th Cir. 1994).

President's Commission for the Study of Ethical Problems in Medical and Biomedical Research (1983). Washington, DC: US Government Printing Office.

Spielman, B. (1994). Collective decisions about medical futility. *American Society of Law, Medicine and Ethics* 22:152–160.

Chapter 60

American Nurses Association (1991). *Nursing and the Patient Self-determination Act.* ANA, Washington, DC: American Nurses Association.

Crego, P.J., and Lipp, E.J. (1998). Nurses' knowledge of advance directives. *American Journal of Critical Care* 7(3): 218–223.

Fade, A.E. (1995). Advance directives: An overview of changing right-to-die laws. *Journal of Nursing Law* (2):27–38.

Jarr, S., Henderson, M.L., and Henley, C. (1998). The registered nurse: Perceptions about advance directives. *Journal of Nursing Care Quality* (12):26–36.

Mezey, L., et al. (1994). The Patient Self-determination Act: Sources of concern for nurses. *Nursing Outlook* 42(1):30–38.

Sabatino, C.P. (1995). 10 legal myths about advance medical directives. *Journal of Nursing Law* (3):35–42.

Schlenk, J.S. (1997). Advance directives: Role of nurse practitioners. *Journal of American Academy of Nurse Practitioners* (9):317–321.

Weiler, K., Eland, J., and Buckwalter, K.C. (1996). Iowa nurses' knowledge of living wills and perceptions of patient autonomy. *Journal of Professional Nursing* 12(4):245–252.

Chapter 61

Cruzan v Director, Missouri Department of Health, 497 U.S. 261 (1990).

Patient Self-determination Act, 42 U.S.C. §§ 1395–1396 (1990).

Chapter 62

American Nurses Association (1994). *Position Statement on Assisted Suicide.* Washington, DC.

Chopko, M.E., and Moses, M.F. (1995). Assisted suicide: Still a wonderful life? *Notre Dame Law Review* 70:519.

Cruzan v Director, Missouri Department of Health, 497 U.S. 261 (1990).

In re: Karen Quinlan, 355 A.2d 644 (N.J. S. Ct. 1976) reversing, 348 A.2d 80 (N.J. S. Ct. 1976).

Scofield, G. R. (1997). Natural causes, unnatural results, and the least restrictive alternative. *Western New England Law Review* 9(2): 351.

Vacco v Quill, 117 S. Ct. 2293 (1997).

Volker, D.L. (1995). Assisted suicide and the terminally ill: Is there a right to self-determination? *Journal of Nursing Law* 2(4):37–47.

Washington v Gluckberg, 117 S. Ct. 2259 (1997).

Index

Expand Your Library
With These Exceptional Texts!

Other Exciting Books in the Quick Look Nursing *Series Include:*

Title	Book #	Price
❑ Quick Look Nursing: Growth and Development Through the Lifespan	25066	$21.95
❑ Quick Look Nursing: Nutrition	25015	$17.95
❑ Quick Look Nursing: Pathophysiology	25031	$21.95
❑ Quick Look Nursing: Pharmacology	25023	$21.95

Subtotal $____

NJ and CA Sales Tax* $____

Handling Charge $ 4.50

Total $____

Name: _____

Address: _____

City: _____ State: _____ Zip Code: _____

Phone: _____ Fax: _____

Charge my: ❑ AMERICAN EXPRESS ❑ MasterCard ❑ VISA   Account#: _____

Exp. date: _____ Signature: _____

Prices are subject to change. Shipping charges may apply.
*Purchases in NJ and CA are subject to tax. Please add applicable state and local taxes.

CODE: 2A556

Mail Order Form To: SLACK Incorporated
Professional Book Division
6900 Grove Road
Thorofare, NJ 08086-9864

Call: 800-257-8290 or 856-848-1000
Fax: 856-853-5991
Email: Orders@slackinc.com

Visit Our World Wide Web: www.slackbooks.com